Our Naked Frailties

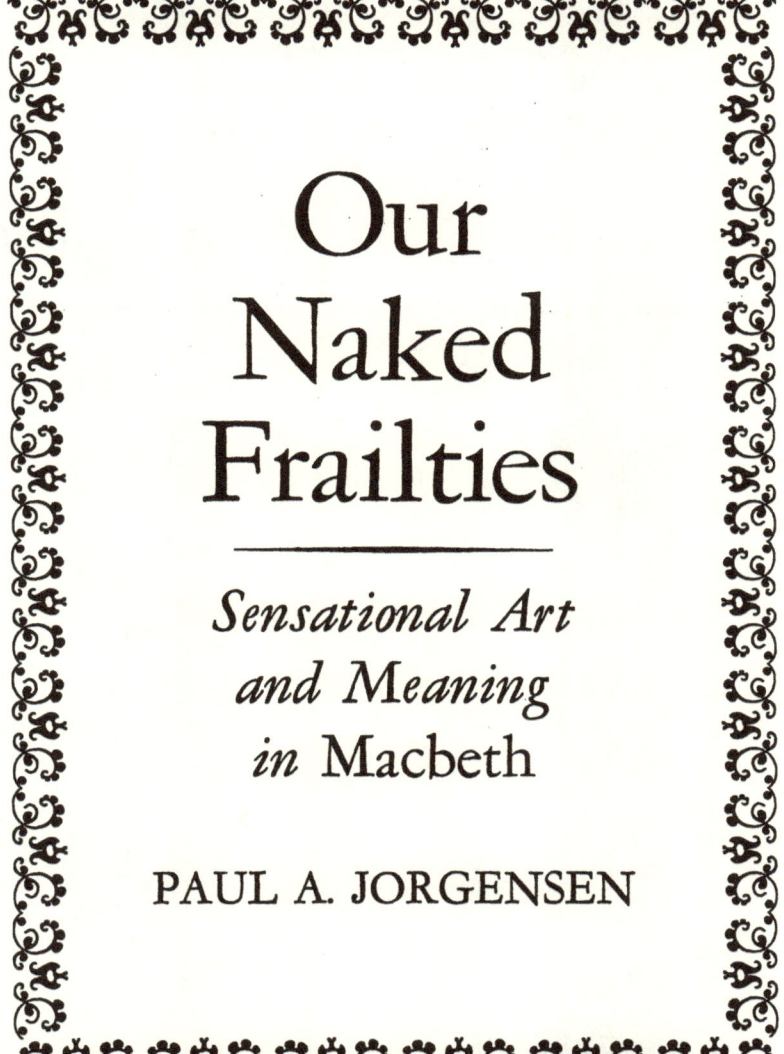

Our Naked Frailties

Sensational Art and Meaning in Macbeth

PAUL A. JORGENSEN

UNIVERSITY OF CALIFORNIA PRESS
BERKELEY, LOS ANGELES, LONDON
1971

University of California Press
Berkeley and Los Angeles, California

University of California Press, Ltd.
London, England

Copyright © 1971 by The Regents of the University of California
ISBN: 0-520-1915-6
Library of Congress Catalog Card Number: 70-1457-88
Designed by Steve Reoutt

to my university

Acknowledgments

At a time when there are distracting pressures of anti-intellectualism and subintellectualism within universities, it is a privilege—I hope not a presumption—to dedicate a book of scholarship to one's university. It is not so much the modest contribution of this book which prompts my dedication as my appreciation of the general pursuit of truth which the climate of this university has so far made possible. However, I have personal indebtednesses within the institution which I think are typical of those enjoyed by my colleagues.

First of all is our admirable University Research Library, which, together with the Huntington Library, has provided most of the books needed for the project.

Equally important are the incentive and assistance to research provided by a sabbatical leave during two quarters of 1970 and by appointment for two summers to the University of California Humanities Institute. Of comparable value were grants by the University Research Committee for student assistance and also the services of Katherine Proppe made possible under a research assistantship from the Center for Medieval and Renaissance Studies. Other students who have assisted me are Maryaurelia Lemmon, Sharon Jaffe (who expertly checked references, gave encouragement, and constructed the Index), and Carol McKay (to whom, among other things, I owe an idea about the Witches).

I am grateful to our distinguished University Press, which has borne with me, through three previous books, in my groping toward a fuller understanding of Shakespeare.

And finally there are my colleagues, who by their search for knowledge have stimulated my own research. I am particularly indebted to the broad learning of my colleagues in the Renaissance: R. W. Dent, Hugh G. Dick, H. A. Kelly, Robert S. Kinsman, Richard A. Lanham, and James E. Phillips. Professor Dent, who was editing *Macbeth* during my work on this book, was an invigorating influence; and Professor Kelly answered questions on demonology out of his considerable knowledge. Though they are not in my "field," Blake R. Nevius and John J. Espey helped me with their comprehensive knowledge of literature and, above all, with their friendship and solace.

But of course my major help in this project has been, as it should be, from a world of scholarship which transcends institutions. Many scholars and critics have been mentioned in text and notes. Here I should like to single out with special admiration a book not devoted to Shakespeare: Douglas Cole's *Suffering and Evil in the Plays of Christopher Marlowe*. And I acknowledge with real appreciation the keen, yet generous, reading of the manuscript by David Bevington.

I cannot overlook my gratitude to my family, especially my wife, whom this book has cost so much and to whom it will mean the most.

P. A. J.

University of California
Los Angeles

Contents

I • *Prologue on Earth* 1
II • *Sensational Background* 14
III • *The Evil* 41
IV • *He Is About It* 59
V • *Bloody Instructions* 70
VI • *Babes Savagely Slaughtered* 94
VII • *More Strange Than Such a Murder Is* 110
VIII • *The Rest Is Labor* 140
IX • *Pestered Senses* 157
X • *Torture of the Mind* 185
XI • *Epilogue in Hell* 217
Index 221

Look to the Lady:—
And when we have our naked frailties hid,
That suffer in exposure, let us meet,
And question this most bloody piece of work,
To know it further.
MACBETH II.iii. 125–129

Chapter I

Prologue on Earth

We meet in thunder, lightning, or in rain. These are the elements, dread and portentous, of "the one half-world" of *Macbeth*. But they are also the elements of our own human earth which we find in the play, the disturbances not of external nature but of our own selves in tumult and in evil that we must recognize as our own. My concern in this study does not exclude the unworldly, the external, sources of the sensational, but it is more anxiously about the sublunary, the human—that part of ourselves which is designed to make us tremble in recognition, through great art, at something disturbingly strange and potentially dangerous within ourselves.

My concern, more precisely, is to get at what I take to be the characterizing human feature of *Macbeth*: its almost uniquely tangible impact, from within us, upon our feelings. For I take "sensational" not so much in its popular meaning of spectacular as in its deeper, interior meaning of causing sensation. All Shakespearean tragedies, of course, powerfully affect the feelings, and I am aware that a part of my methodology could be applied to any of them; indeed we need to know more about the serious, poetic use of the sensational in Elizabethan drama generally. But there is in *Macbeth*, as most critics have noted, a peculiar quality in the language and imagery, one which seems to me to be responsible for making the play violently vivid, tactile, and generally sensory. According to G. K. Hunter, for example, the imagery is "lurid and violent" and we have "the sense of an inferno barely controlled beneath the surface crust."[1] I am also concerned—and this will perhaps be the strongest assertion of an assertive book—to show that the function of sensation in the play is organic in a way that it is not in any other Shakespearean tragedy. In other words, I shall try to show that in *Macbeth* Shakespeare disturbs us throughout our nervous system, by exposing to each of us what is within us, by exposing what Banquo calls our "naked frailties," and that Shakespeare does so not by techniques alone (though I am of course constantly interested in the poetic mechanism of the sensational results). Rather, the *meaning* of the play dictated for Shakespeare the texture which his most sensational play would take. (At this point I hope for, because I will presently undertake to meet, the objection that surely *Titus Andronicus* is more sensational.)

II

I begin, therefore, with the problem presented by the meaning of a play presumably so simple—and also presumably so exciting—that it is commonly taught in high schools. The other major tragedies, notably *Hamlet* and *King Lear*, are predictably much richer in problems, and their meaning, if there is a single one, is not easily formulated. In *Macbeth*, which is often traced to the morality play, one is inclined to expect a stable and reassuring moral, or at least an awareness of some firm comment upon good and evil in terms of human action. I have accordingly, in good faith, sought, in major modern critics who have been lucid and forthright enough to commit themselves, the expected statement of edifying meaning. They are generally all good statements, and my purpose in presenting them here is not to regret their baffling diversity but rather to show that *Macbeth* is a very difficult play and that perhaps we are in need of a new approach more germane to its peculiar nature. After all, only four considerable books have been devoted to the play,

---

[1] Introduction to his edition of *Macbeth* (New Penguin Shakespeare), (Harmondsworth, England, 1967), p. 28.

Prologue on Earth · 3

a small number for one of the major tragedies, and three of these books have been valued more as comment, often controversial, than as central interpretation.[2] The best criticism is to be found in works not devoted exclusively to this play.

Here are only a few of the statements I have culled. *Macbeth* is "a study in the complementary pair of passions of rash courage and fear."[3] It is "the shortest of Shakespeare's tragedies and the simplest in its statement: *Thou shalt not kill*. In the words of Coleridge, it contains 'no reasonings of equivocal morality,... no sophistry of self-delusion'."[4] It is "the culmination of a long development of tragic writing on the theme of the rise and fall of an ambitious prince...."[5] "In short, Macbeth's spiritual experience is a representation on the stage of the traditional Christian conception of a human soul on its to the Devil."[6] "In a final judgement the whole play may be writ down as a wrestling of destruction with creation:... there is a wrenching of new birth, itself disorderly and unnatural in this disordered world, and then creation's more firm-set sequent concord replaces chaos."[7] *Macbeth* is "a statement of evil" and comprises three themes: "the reversal of values," "unnatural disorder,"

---

[2] Roy Walker, in *The Time Is Free: A Study of Macbeth* (London, 1949), colorfully retells the play, with many good insights. G. R. Elliott, in *Dramatic Providence in Macbeth* (Princeton, 1960), also vividly retells the play, but mainly in order to show that the big issue is the potential salvation of Macbeth. Henry N. Paul, in *The Royal Play of Macbeth* (New York, 1950), is primarily interested in the relationship of the play to James I. In *Macbeth and the Players* (Cambridge, 1969), Dennis Bartholomeusz has provided many valuable comments of his own, but the primary contribution of the book is in recording theatrical interpretations.

[3] Lily B. Campbell, *Shakespeare's Tragic Heroes: Slaves of Passion* (New York, 1952; first published 1930), p. 238.

[4] Alfred Harbage, in his Introduction to *Macbeth*, in *William Shakespeare: The Complete Works* (The Pelican Text Revised), (Baltimore, 1969), p. 1107.

[5] R. A. Foakes, in the Introduction to his edition of *Macbeth* (Indianapolis, 1968), p. ix.

[6] Walter Clyde Curry, *Shakespeare's Philosophical Patterns* (Baton Rouge, La., 1959; first published 1937), p. 105.

[7] G. Wilson Knight, *The Imperial Theme* (corrected edition), (London, 1961), p. 153. The stress upon the destruction and restoration of order is also made by D. A. Traversi, *An Approach to Shakespeare* (New York, 1956), p. 152. In *The Wheel of Fire* (Cleveland and New York, 1963; first published 1930), p. 140, Knight takes the thesis that *Macbeth* is "Shakespeare's most profound and mature vision of evil."

and "deceitful apearance."[8] It concentrates upon "the very essence" of Shakespeare's tragic vision—"upon the fact that the *infernal* evil working in man more instantly than his *natural* goodness . . . can ruin his humanity—so glorious at its best—unless it is sustained by the *supernal* power of Grace."[9]

There is nothing disprovable about any of these statements, and I would emphasize that they all become more impressive in their context of argument and elaboration. But from the point of view of the present study, they are generally wanting in an adequate and central explanation of what seems to me to be the distinctive feature of the play, its dark and painful power resulting from unparalleled sensational artistry.

Critics have tended to be much more impressive on the subject of the play's power than they have been upon its meaning. From the first recorded critic, Simon Forman, through De Quincey, Hazlitt, and Bradley, there has been recognition of the aesthetics of the tumult and agitation of the play, its dark happenings, its romantic qualities. Indeed it is significant that the Romantic critics—and here Bradley and perhaps G. Wilson Knight must be numbered among them—have written interpretive prose that is in its own beauty and feeling most adequate to the power and thereby the distinction of *Macbeth*. But De Quincey, though he explains much aesthetically, treats a limited segment of the play, and Bradley, to the indignation of L. C. Knights and others, was damagingly influential in trying to relate all to character.

I should also say something about a tendency, found first in the Romantic critics, to attribute much of the sensation in the play to Macbeth's poetic imagination. This approach was particularly congenial to Bradley's penchant for character criticism. But in limiting most of the poetry of the play to the temperament of one character, this approach has drawn fire from, predictably, L. C. Knights and F. R. Leavis, and also from S. L. Bethell. My own feeling is still, despite the cogent protests of these critics, that Bradley was not entirely wrong, but that he did not make enough allowance for factors in Macbeth and his situation other than poetic temperament which produce the

[8] L. C. Knights, *Explorations* (London, 1946), p. 18.
[9] G. R. Elliott, *Dramatic Providence in Macbeth*, p. 11.

poetry, particularly the poetry of sensation. But I shall have more to say about imagination in subsequent chapters.

Here I would emphasize that the interpreters of the power of the play err in much the same way as the interpreters of its meaning: they fail to account for why Shakespeare, apart from his supreme ability to do so, made this play, in terms of meaning, especially forceful in a sensational way. It is well enough to say, as Hazlitt has done so expressively, of the uniqueness of this play:

> The action is desperate and the reaction is dreadful. It is a huddling together of fierce extremes, a war of opposite natures which of them shall destroy the other. There is nothing but what has a violent end or violent beginnings. The lights and shades are laid on with a determined hand; the transitions from triumph to despair, from the height of terror to the repose of death, are sudden and startling. . . .[10]

But why? And, also central to this study, how?

Since I have subjected several critics to exposure, in a sentence or two, of their interpretation of the play, it is only just that I attempt here my own statement. Profiting from the results of their forthrightness, I shall do so warily. *Macbeth* depicts man's primal ordeal of temptation, crime, and punishment, here upon this bank and shoal of time—in this case an ordeal of one who is more heroic in proportion and potentially more terrible than most of us but who nevertheless sees and feels in a way that compels us to see and feel, yet not always to agree, with him. And the extent to which he does so is determined not so much by his poetic nature as by the special quality of his ordeal and by Shakespeare's own ability to express it in suitable language.

Such a statement (perhaps unfairly long) has one virtue. It would make Macbeth not a psychotically sensitive man, with its resultant limitation of tragic meaning. (To take parallel cases, we prefer not to make Hamlet or Lear abnormally susceptible to madness.) This is not of course to say that Macbeth may not be unusually subject to imagination, as Hamlet is to

[10] *The Complete Works of William Hazlitt*, ed. by P. P. Howe (London and Toronto, 1930), IV, 191.

melancholy. But the larger part of what he sees and feels, even the manner in which he expresses his perceptions, can most simply be accounted for by the nature of his ordeal. Much the same thing can be said for Lady Macbeth, but not to the same degree. I have chosen to center my analysis upon the man rather than the woman, viewing her mainly as a major part of the temptation. But she is far from being without poetry of the most vivid sensation, even though no one has thought fit to call her a poet. Even with her supposedly practical nature, her own ordeal is such as to call forth the scene of most painful and exposed feeling in the entire play.

For the poetry and sensation of the play as a whole, my statement of meaning is also largely, I think, adequate. Not only through the two protagonists—though predominantly through them—but also with all his resources of language, stagecraft, and command of the supernatural, Shakespeare commits himself fully to one of the most terrifyingly fundamental problems he ever undertook. He is dealing with an evil, one which I shall later attempt to define more clearly, which to him and to his era was probably unparalleled. And that evil, with its tempting qualities and the resultant punishment, informs the texture and structure of the whole play.

But another reason for the sensational distinction of the play must be considered. It is possible that here there was something more than the subject dictating the manner. Perhaps Shakespeare's kind and degree of artistry had reached, when he came to write *Macbeth*, a condition that impelled him to write about a subject that served as a worthy vehicle for sensational action and poetry. This is not the biographical fallacy; it is, at worst, the fallacy of artistic readiness. Although I do not consider it so important as the explanation given earlier, it is always good to consider the peculiar phenomenon claimed especially for one play in relationship to Shakespeare's artistic (not biographical) development. Such is, in part, the approach taken by Willard Farnham in his radical re-evaluation of the play, defining the nature of *Macbeth* as a tragedy and answering fundamental speculations about the kind and limits of our identification with its protagonist.[11] My own survey is quite different and necessar-

[11] *Shakespeare's Tragic Frontier: The World of His Final Tragedies* (Berkeley and Los Angeles, 1950). By placing Macbeth among Shake-

ily brief. In subsequent chapters I will place particular kinds of sensation in the context of Shakespeare's development in the art of sensation.

III

In the *Henry VI* plays Shakespeare makes some rather tame use of witchcraft and he also stages a number of murders, rather perfunctorily executed, and there is some hint of mutilation. But most of the felt sensation lies in an incessant and shrill rhetoric of defiance and, subsequently, lament. The emotional emphasis is upon what is variously called "saddest spectacle" and "O piteous spectacle."[12]

Viewed simply in the number and kinds of atrocities, *Titus Andronicus* would fully merit both the distinction and the ignominy of being Shakespeare's most sensational play. Before Eugene M. Waith's perceptive essay, giving it a serious purpose by relating it to Ovid,[13] it had usually been written off as an early aberration or "Senecan" exercise capitalizing upon the kind of sensationalism found in Kyd's *The Spanish Tragedy*. There is certainly too much pointless shock here, and too much dependence upon action, rather than on poetic emphasis, for effect. If this were a play with more credible human involvement, Aaron's summary of his villainies would be a grossly inadequate statement of its sensationalism, but I suspect that it is close to what original audiences found in the action:

---

speare's later tragic heroes, whom he shows to be deeply flawed and in whom it is difficult to separate what we admire from what repels us, Farnham raises problems of tragic identification only partially dealt with in this study; he also makes it thereby clear why *Macbeth* is not a simple play.

[12] *3 Henry VI* II.i.67; II.v.73. Except for *Macbeth* all Shakespeare references are to *The Complete Plays and Poems*, ed. by William Allan Neilson and Charles Jarvis Hill (Cambridge, Mass., 1942). All *Macbeth* citations are to the new Arden Shakespeare, ed. by Kenneth Muir (New York, 1964; first published 1951). For the sake of uniformity, I have normalized two of Muir's words, preferring *murder* and *weird*.

[13] "The Metamorphosis of Violence in *Titus Andronicus*," *Shakespeare Survey 10* (Cambridge, 1957), pp. 39–49. The most recent study of the play also discounts any sheerly horrific intent. In fact, writes Jack E. Reese, "*Titus Andronicus* represents, not a deliberate effort to shock an audience, but a fascinating and partially successful attempt to subdue the sensationalism of the most shocking material imaginable." "The Formalization of Horror in *Titus Andronicus*," *Shakespeare Quarterly*, *XXI* (1970), 77–84.

> Why, assure thee, Lucius,
> 'Twill vex thy soul to hear what I shall speak,
> For I must talk of murders, rapes, and massacres,
> Acts of black night, abominable deeds,
> Complots of mischief, treason, villainies,
> Ruthful to hear, yet piteously perform'd.
>
> *(V.i.61-66)*

One notes here also the early Shakespeare's tendency, expressed in the last line, to favor pity over power, and the terror that requires power. But there is more than sensation of action in the play. Occasionally, but not often, Shakespeare achieves genuine poetic sensation. There is a chilling, sensory force, anticipatory of the "uncouth fear" of *Macbeth*, in the description of Titus's two sons of the nightmarish scene and place of the discovery of the dead Bassianus:

> *Quin.* I am surprised with an uncouth fear;
> A chilling sweat o'er-runs my trembling joints;
> My heart suspects more than mine eye can see.
> *Mart.* To prove thou hast a true-divining heart,
> Aaron and thou look down into this den
> And see a fearful sight of blood and death.
> *Quin.* Aaron is gone; and my compassionate heart
> Will not permit mine eyes once to behold
> The thing whereat it trembles by surmise.
> O, tell me who it is; for ne'er till now
> Was I a child to fear I know not what.
>
> *(II.ii.211-221)*

The vague namelessness of the terror also anticipates *Macbeth* in a way that perhaps no intervening play, except *Hamlet*, will do. But if one turns to other passages of atmospheric suggestiveness (e.g., I.i.141-145; II.iii.91-104; III.i.81-86, 253-267), one notes a lyrical rather than dramatic quality, and the lyricism is sometimes too sweet. One cannot hold excessive description, per se, against the play, for there is much of this in *Macbeth*, and even the famous "silver skin lac'd with his golden blood" (II.iii.112) is not markedly different from most of the pictorial manner of *Titus*. But one can object to the absence of poetry that really thrills the reader in a dramatic context and to a technique that excites more pity than terror. It is still, like *Henry VI*, a play of lamentation; and horrified reaction, as we shall see in the discussion of blood, is sometimes merely picturesque. Shakespeare was not yet ready to write poetry of the intensity he was seemingly impelled to write in *Macbeth*. But I would still insist that meaning comes before technique. What is lacking is a worthy subject for sensation. If the hideous torment has any purpose, it is to express the play's mood of a wilderness of inhuman evil. We do not receive the powerful sensation of *Macbeth*, where we participate in the evil as well as in the torment. *Macbeth* is fundamentally a more sensational play than *Titus* because its subject, probing to the deeps of human evil with its subsequent guilt and torment, can almost compel the Shakespearean artistry needed to shake the reader.

What, in a more positive sense, is noteworthy about *Titus Andronicus* as an early sensational play is that it has, compared with *Henry VI*, as great a moral impact in the sensational passages as it does. Similarly in a play written at about the same time, *Richard III;* although there is much that is rather pointlessly shocking in the action, perhaps this is due again to having the action initiated by men without feeling. And when Shakespeare does make us respond to sought sensation—apart from the truly remarkable dream of Clarence, also a moral recital—he does so by momentarily giving a moral stature to *Richard III* as he awakes in cold sweat from his nightmare. But I need not elaborate upon the acknowledged usefulness of *Richard III* as an early experiment in some of the artistic strategies given mature form in *Macbeth*.

Julius Caesar, despite ingredients of the supernatural and a profusion of blood, does not have much excitement in its poetry. It has always been regarded as a rather cold, unimaginative play. In *Hamlet*, on the other hand, we have another "Senecan" play, and an occasional high level of intense poetry. There are also suspense and foreboding atmosphere. But again, as in *Titus*, much of the sensationalism must be sought in the animated action and intrigue. Horatio's summary of the action is disturbingly reminiscent of Aaron's:

> And let me speak to th' yet unknowing world
> How these things came about. So shall you hear
> Of carnal, bloody, and unnatural acts,
> Of accidental judgements, casual slaughters,
> Of deaths put on by cunning and forc'd cause,
> And in this upshot, purposes mistook
> Fall'n on the inventors' heads....
>
> (V.ii.390–396)

There is also sometimes, and especially in the protagonist, an amplification rather than an intensification of expression. What Hamlet says of the actor is often only too true of himself:

> What would he do,
> Had he the motive and the cue for passion
> That I have? He would drown the stage with tears
> And cleave the general ear with horrid speech,
> Make mad the guilty and appall the free,
> Confound the ignorant, and amaze indeed
> The very faculty of eyes and ears.
>
> (II.ii.586–592)

Too seldom do we feel in *Hamlet*, literally as we do in *Macbeth*, the amazement of eyes and ears. We do so, I think, in the scenes on the battlements. These are not the best scenes in the play, nor am I suggesting that *Macbeth* is a better play than *Hamlet*. But these scenes do succeed in their own way. They alert the full sense of apprehension in an audience. They awaken the whole nervous frame of the reader. And they are anything but sensation for the sake of sensation, for they impart — far more evocatively and truly than the more celebrated indoor scenes — the terrible, raw nature of the play's evil.

Othello and *King Lear* are not notable for sensationalism as are *Titus Andronicus* and *Hamlet*, though *King Lear* has a more massive and tumultuous kind of sensory impact than any of the other plays. But as in *Hamlet*, there is an occasional vehemence and agitation of style premonitory of the kind of nervous energy that finds most concentrated expression in *Macbeth*. Shakespeare's tragic career before and during these plays shows a continual, though not steady, development of what in *King Lear* and *Macbeth* can be considered to be his most unapproachable language of sensation and of tragedy, just as during this period his tragic subjects grow in power, profundity, and difficulty.

After *Macbeth* there is a kind of relaxing of the high tension; though syntax is still brilliantly unpredictable in *Antony and Cleopatra*, it lacks the nervous force of *Macbeth*. *Macbeth* may in fact represent, not only for Shakespeare but for his fellows, the ideal of Jacobean tragedy in terms of its sensational artistry. Thereafter, the action and the intrigue and the spectacle become both cheaper in poetic expression and less organically related to a worthy subject. One has sensationalism without the kind of sensation that is conducive to the highest purpose of tragedy.

But this is speculative only, and certainly is not intended to reflect adversely upon the importance of sensationalism, however it may be achieved, in the deeply stirring tragedies of the Jacobean era. What, rather, I should like to do is to find in *Macbeth* a kind of technique and purpose that may provide a vindication, by serving as a model, for the often maligned and misunderstood sensational nature of the later drama.

In the next chapter, accordingly, I explore sensationalism in the English Renaissance, seeking the kind of serious meaning that the age may have given to it and justifying much of the discussion that follows in the chapters on *Macbeth*. In these chapters I take up the sensational topics and techniques that the age would have found both especially powerful and especially meaningful in the play. These also, in large part, happen to be the staples of sensational nondramatic writing of the age. I should mention in advance that my survey in the next chapter, and therefore throughout the remainder of the book, will minimize Senecan influence in favor of Biblical and English religious background. Since Howard Baker's *Induction to Tragedy* (1939), and since Willard Farnham's *The Medieval Heritage of Elizabethan Tragedy* (1936), which influenced it, there has been less confident insistence on the direct impact of Seneca. But there are Senecan lines in *Macbeth* and I have occasionally called attention to Senecan analogues for many of the techniques and ideas, notably those which, in one way or another, had found stage expression earlier in England.

The major sensational features, however, are explicable in terms of native tradition and, especially, in terms of the Bible and Biblical lore in English religious writings. For the Bible was at once the most widely read, the most sensational, and the most moral book the English had. But I do try, not always successfully, to make only a controlled use of allegorical and anagogical interpretation. *Macbeth* lends itself, partially because of its descent from the morality play, to allegorical ecstasy in the critic. There are characters, including Old Man, so vaguely individualized that they seem to be personified abstractions. And even in the protagonists there is a quality, one which I have never seen critically recognized, that lessens their individualization and baffles character analysis. They tell us what they are suffering and feeling, but not what or who they are. And I shall later argue that what they feel does not, as it does with Hamlet and Lear, lead to insight into identity. These dark, proud figures hold us always at a distance. But there is more than pride in the distancing; through it Shakespeare achieved unprecedented power by extending the possibility of fearful participation to almost all sinful readers.

Struggling against strong eschatological implications in the play, I try to hold it firmly on earth. This is not always easy or desirable. The supernatural, as Bradley noted, is a source of mystery and power in Shakespeare's greatest tragedies, distinguishing them from *Antony and Cleopatra* and *Coriolanus*. In *Macbeth* there are, in unsurpassed degree, portents, hints of Doomsday, and references to angels, God, the Devil, and the immortal soul. But all of this is achieved without a descent into hell and without the appearance of the Devil onstage. The supernatural takes earthly embodiments. If God is physically present, it is in the voice which Macbeth hears; demons are incarnate in the Witches; and supernatural comment upon man's activities is expressed in the shaking of the earth. No fiends come to fetch away Macbeth; his terrible future is not commented upon, and instead, he suffers a hell on earth. The play, in short, achieves a remarkable expression of cosmic implications without leaving the stage of the world. No other tragedy has so many strange, disturbing phenomena that, like the Witches, "look not like th' inhabitants o' th' earth, / And yet are on' t" (I.iii.41-42).

Chapter II

Sensational Background

Present-day critics of the Elizabethan-Jacobean drama have been, at best, indulgent to the various excesses of violence and horror which they generally take to be the essence of sensationalism in the period. Symonds typically takes it to be an inevitable and characteristic ingredient of the drama, but one which certainly cheapens it:

> The reserve of the Greek Drama, the postponement of physical to spiritual anguish, the tuning of moral discord to dignified and solemn moods of sustained suffering, was unknown in England. Playwrights used every conceivable means to stir the passion and excite the feeling of their audience. They glutted them with horrors; cudgelled their horny fibres into sensitiveness.[1]

If there is purpose in it, Symonds seems to say, it must be in making an insensitive audience feel. Phoebe Sheavyn relates the literary kind of horror to the temperament of the Elizabethans, "a people familiarized with violence and bloodshed, by the perils of street life and travel, and by the spectacle of public sanguinary whippings and executions." To these people "there was nothing revolting, but rather something boldly great, in the excesses shown at times upon the stage."[2] A more recent writer,

---

[1] John Addington Symonds, *Shakespeare's Predecessors in the English Drama* (London, 1924), p. 387.
[2] *The Literary Profession in the Elizabethan Age* (Manchester, 1909), p. 202.

Maurice Charney, has seen the need to assess the moral and aesthetic purpose of violence on the stage. Although he believes that "the moral force of violence in Elizabethan drama should not be exaggerated" and that "there is a sense that the violence is performed for its own sake and is to be judged by esthetic rather than moral criteria," he perceptively recognizes that "the direct presentation of violence on stage could also powerfully evoke the emotions of pity and fear that Aristotle tells us are the proper effects of tragedy."[3] Wolfgang Clemen also finds an Aristotelian justification in terms of Renaissance interpreters of the Greek critic. The "famous doctrine of catharsis was construed as meaning that tragedy purges the onlooker of the emotions of pity and terror in that it gets him used to the sight of suffering by piling on the horror, and thus teaching him to accept it with composure."[4]

Surprisingly, though, little has been written about the notorious sensationalism of the Elizabethans, and most of what has been written concerns it in the limited and least rewarding sense of violence and horror, without an attempt to probe beneath it to the subtler artifices of sensation. The kind of sensationalism usually described would, for example, apply only to the blood and perhaps the Witches and the Ghost of *Macbeth*, whereas there are violences of imagery, atmosphere, stress, and sensory and mental torment—to name only a few—which must be considered if *Macbeth* and comparable works are to rank as sensational and hence dignify the stereotype of Elizabethan sensational drama.

Even more important is the need to discover—beyond the questionable clichés of sanguinary behavior and appetites—exactly what the role of sensationalism was in the age. What, so far as we can tell, did the age really think of the sensational, especially in terms of what use was made of it? What serious purpose did it have for a people whom we otherwise know not as frivolous but as morally anxious in their taste? And if it did, in its ideal form, serve some purpose beyond providing thrills, how

[3] "The Persuasiveness of Violence in Elizabethan Plays," *Renaissance Drama*, New Series, II (1969), 59–70.
[4] *English Tragedy before Shakespeare: The Development of Dramatic Speech*, trans. by T. S. Dorsch (London, 1961; German original, 1955), p. 39.

does that purpose relate to a tragedy like *Macbeth?* We can say at once that there must be something more specific than sensation as emotional therapy or as a simple bludgeoning of insensitive people, though both of these functions may be present.

II

The word *sensation* was unfortunately not in Shakespeare's, or his age's, vocabulary, but *sensible,* with the meaning of bodily feeling, prominently was; and the word was highly important to the way in which the age looked upon what we would today call sensation. Contrary to any easy generalization that the Renaissance was addicted to all that stimulated feeling, we must observe that there was, partly as a result of faculty psychology and partly because of influences like Neoplatonism, a distrust of feeling. Although the "soule sensible that giveth feeling" was considered more noble than the vegetable soul, it was firmly placed beneath "the soule Rationalis, that giveth reason. For the being and the working of the soule, that is Sensibilis, is dependent of the bodie, that it is in, and maketh it perfect."[5] There was a general distrust of the senses, in that they could lead to sensuality and in that they "doe deceive and enforce the understanding" and are conducive to that Renaissance demon, passion.[6] On the other hand, the sensible soul is potentially, though limited to the body, capable of "many noble workings and dooings. For it maketh the bodies of beastes to have feeling, and maketh perfect the inner kinde and the utter knowing.... Also it dealeth & spreadeth his vertue into all the parts of the body."[7] Sensation was, then, hazardous but necessary and valuable, at least according to the psychology that for so long influenced the aesthetic of the age. We must not expect to find it endorsed without some responsible force such as reason or moral purpose.

Not only because the concept of the imagination is so important to an appreciation of *Macbeth,* but because the imag-

[5] *Batman uppon Bartholome, his Booke De Propietatibus Rerum* (1582), fol. 15r.

[6] Pierre Charron, *Of Wisdome, Three Bookes,* trans. by S. Lennard (*ca.* 1612; entered 1606), p. 42.

[7] *Batman,* fol. 15r.

Sensational Background · 17

ination was commonly classified under the sensible soul, we may profitably inquire how this faculty was regarded by the Renaissance. Moral and psychological treatises tend to equate it in function and irresponsibility with the senses, and thus to give it both their virtues and their dangers. It is recognized as a faculty that can make distant things close and present, and can animate what we perceive.[8] Most valuably, it "printeth in the body, the images of those things which it doeth vehemently thinke of and apprehend."[9] But its hazards were great. One of the dangers most applicable to *Macbeth* was that the Devil worked principally through the imagination.[10] According to Robert Burton, "the Devil commonly suggests things opposite to nature, opposite to God and his word, impious, absurd, such as a man would never think of himself, or could not conceive, they strike terror and horror into the party's own heart." The terrible thoughts that assail his imagination "are not his own, but the Devil's."[11] Still another and allied reason, attributable principally to Calvinists, makes the imagination suspect. The very influential William Perkins, for example, devotes much of an entire book to detailing the innate evil of man's imagination since the Fall: the "thoughts of the Imagination are all naturally wicked."[12]

These strictures upon the imagination help to explain some of the temptations and innate fallibilities Macbeth must confront, and perhaps a part of his downfall and suffering is due to his yielding directly to the imaginative faculty rather than to the reason and conscience that should control it. But at this point it is more important to explain why, if the age regarded the imagination so distrustfully, Shakespeare would produce a greatly moral work which depends so constantly for its power upon this faculty linked to the body. First, even the psychol-

[8] For the vividness which the imagination can give to experience, see Charron, pp. 68–69.
[9] Pierre de La Primaudaye, *The French Academie*, trans. by T. B[owes] (1594), II, 157.
[10] Ibid., I, 156.
[11] *The Anatomy of Melancholy*, ed. by Floyd Dell and Paul Jordan-Smith (New York, 1941), p. 958.
[12] *A Treatise of Mans Imaginations. Showing His Naturally Evill Thoughts: His Want of Good Thoughts: The Way to Reform Them* (Cambridge, 1607; preached in 1606), p. 22.

ogists acknowledged the necessity of the imagination in the faculty hierarchy, just as they did for the senses. The imagination was essential in informing the "Minds Intelligence,"[13] and it could do so in a vivid way unique to itself. Secondly, two modern scholars have offered reasons for Renaissance acceptance of the faculty. M. D. Bundy suggests that the influence of rhetoricians, who associated the imagination with "invention," helped to dignify the former, and a distinction was made between useful poetic imagination and the pathological sort. Puttenham, for example, one of the rhetorical defenders of the imagination, argued that the imagination, if not "disordered," can represent "the best, most comely, and bewtifull images or apparances of thinges to the soule and according to their very truth."[14] But William Rossky, a more recent scholar, who apparently was unaware of Bundy's article, has presented an explanation which, while not rendering Bundy's invalid, is more in accord with what the Renaissance would find valuable in defending the imagination. He contends that the very defects commonly alleged against it, its excessive emotional power and distortion, could be effective in persuasion to virtue.[15] I am especially inclined to agree with Rossky because most of what I have found generally in sensational works of the age shows that they were valued primarily, or at least ostensibly, for their moral purpose. But I hope that "moral purpose" will not be here interpreted too narrowly or too somberly. I am obviously pointing toward *Macbeth*, and I recognize not only that there is much sensation in the play which is, at best, amoral (or such that I have not been able to find a moral meaning in it) but that moral purpose in tragic drama can be an enlargement of the sensibilities so as to make us more humanly and universally aware of man's plight. Moreover, agents of literary power, such as metaphor and the imagination, howsoever they came to be

[13] John Davies of Hereford, *Mirum in Modum* (1602), in *The Complete Works of John Davies of Hereford*, ed. by A. B. Grosart (Edinburgh, 1878), I, 9.

[14] "'Invention' and 'Imagination' in the Renaissance," *Journal of English and Germanic Philology*, XXIX (1930), 536. The quotation from Puttenham is from *The Arte of English Poesie* (1589), in *Elizabethan Critical Essays*, ed. by G. Gregory Smith (Oxford, 1904), II, 20.

[15] "Imagination in the English Renaissance: Psychology and Poetic," *Studies in the Renaissance*, V (1958), 49–73.

defended, were obviously accepted, and with them was accepted for literary purposes the value of the bodily senses in emotional response. Thus Thomas Wilson, writing of figurative language (which he calls "translation"), speaks approvingly of it as a device which refers meaning "to the senses of the bodie." We "alter a word from that which is in the mind, to that which is in the bodie" especially "when we talke earnestly of any matter."[16] Obviously the literary critics, whatever their elevated reasons for defending poetry, knew that it had to make reference to the senses and to the imagination. But this did not mean that the most effective use of the senses and the most valuable kind of sensational writing would not be that which sought the virtuous and edifying kind of delight described so well by Sidney and still acceptable to a less religiously minded audience today.

III

There were many kinds of sensational writing in the Renaissance, far more than have heretofore been considered in a study of the drama; and almost all of these, even those by Thomas Dekker on the plague, have some applicability to *Macbeth*. They all, moreover, with their animated and graphic language, and in view of their neglect by scholars, are especially conducive to quotation. I must, however, restrict their prominence here to those which most helpfully illustrate the purpose of sensational writing and point toward the uses of it in *Macbeth*. These purposes happen, as I have said, to be moral and usually Christian.

But the writer known to the Renaissance who is most commonly associated today with its sensationalism was the heathen Seneca, and whatever the precise extent of his influence on the drama, it is interesting to see what features drew the Renaissance to his writings. In the most recent statement of his influence on Renaissance England, Gareth Lloyd Evans writes that "Seneca's most compelling appeal for the Elizabethan playwrights lay in his exploitation of the themes and usages of blood,

---

[16] *Arte of Rhetorique* (1560), ed. by G. H. Mair (Oxford, 1909), pp. 171–173.

revenge, and cruelty."[17] This is questionable in view of Baker's disclosure that these themes were more readily available in Ovid and especially in native English writings such as the metrical tragedies and in view of the exemplary sensational use that Elizabethans tended to make of Seneca. Sidney praised the fervently didactic *Gorboduc* for "clyming to the height of *Seneca* his stile, and as full of notable moralitie, which it doth most delightfully teach, and so obtayne the very end of Poesie,"[18] associating both the English tragedy and Seneca in their moral eloquence, and certainly showing that Seneca was valued for some quality in his style, perhaps decorous power, that is something more sober than blood, revenge, and cruelty. Another Elizabethan reaction to Seneca is to be found in Thomas Newton's introduction to the translation of the ten plays, published in 1581:

> For it may not at any hand be thought and deemed the direct meaning of Seneca himselfe, whose whole wrytinges [penned with a peerlesse sublimity and loftinesse of Style,] are so farre from countenauncing vice, that I doubt whether there bee any amonge all the Catalogue of Heathen wryters, that with more gravity of Philosophicall sentences, more waightynes of sappy words, or greater authority of sound matter beateth down sinne, loose lyfe, dissolute dealinge, and unbrydled sensuality: or that more sensibly, pithily, and bytingly layeth doune the guedon [sic] of filthy lust, cloaked dissimulation and odious treachery: which is the dryft, whereunto he leveleth the whole yssue of ech one of his Tragedies.[19]

[17] "Shakespeare, Seneca, and the Kingdom of Violence," in *Roman Drama*, ed. by T. A. Dorey and Donald R. Dudley (London, 1965), p. 125. The essay is good for its analysis of the psychology of audience reaction to excitement and revenge. But there is almost nothing on *Macbeth*. The best study of Senecan influence on the language of *Macbeth* is still F. L. Lucas, *Seneca and Elizabethan Tragedy* (Cambridge, 1922), particularly p. 121. For Senecan influence through Italian and French intermediaries, see H. B. Charlton's Introduction to *The Poetical Works of Sir William Alexander*, ed. by Charlton and L. E. Kastner (Manchester, 1921), pp. xvii–cc; also A. M. Witherspoon, *The Inflence of Robert Garnier on Elizabethan Drama* (New Haven, 1924). I have not found these intermediaries to have had much bearing on *Macbeth*, though they certainly had their special brand of heightened language, especially in the form of the lament.
[18] *Apologie for Poetrie* (ca. 1583; printed 1595), in *Elizabethan Critical Essays*, ed. by G. Gregory Smith, I, 197.
[19] *Seneca: His Tenne Tragedies Translated into English*, ed. by

Here, as in Sidney, is a tribute to qualities of style, among which are to be noted "sensibly" and "bytingly." But even more prominent is the appreciation of Seneca for his potent moral lesson, particularly in the "guedon" of vices, which he makes "the whole yssue" of each of his tragedies. This influential statement is invaluable for my purposes since I feel that what was most Senecan about *Macbeth* to Jacobean audiences was not the Ghost but the spectacular manner in which evil was rewarded. But this is to anticipate somewhat the discussion of punishment to come later in this chapter. Here it is more relevant to note that the obvious English beneficiaries of Seneca— partially *Gorboduc* and certainly *The Misfortunes of Arthur*— seek the same "sensible" power of style and are impeccably moral in the sense that they mete out punishment with the same kind of judicious sensationalism found in Seneca.

It is tempting to dwell on Foxe's *Book of Martyrs*, the most popular sensational book of English origin, for not only was the purpose of the horrors in it spectacularly instructional, but the iconography of the gruesome woodcuts probably impressed the imaginations of English readers more than words. In a woodcut called "The Image of the true Catholicke Church of Christ," one man in the background is being burned alive, another eaten by a lion, another crucified upside down, while still another's head is about to be cut off. In the foreground, in the presence of some dignitaries, a man with a drill-type instrument is in the process of drilling another man's eye out, while in the lower right of the foreground a third man is being whipped with barbed scourges and is bleeding copiously.[20] Not only this heavily imaged woodcut but the volume as a whole in its message bears some resemblance to a theme, almost an iconographical one, which we shall notice in *Macbeth*: the torment but ultimate triumph of Innocence.

More directly germane to *Macbeth* is the substantial and sometimes impressive body of tracts and plays dealing with celebrated contemporary murders. Though most of these were

---

Thomas Newton, Anno 1581. With an introduction by T. S. Eliot (London, 1927), I, 5.

[20] John Foxe, *The Volume of the Ecclesiastical Historie, Conteining the Acts and Monuments of Martyrs* (1583), p. 780.

gotten out hastily, they have the advantage of journalistic verve, and some of their graphic artistry will be apparent in subsequent chapters. The tracts are moral in both outcome and in commentary. Murders which did not yield a satisfactory kind of lesson were simply not chosen as subjects for tracts. There were certainly hundreds of brutal, morally artless, and pointless murders committed in England, yielding at least equal value in horrible appeal. But the artists in the genre, and in the corresponding drama, had a concept of their craft which ruled out meaningless brutality. They even, it would seem, considered their stories to be tragedies. Thus a pretentiously styled tract by one W. R., a servant of the victim, is called *The Most Horrible and Tragicall Murther of the Right Honorable, the Vertuous, and Valerous Gentleman, John Lord Burgh* (1591). And Robert Yarington dramatizes two such murders in *Two Lamentable Tragedies* (1601). The only possible tragic meaning in these works must be sought in the impressiveness of the providential retribution, for the human agents are humble citizens without heroic stature and the actual murders are without any frightening qualities.[21]

What is awesome is the way Providence works. In *The Most Horrible and Tragicall Murther*, Cosby, the murderer, got on his "lustie strong Geldinge . . . , but he was no sooner on his backe, but he presently fell lame, and was not able to carie him, suche is the just judgement of God that abhorreth murderers, and wil not theyre villainie be concealed" (sig. A 4ʳ). In another tract, a child who had had her tongue cut out so that she could not reveal the murderers of her brother miraculously regained her speech and reported the murder.[22] The retribution in this tract is extended to more than the judicial outcome of the action, for the author comments that "a guilty conscience Salamander-like lives always in fire, that his dayes are dreadfull, his nights terrible" (sig. B 4ᵛ).

Two of the murder tracts avow that they were published

[21] A basic survey of the genre and its artistic limitations is to be found in Henry Hitch Adams, *English Domestic Or, Homiletic Tragedy 1575 to 1642* (New York, 1943).

[22] *The Most Cruell and Bloody Murther Committed by an Inkeepers Wife, Called Annis Dell, and Her Sonne George Dell, Foure Yeeres Since* (1606).

for example's sake.²³ But the inevitable luridness of their titles (e.g., *A Horrible Creuel and Bloudy Murther*, 1614) and their delight in the details of bloodshed make their purely pious motive suspect. Shakespeare is perhaps influenced by the titles and the manner when he has Macbeth say that "murders have been perform'd / Too terrible for the ear" (III. iv. 76–77). Nevertheless, if Shakespeare read them, he was also influenced by the tracts in a manner more valuable than simple shock at their horror. They represent, in the minor artistry of their concept of murder tragedy, a lesson that he invariably incorporates in the moral design of his tragedies, possibly, as we shall see, in the amazing appropriateness of the punishment and certainly in the more than proverbial lesson that murder, like the tongueless child, will speak with most miraculous organ. At the very least, since some critics feel that *Macbeth* is fundamentally a play about murder, and because these tracts and their comparable plays achieved notoriety and a certain conventional, if limited, artistry of murder depiction, they are worthy of attention. And they are decidedly one of the most popular kinds of secular sensationalism in the period.

Another large segment of the sensational literature was that dealing with witches, and because the subject is so important to *Macbeth* I shall have more to say later about this body of popular writings. Like the murder tracts, these are primarily detailed, journalistic accounts. All of the clinical symptoms of possession, usually of children, are tirelessly given, and they must have been more fascinating to the Elizabethans in their tone of earnest conviction than they are today. Shakespeare probably, however, gleaned from them some physical details in his depiction of the Witches, and I suspect that he depended upon their notoriety, more than upon the favor of King James, for audience response to the Witches in *Macbeth*.

One way in which these tracts contributed to his purpose was to make witchcraft a subject of frightening spiritual concern. Shakespeare could be confident that his Witches would be viewed as more than spectacle (they are little more than

---

²³.*Two Most Unnaturall and Bloodie Murthers* (1605), p. 1; *A Most Horrible & Detestable Murther Committed by a Bloodie Man upon His Owne Wife* (1595), sig. A 2ʳ.

24 · OUR NAKED FRAILTIES

this in Middleton); they would serve worthily a moral function in a morally sensational play.

One of the largest spiritual aspects of witches was their place in a scheme of divine punishment. They do not meaninglessly proliferate in "these our desperate daies" but are the result of God's permitting Satan to multiply "the broude of them" as a scourge for our sinns."[24] But the treatises seek their edifying aims not primarily in the metaphysics of demonology but in the simpler techniques of reporting the horrors witches have been responsible for. Thus one tract asserts:

> There is not anie Christian (I am sure) but in heart will relent, and with great admiration, lift up his eyes toward heaven, and stande amazed at the wicked practises of six of the most notorious wicked Witches that ever they heard of: who (giving both bodyes and soules to eternall damnation) committed so many inhumaine Murders..., causing strange hayle and tempest..., that I thinke it a matter worthy to be kept in memorie, whereby the shamefull end of such malafactors, may serve as a notable example to our eyes, a griefe to the godly, and a terrour to the wicked and reprobate people.[25]

It is not impossible that Shakespeare's Witches had a comparable effect upon the audience and because of their uncommonly awesome nature served as a terror to sinners in the pit as they seem unable to do to sinners today. Another tract, emphasizing the strangeness of the moral lesson miraculously conveyed by possessed children in their fits, is confident that if the reader could have heard it, "he would not have thought himself better edified at ten Sermons."[26]

All three of the witch tracts referred to have *strange* in their title, testifying to more than an attempt at matching "ten sermons" (though sermons, too, could be strange). Murders, witches, and other disturbing and exciting phenomena were

---

[24] *A Rehearsall Both Straung and True, of Hainous and Horrible Actes Committed by Elizabeth Stile* [1579], sig. A 2ʳ. For a fuller account of "why God permits the Devil so to busy himself with witchcraft," see Francesco Maria Guazzo, *Compendium Maleficarum* (1608), trans. by E. A. Ashwin; ed. by Rev. Montague Summers (London, 1929), p. 111.

[25] *A Strange Report of Sixe Most Notorious Witches* (1601), sig. A 2ʳ.

[26] *The Most Strange and Admirable Discoverie of the Three Witches of Warboys* (1593), sig. F 4ʳ.

grouped by writers in a classification that suggested a dark, foreboding kind of mystery, threatening to man's sense of security in his sinful state. Indeed, one of the age's largest bodies of popular writing concerned "strange" happenings. Many of these, like those on murder and witchcraft, are so germane to *Macbeth* that the suspicion is warranted that Shakespeare, for motives which were doubtless of the highest, seems to have knowingly drawn upon almost the entire repertory for his play. The subjects range from unusual babies and births (perhaps relevant to the mysterious role of babies in *Macbeth*) to portents of Heaven's displeasure. The commonplaces of subject matter are described in *A True and Most Dreadfull Discourse of a Woman Possessed with the Devill* (1584):

> Many are the woonders which hath lately happened, as of suddaine and straunge death upon perjured persons, straunge sights in the Aier, straunge birthes on the Earth: Earth quakes, commetts and fiery Impressions, and all to put us in mynde of God, whose woorkes are wonderfull.[27]

The purpose of the tract is also conventional: to alert sinners to threatened Doomsday. And although Doomsday is strongly suggested in the imagery of *Macbeth*, perhaps the message of another tract better expresses the sensational value generally of this disturbing genre:

> As nothing can moove or stirre man more effectually, unto the feeling of his owne sins, then the lawe of God, thundred out, & threatned against the conscience of his iniquity: so, nothing can draw him, more forcibly unto repentance, then the sencible sight and feeling, of fearefull and mighty plagues, heavenly threatninges, and strange and prodigious wonders, drawn by the efficient cause (God) from the operations of earthy, ayrie, watry, & heavenly supernal Elementes.[28]

The pious justification of sensationalism is conspicuous here,

[27] Sig. A 3ᵛ. See also Anthony Mundy, *A View of Sundry Examples Reporting Many Straunge Murthers, Sundry Persons Perjured, Signes, and Tokens of Gods Anger Towards Us. What Straunge and Monstrous Children Have of Late Been Borne* (1580).
[28] Thomas Day, *Wonderfull Straunge Sightes Seene in the Element, over the Citie of London and Other Places . . . : Most Strange and Fearefull to the Beholders* [1583], [p. 2].

in that man's "sencible sight and feeling" of strange phenomena are unparalleled in drawing him to repentance. Similarly in *The Strange Newes* (1561), the imminence of such "great evil" will make it "perse the eies and mindes of all men," illustrating the tendency of these didactic tracts to prove that "for the most part the calamities of mankind be sermons of repentence" (sig. B 5). Obviously, even if the literary critics could not of themselves do so, the writers of these alarming treatises gave the most respectable of credentials to man's sensible soul.

Thomas Day, we also recall, had asserted that nothing can stir man to a feeling of his own sins like God's laws "thundred out, & threatned against the conscience of his iniquity." Probably the most influential kind of sensational writing produced by the age was that of published sermons. As one preacher observed, doubtless from personal experience,

> when thou hearest the preacher declare the glorious majesty of God, his sharp punishing of sin, the wretched estate of man, that of himself can do nothing but sin, and the everlasting pains appointed for all hard-hearted sinners; it maketh him to quake, to enter into himself, condemn himself. . . .[29]

There was in these sermons a kinship with sensational tragedy in their emphasis upon guilt and punishment and in the way they made the auditor "to quake, to enter into himself." Robert Burton, uneasy about the psychological effect of their "horror" upon congregations, even referred to them as "tragical."[30] These thundering utterances were considered inferior only to the Bible in the terror of their hold upon the sense of guilt in all listeners.[31] Edmund Rudierd compares his admonitory book to the Bible in "that it is so full of terror against both the doer, and sufferer of sinne, that it will make any Christian heart to feare, and tremble: for feare, you may find many wonderfull and unwonted judgments, not only against wicked sinners, but also

---

[29] James Pilkington, "Exposition upon Certain Chapters of Nehemiah" (1562), in *The Works of James Pilkington, B. D.*, ed. by Rev. James Scholefield (Parker Society), (Cambridge, 1842), p. 291.

[30] *The Anatomy of Melancholy*, p. 942.

[31] See, for example, John Hooper, *Certeine Comfortable Expositions*, ed. by Rev. Charles Nevinson (Parker Society), (Cambridge, 1852), p. 322.

against such as have bin favourers of sinne."[32] Both the Bible and the sermons were full of examples of God's wonderful judgments upon sinners, and surely these judgments were a primary source of their appeal. This may have been at least partially the case with sensational tragedy. One amateur but talented Renaissance dramatist, we know, had seen his tragedy as the thing to catch the conscience of the King. Though this purpose of tragedy is today critically unfashionable, I suspect that our more sophisticated aesthetics of tragic power are not much more satisfactory than Hamlet's and that for a play like *Macbeth* there may be a lesson to be learned from the types of speaking and writing which demonstrably made the greatest emotional impression upon the people. Catching the conscience of Macbeth and, through him, of the audience was surely a major source of the play's power and a source that helps immensely to explain why there is so much sensational art in the play.

IV

What especially links *Macbeth* and the religious works in this kind of power is the concentration upon wonderful judgments and punishment. In the next chapter I shall take up the specific kind of evil and, in part, the punishment for it which we find in *Macbeth*. Here I shall prepare for that presentation by describing punishment as it appears, less subtly but with some power, in the religious literature.

The principal and ultimate form that punishment took was of course hell. Thomas Nashe tells how "Preachers threaten us for sinne with thys adjunct, eternall, as paynes eternall, eternall damnation, eternall horror and vexation."[33] In their description of hell, what is artistically relevant is the importance put upon the necessity for feeling its horrors with the senses. Arthur Dent praises the Bible for speaking "terribly to our senses, concerning the estate of the damned persons calling it hel fire damnation, the lake that burneth with fire & brimstone

[32] *The Thunderbolt of Gods Wrath against Hard-Hearted and Stiff-Necked Sinners* (1618), Epistle Dedicatorie.
[33] *Christs Teares over Jerusalem* (1593), in *The Works of Thomas Nashe*, ed. by Ronald B. McKerrow, with corrections and supplementary notes by F. P. Wilson (Oxford, 1958), II, 168.

for ever."[34] The purpose of hell, after all, was to make sinners feel. One of the best accounts of the aesthetics of punishment in hell is given by Jeremiah Dyke. "Seared consciences" may be quiet now,

> yet there will come a day that this seared crustinesse shall bee scaled off, & those consciences which were not sensible of sinne, shall be most sensible of paine: though they were past feeling in the committing of sinne, yet they shall bee all feeling in suffering punishment for sinne. God will pare off that brawninesse from their consciences, and will pare them so to the quicke, that they shall feele and most sensibly feele that which here they would not feele.[35]

Perhaps a major purpose of sensational drama was to pare off "brawniness" from the consciences of the audience. And this is a less naive purpose than may at first appear. Guilty souls (as most audiences are) sitting at a play can, as Hamlet declared, be struck so to the soul that they will proclaim, not publicly but most painfully to themselves, their malefactions. Most modern readers, and even modern scholars, are aware of hell-fire sermons only by hearsay. These sermons are a cliché of intellectual history, yet few scholars can name even one of them, and I have never seen them listed in print. We would do well to read some of them for the light they shed not only upon the Elizabethan art of sensation but upon the ethics of punishment reflected in the drama.[36] Shakespeare seems to have been aware of at least the sensory impact of these sermons. The Ghost tells Hamlet:

---

[34] *A Sermon of Repentaunce* (1583), sigs. D 1ᵛ-D 2ʳ.

[35] *Good Conscience: or a Treatise Shewing the Nature, Meanes, Marks, Benefit, and Necessity Thereof* (1624), p. 42.

[36] A few of the religious writings on hell are the work by Arthur Dent mentioned above; George Gascoigne's *The Droomme of Doomes Day* (1576; trans. from Innocent III), in *Works*, ed. by John W. Cunliffe (Cambridge, 1907), particularly, p. 436; Hugh Latimer, *The Seven Sermons of the Reverend Father M. Hugh Latimer* (1562), in *Sermons of Hugh Latimer*, ed. by Rev. George E. Corrie (Parker Society), (Cambridge, 1844), the seventh sermon; Thomas Tymme, *A Silver Watch-Bell* (1605), Chapter IV (more than eighteen printings between 1605 and 1640); and especially Myles Coverdale, *The Hope of the Faithful* [1579], in *Remains of Myles Coverdale*, ed. by George Pearson (Parker Society), (Cambridge, 1846), Chapters XXVI-XXVIII. Coverdale cites virtually every possible Biblical hint of hell.

> But that I am forbid
> To tell the secrets of my prison-house,
> I could a tale unfold whose lightest word
> Would harrow up thy soul, freeze thy young blood,
> Make thy two eyes, like stars, start from their spheres,
> Thy knotty and combined locks to part
> And each particular hair to stand on end,
> Like quills upon the fretful porpentine.
>
> *(I.v.13-20)*

This tale is actually told, in a specific manner that demonstrates Shakespeare's detailed knowledge of a physical hell, by Claudio in *Measure for Measure* (III.i.118–128),[37] and the passage is justly valued as the most intense poetry in the play. But what probably impressed him most in the writings and preachings on hell was the way they forced sinners to feel. In the 1616 version of *Doctor Faustus* Marlowe displayed a similar awareness in Faustus's vision of hell. The Bad Angel orders Faustus to "let thine eyes with horror stare / Into that vast perpetual torture-house" and proceeds to a terrifying description of it. When Faustus complains that he has seen enough to torture him, the Bad Angel insists: "Nay, thou must feel them, taste the smart of all."[38]

A physical hell looms fairly large in the imagery and meaning of *Macbeth*, but the conventional features of its kind of punishment—notably the fire—are of course far less evident than in *Doctor Faustus*. Macbeth himself does not seem to be so much concerned with the life to come, and one of the finest features of the play is the power and adequacy with which retribution for sin is meted out during this life. But we shall see that certain penal aspects of hell are of utmost importance in the play, and they can reasonably be shown to be so only if we attribute to the age at least an emerging concept that hell, for the sinner, exists here and now. Marlowe's Mephostophilis, speaking on the earth, tells Faustus, "Why, this is hell, nor

---

[37] For Shakespeare's knowledge of hell in this passage, see John E. Hankins, "The Pains of the Afterworld: Fire, Wind, and Ice in Milton and Shakespeare," *PMLA*, LXXI (1956), 482-495.

[38] Christopher Marlowe, *Doctor Faustus*, ed. by John D. Jump (The Revels Plays), (London, 1962), scene XIX, ll. 116-117, 129.

am I out of it" (scene iii. line 78). Calvin and Luther both held that "hell is a state of mind, the condition rather than the location of those doomed by God to destruction."[39] Although hell was thought to be under the earth, Gascoigne was typical in affirming that "all places are penall unto the reprobate. Which doe alwayes carry torments and vexation against themselves."[40] "What is everlasting death, or hell?" Thomas Becon asked. "In this life it is the perpetual grudge and horrible fear of conscience, the distress and tediousness of the mind, dreading the wrath of God, which the devil increaseth in the unfaithful; as it is plainly declared. Also hell is taken for extreme temptation, which almost leadeth us down to desperation."[41] Many other writers equate present hell with the pains of conscience. Jeremiah Dyke calls conscience the greatest of torments and "farre more truely the suburbes of Hell, then is the Popish Purgatory."[42] John Woolton demonstrates how far the age had progressed from the conventional horrors of hell:

> For assuredly furies doe always pursue and chase the wicked, not with burning torches and firebrandes, as interludes and playes sette out, but with horrores of Conscience, and anguish of minde, wayting always upon mischievous men, even as the shadowe foloweth the body, not sufering them to breath and as it were, to pause one momente from trembling and feare.[43]

Hell, therefore, could be viewed as a present state of "extreme temptation," leading through horrors of conscience

[39] Susan Snyder, "The Left Hand of God: Despair in Medieval and Renaissance Tradition," *Studies in the Renaissance*, XII (1965), 27.

[40] *The Droomme of Doomes Day*, p. 266. John Donne preached that the conventional torments of hell are preferable to those in this life, such as "a spirituall burthen, a perplexity that sinks our understanding, or a guiltinesse that depresses our conscience." *The Sermons of John Donne*, ed. by G. R. Potter and Evelyn Simpson (Berkeley and Los Angeles, 1959), V, 336. An excellent modern study of punishment here, especially in terms of "psychological infelicity," is to be found in Roy W. Battenhouse, *Marlowe's Tamburlaine: A Study in Renaissance Moral Philosophy* (Nashville, 1941), pp. 99-113.

[41] "The Demands of Holy Scripture," in *Prayers and Other Pieces by Thomas Becon, S.T.P.* [1563], ed. by Rev. John Ayre (Parker Society), (Cambridge, 1844), p. 604.

[42] *Good Conscience*, p. 258.

[43] *A Discourse of the Conscience* (1576), sig. E 4r.

Sensational Background · 31

(which could pursue like furies) to "anguish of minde" and to desperation. The disastrous chain of consequences, with temptation implied, leading to hell on earth is well described in one of the most secular and popular plays of the period:

> There is a path upon your left-hand side,
> That leadeth from a guilty conscience
> Unto a forest of distrust and fear,
> A darksome place and dangerous to pass:
> There shall you meet with melancholy thoughts,
> Whose baleful humours if you but uphold,
> It will conduct you to despair and death. . . .[44]

In the hell on earth it is also important to differentiate between two important functions. According to Calvin, "Such weeping and gnashing of teeth is in that verie [i.e., true] Hell, not that whiche stirreth up the reprobate to seeke after God, but which only vexeth them with blinde tormentes."[45] There is, I think, an important difference in the hell which Macbeth inhabits between the comparatively benign horror of temptation and conscience which he at first undergoes and that part of his worsening career in which he is merely subject to "blinde tormentes." Further, in the hell on earth he would be at the mercy of the same spirits that would torment him below, and these could both tempt and punish. Their aim would of course not be to lead him "to seeke after God." Rather, according to one divine,

> there is a double worke to be considered in the evill ministring spirits, for either they are ministers of outward punishments onely, as in vexing and afflicting the bodie, so they worke by *immission*, and sending from God, or they also egge and tempt unto evill, so they worke onely by the *permission* and sufferance of God: . . . both these waies was Saul assaulted by Sathan: for both his bodie was vexed, and his minde tempted.[46]

For Macbeth, then, it should be possible to show that vir-

---

[44] Thomas Kyd, *The Spanish Tragedy*, ed. by Philip Edwards (The Revels Plays), (London, 1959), III.xi.13-19.
[45] *A Commentarie of John Calvin upon the First Booke of Moses Called Genesis*, trans. by Thomas Tymme (1578), Chapter 27, p. 582.
[46] Andrew Willet, *An Harmonie upon the First Booke of Samuel* (1607), p. 141.

tually his entire career in the play, from the tempting of his mind to the vexing of his body, is understandable in terms of demonic forces from hell, acting in a present hell on earth[47] and permitted by God. But our immediate concern is *punishment* here and now, and two aspects of the Renaissance doctrine of providential punishment remain to be considered.

One of the most deeply held and influential Renaissance theories of punishment was that it should fit, in kind as well as in degree, the crime. Secular crimes found such condign punishment as the loss of a hand for a writer of treasonable material. Divine punishment, more mysterious, was not always so explicably accurate, but in its sometimes allegorical appropriateness it lent itself admirably to poetic drama. It may also, in its surprising fitness, be conducive to the highest kind of tragic irony, a quality for which *Macbeth* is famous. (According to Aristotle, the "sensation" of apparently accidental events is greater if they appear to have a purpose, as when the statue of Mitys at Argus killed the man who caused his death, by falling on him.)

This kind of punishment, a religious sophistication of the primitive *lex talionis*, derives partially from the Old Testament, and though it was considerably modified in stage comedy by the Christian doctrine of mercy, it remained inexorably firm in tragedy and judicial practice.[48] The Hebraic admonitions were often cited in the Renaissance:

---

[47] Irving Ribner comes helpfully close to my view of the play, including a hell on earth, in a brief but suggestive comment: "In this play Shakespeare explores the damnation of a human soul, a man of heroic proportions, with whom we can have a full measure of sympathy, who, by his own deliberate and knowing moral choice, commits a crime in violation of his own natural feelings, suffers in his isolation a hell on earth, and is finally damned." *The Tragedy of Macbeth*, ed. by George Lyman Kittredge (revised by Irving Ribner), (Waltham, Massachusetts, 1966), p. xiv. I am not sure of our "full measure of sympathy" unless the reference is to the Macbeth who puts down the rebellion, the Macbeth whom we have not seen.

[48] According to Sister Mary Bonaventure Mroz, "The Christian dispensation repeated with emphasis the Divine sanctions of the Mosaic law," yet "the God Who by redeeming love raises men to Divine sonship remains no less the God of Justice, the avenging custodian of the moral law." *Divine Vengeance: A Study of the Philosophical Backgrounds of the Revenge Motif as It Appears in Shakespeare's Chronicle History Plays* (Washington, D. C., 1941), pp. 10-11.

> Hee that diggeth a pit shal fall therein, and he that rolleth a stone, it shal returne unto him.[49]

And again:

> The heathen are sunken downe in the pit, that thei made: in the net that they hid is their fote taken.
>
> The Lord is knowen by executing judgement: the wicked is snared in the worke of his owne handes.
>
> *(Psalm 9:15–16)*

The Geneva commentator has appended approvingly to the first of these verses: "For God overthroweth the wicked in their enterprise." Partially, however, the tradition goes back to classical forms of punishment, such as that of Midas, and especially that of pagan hell. *The Spanish Tragedy* draws upon Virgil for its picture of condign punishment. Andrea tells of the "deepest hell"

> Where bloody furies shakes their whips of steel,
> And poor Ixion turns an endless wheel:
> Where usurers are chok'd with melting gold,
> And wantons are embrac'd with ugly snakes,
> And murderers groan with never-killing wounds. . . .
>
> *(I.i.64–69)*

The major Elizabethan authority for this theory of punishment, drawing upon contemporary as well as classical and Biblical examples, was Thomas Beard's *The Theatre of Gods Judgements: Or, a Collection of Histories out of Sacred, Ecclesiasticall, and Prophane Authours, Concerning the Admirable Judgements of God upon the Transgressours of His Com-*

For *lex talionis* see especially pp. 20-22. Edmund Spenser, however, as it has just recently been shown by James E. Phillips, gave structure and meaning to Book V of *The Faerie Queene* by representing several levels or kinds of justice. See "Renaissance Concepts of Justice and the Structure of *The Faerie Queene*, Book V," *Huntington Library Quarterly*, XXXIII (1970), 103-120.

[49] Proverbs 26. My Scriptural quotations are all from a 1560 copy of the Geneva Bible, the version which Richmond Noble argues Shakespeare used in his mature plays. See his *Shakespeare's Biblical Knowledge* (London, 1935), pp. 75-76.

mandements (1596). So profusely and consistently does Beard demonstrate the inevitable punishment of evil that even a modern sinner cannot escape the overwhelming sense of unfailing and reassuringly adequate justice in the universe. What contributes most to this effect is not only the monumental scope of the work but Beard's purpose of producing "examples of those punishments that have fallen upon the heads of the transgressors of the same, according to the manner of their transgressions, of what sort soever" (p. 18). Examples appropriate to *Macbeth* will be noted later, but a good general example is that of the fate of Thomas Arondell, Archbishop of Canterbury, who, having "sought to stop the mouth of God in his ministers, and to hinder the passage of his Gospel, had his tongue so swollen that it stopped his owne mouth, that before his death he could neither swallow nor speake, and so through famine died in great despaire" (p. 46). This example has the advantage of showing that a certain amount of poetic symbolism and reach of the imagination was permitted and encouraged in this kind of essentially literary reinterpretation of human evil. In addition to Beard, perhaps most other Renaissance nondramatic writers on crime and punishment took advantage of this convention,[50] and it is difficult to see how, despite flagrant violations of modern notions of poetic justice in Shakespeare, it could miss impact upon the drama, especially since the retribution tended to be both sensational and amenable to imaginative shaping and symbolical interpretation.

Many of the nondramatic interpretations of the convention are of a subtlety not unworthy of literary attempts. An aspect that could apply to *Macbeth* concerns the punishment of and through the imagination. According to the Wisdom of Solomon (3:10), "the ungodlie shalbe punished according to their imaginacions." St. Thomas Aquinas is cited by a Renaissance writer to prove that "a man's body can be affected by his imagination in every way which is naturally correspondent

---

[50] Lily B. Campbell shows, for example, its importance in *The Mirror for Magistrates. Shakespeare's Tragic Heroes: Slaves of Passion* (New York, 1960; first published 1930), p. 8. See also John Woolton, *A Treatise of the Immortalitie of the Soule*, sigs. L 2ʳ–L 2ᵛ: "But it is fit that they should be afflicted with those things wherein they have offended."

with the imaginative faculty."[51] This theory would support the rightness of punishing the body through the imagination in terms of the condition of the imagination. But the imagination itself could also be the direct object of punishment. A favorite Biblical example of the tortured imagination was Nebuchadnezzar. According to John Woolton, he was divinely punished for his intolerably proud imagination by madness, "Which punishment many of the auncient Hebrues, and latter writers referre to the imagination of the king," though Woolton typically offers other explanations than the "stroke of God," including "witchecrafte and aboundance of melancholy humors in mannes body, wherewith the divill conjoyneth him selfe often times."[52] If, as Woolton suggests, the Devil may be the instrument of punishment, it is important to note that the Demon, "knowing the constitutions of men, and the particular diseases whereunto they are inclined, taks the vantage of some, and secondeth the nature of the disease by the concurrence of his owne delusion thereby corrupting the imagination...."[53] One may infer from this that if the imagination is, as it so often was, the most actively evil part of man, the Devil would concentrate both his temptation and his punishment upon this faculty. I suspect that this is what happens in *Macbeth*. It was certainly true that, as Aquinas's statement would imply, the Devil-tormented imagination would affect the body, too, if only because the imagination was part of the soul sensible.

Still another dominant human evil in *Macbeth* was seen as subject to this satisfyingly accurate kind of punishment. This was ambition. This, "the strongest and most powerfull passion that is," shows its self-penal nature by being

> a fire which encreaseth by that nourishment that is given unto it. Wherein it truly paieth his master: for ambition is only just in this, that it sufficeth for his owne punishment, and is executioner to it selfe. The wheele of Ixion is the motion of his desires, which turne and returne up and downe, never giving rest unto his minde.[54]

---

[51] Guazzo, *Compendium Maleficarum*, p. 1. The reference is to *Contra Gentiles*, III.103.

[52] *A Treatise of the Immortalitie of the Soule*, sigs. K 1ᵛ–K 2ʳ.

[53] William Perkins, *A Discourse of the Damned Art of Witchcraft* (1608), p. 24.

[54] Charron, *Of Wisdome*, pp. 79, 82.

36 · OUR NAKED FRAILTIES

I shall devote a chapter, the eighth, to the full working out of this kind of onerous punishment, fraught with the most hopelessly painful kind of sensation suffered by Macbeth.

Punishment of the evil imagination and of ambition are, however, only special examples of a larger concept of condign punishment. At midcareer in crime, Shakespeare's Richard III states: "But I am in / So far in blood that sin will pluck on sin" (IV.ii.64-65). The full meaning of this statement has apparently not been recognized. It means not only that now Richard feels himself hopelessly committed to a chain of sins so that return is impossible. It also suggests something much more painful for Richard, in that all the ensuing sins take the form of punishment for the preceding ones. Thomas Becon had written:

> That God punisheth sin with loss and danger both of body and goods, with sickness, pestilence, and such other, none I think doubteth; but that he punisheth sin by sin, and sin by errors and heresies, the world cannot so clearly perceive.[55]

John Donne also preached on sin plucking on sin:

> Are not the judgements of God speedily enough executed upon thy soule and body together, every day, when as soon as thou commitst a sin, thou art presently left to thine Inpenitence, to thine Insensibleness, and Obduration? Nay, the judgement is more speedy then so: for, that very sin it self, was a punishment of thy former sins.[56]

The doctrine has solid foundation in Aquinas, who explains the punishment as follows:

> For passions, temptations of the devil, and the like are causes of sin, but are impeded by the help of Divine grace which is withdrawn on account of sin. Wherefore since the withdrawal of grace is a punishment, and is from God, as stated above, the result is that the sin which ensues from this is also a punishment

---

[55] "The Demandes of Holy Scripture," in *Prayers and Other Pieces of Thomas Becon, S.T.P.*, ed. by Rev. John Ayre (Parker Society), (Cambridge, 1884), p. 605.
[56] "A Sermon Preached at White-hall, April 21, 1616," in *The Sermons of John Donne*, ed. cit., I, 177.

accidentally ... because, to wit, when men are deprived of the help of Divine grace, they are overcome by their passions.[57]

The explanations of both Donne and Aquinas are useful to the student of *Macbeth*: punishments by both moral insensibility and passion are found in the play, and the withdrawal of divine grace has more than an abstract and dimly theological impact upon the suffering of Macbeth.

As we draw nearer to a concentration upon *Macbeth* itself as a tragedy of sensation in which a peculiarly appropriate kind of punishment operates, we would do well to inquire whether there is any evidence, beyond the apparent prevalence of this theory of punishment, that Shakespeare used it in his other plays. It appears rather faintly in *Richard III*, considered in isolation from the preceding histories, but in relation to those plays it demonstrates a fairly appropriate kind of punishment for the three Yorkist brothers. Beard, moreover, had chosen the story of Richard as a prize example "Of such as have murdered their rulers or Princes" to show that these malefactors cannot enjoy any of the fruits of their crime.[58] In the major tragedies the theory invites larger and more symbolic interpretation. Hamlet is especially dedicated to the satisfying artistry of having "the enginer / Hoist with his own petar." And Providence in the play seems to cooperate with his sense of condign punishment, for Laertes confesses, "I am justly kill'd with mine own treachery" (V.ii.318); and Claudius, that artist in poisoning, has finally forced on him the poisoned chalice he has prepared, and he finds punishment in the way his sin unexpectedly multiplies even to the unintended poisoning of his Queen. Horatio finally summarizes the actions of the play as "purposes mistook / Fall'n on the inventors' heads" (V.ii.395-396). Othello can be seen as suffering primarily through his imagination because of the foul ideas and images nurtured in his imagination by a demidevil. And in *King Lear* it is a commonplace of criticism, though the penal theory behind it has not been understood, that the sensual Gloucester suffers

[57] Thomas Aquinas, *The Summa Theologica*, trans. by Fathers of the English Dominican Province (London, 1915), Second Number (QQ. XLIX-LXXXIX), vol. VII, pt. II, 462, Q. 87. Art. 2.
[58] *The Theatre of Gods Judgements*, p. 230.

through the body, just as the spiritually flawed King must suffer through the mind and do so by exchanging the proud, insensible control of sanity for the humble, feeling instruction in mortality which he finds in madness. This is not, of course, to insist upon complete poetic justice in these plays, notably in *King Lear*. Poetic justice would demand that the virtuous receive temporal reward or continued life on earth. This is too shallow for Shakespeare. My insistence is rather upon something special in *Macbeth*, that which derives from its being so centrally a tragedy of crime and punishment. There is probably, in fact, no major Elizabethan tragedy comparable to *Macbeth* in "judgment here," specifically in the way bloody instructions return to plague the inventor and the poisoned chalice is commended to the lips of the criminal.

The final aspect of punishment to be considered is commonly based in hell, but *Doctor Faustus* offers dramatic proof that it could be found on earth.[59] I refer to the two ultimate kinds of punishment, most influentially enunciated by Aquinas: pain of sense (*poena sensus*) and pain of loss (*poena damni*). According to Aquinas the pain of sense is the punishment for turning to a mutable good, and the pain of loss is the punishment for turning away from the immutable good.[60] The exact symptoms of these torments are never fully or invariably given. Gascoigne, translating Pope Innocent III, describes the pain of loss as "extreame miserie and lack of the heavenly fruition" and the pain of sense as "the sencible paynes of hell which are the punishmentes of eternall fyre."[61] But these were more liberally interpreted in the Renaissance so as to apply, respectively, to the major torments of mind and body suffered here as well as in hell. Although Shakespeare did not try to apply them with precision to *Macbeth*, their traditional force, strengthened by Renaissance interpretation, provides the best explanation for the structure of the play and the twofold nature of the suffering in it. The pain of sense is especially applicable to the major kind

---

[59] Indeed, for a part of this concept I have been much helped by Douglas Cole's excellent application of *poena damni* to *Doctor Faustus* in *Suffering and Evil in the Plays of Christopher Marlowe* (Princeton, 1962), Chapter V.

[60] *The Summa Theologica*, vol. VII, pt. II, 466, Q. 87. Art. 4.

[61] *The Droomme of Doomes Day*, p. 283.

of torment received throughout approximately the first four acts of the play, and the pain of loss, though operating as early as the murder of Duncan, is not felt fully until the fifth act.

These two modes of suffering are, moreover, not only amenable to but also the ultimate form of the doctrine of condign punishment. Indeed, they are required in order to dignify the doctrine humanely and not simply supernaturally. They lift it from the vindictive to the regretful but necessary. He who willfully chooses to reject God loses, in a sense that is more than punishment, the presence of God. And he who chooses something less than God is given, but not primarily punished by, the painful aspects of what he has chosen. There is, I think, this sadness of willfully espoused pain in *Macbeth*; and the play is the greater and the wiser for it.

V

In this chapter we have studied various kinds of sensational writing prevalent in the age, particularly those that might help to illuminate *Macbeth*, and we have seen how these writings helped, by their moral purpose and moving power, to justify for the Renaissance an appeal to the senses which might otherwise have been suspect. We have studied, as perhaps the most important kind of sensational writing, that which bears upon punishment, for punishment is the occasion, though not the only cause, of the most meaningful kind of sensation in *Macbeth*.

It would be interesting to speculate further upon the fuller meaning of punishment in the Renaissance. The era was obviously unusually given to the most violent and sanguinary kinds of pious retribution, and the popularity of revenge tragedy affords further evidence that "Vengence is mine: I will repay, saith the Lord" (Romans 12:19) could produce more violently satisfying punishments than could human agents. But we must be limited to the question of how the punitive torment of the hero is conducive not merely to the ethical doctrine of the age, but to the aims of tragedy. A part of the answer to this question has been given in the present chapter. We are dealing here with an unusual kind of play, one in which the protagonist is the criminal. In *Othello* only a brief attention can be given to the punishment of Iago. But in *Macbeth* the very soul and power of the play must be in the significance and adequacy and wisdom of the punishment. These must be deeply felt, not from a distance but from the closest participation with the hero. And their immediacy must be enforced by the highest artistry and meaning of sensation. John Reynolds, the Jacobean writer of a work like Beard's, gives through his description of the artistic aims of his book a clue to what might be the foundation for the kind of power found in sensationally punitive works of higher artistry. Considering, he writes, the foulness of the crimes against the virtuous victims,

> some through blood, others through poyson, as also Gods miraculous detection, and severe punishment thereof, in revenging blood for blood, and death for death, yea, many times repaying it home with interest, and rewarding one death with many, that the consideration of these bloudy and mournefull tragedies may by their examples, strike astonishment to our thought, and amazement to our senses.[62]

These works of condign retribution are confidently labeled tragedies, and their power lies in astonishing the mind and amazing the senses. Reynolds cannot compare with Shakespeare in either of these functions, but much of the sensory immediacy of *Macbeth* may derive from a comparable purpose and method.

But an Elizabethan dramatist has explained the compelling power that we feel in *Macbeth*, in terms of its grip upon audience guilt, perhaps as well as can be done. One of the major functions of tragedy, he writes, is "attaching the consciences of spectators, finding themselves toucht in presenting the vices of others."[63] Probably no other English play attaches our conscience so deeply as *Macbeth;* and, because of the immediacy and inevitability of the punishment, we yield to it emotionally, even while resisting the evil of the play, and undergo the catharsis of having indulged fully in the primal drama of sinful humanity: crime and punishment.

---

[62] *The Triumphs of Gods Revenge* (1621), "The Author his Preface to the Reader," sig A 2ʳ.

[63] Thomas Heywood, *An Apology for Actors* (1612), sig F 3ʳ.

Chapter III

The Evil

If *Macbeth* is a drama of crime and punishment, the nature of the evil in the play is of first importance. But the generally acknowledged mysteriousness of the evil also is important in defining the sensational artistry of the play, for in no other work does Shakespeare succeed in creating—nor does he try to create—a more disturbing, more pervasive, or, I think, more darkly fundamental kind of evil. And it is significant that almost all critics of the play, baffled by the meaning of the evil, have elected to ascribe their bafflement to Shakespeare's art.

G. Wilson Knight, praising *Macbeth* as "Shakespeare's most profound and mature vision of evil," admits that analysis of the play is for this reason of great value, "but it is not easy."[1] Our reaction to this elusive evil, he proposes, is that of a fear that follows nightmare, "wherein there is an experience of something at once insubstantial and unreal to the understanding and appallingly horrible to the feelings: this is the evil of *Macbeth*" (p. 149). This evil cannot be explained in terms of the will or causality, nor is it responsive to the critical intellect (p. 158). Knight's essay owes much of its suggestive power to its renunciation of the critical faculty in favor of emotional awe at something not meant to be grasped logically. His own artistic tech-

---

[1] *The Wheel of Fire* (Cleveland and New York, 1963; first published 1930), p. 140.

nique is modeled upon that which he attributes to Shakespeare. Next to Knight, the most impressionistic artist of interpretation of the evil is Bradley. Commenting beautifully upon the dark and supernatural forces in the play, Bradley generalizes that Shakespeare has "concentrated attention on the obscurer regions of man's being, on phenomena which make it seem that he is in the power of secret forces lurking below, and independent of his consciousness and will."[2] All this, Bradley concludes, gives us "a dread of the presence of evil not only in its recognized seat but all through and around our mysterious nature." Even Granville-Barker, who is noted more for theatrical than for impressionistic explanations, when commenting upon the lines,

>   Light thickens; and the crow
>   Makes wings to th' rooky wood,
>
>   *(III.ii.50–51)*

asks: "How explain the sense of chill, mysterious evil with which that fills us? It is a dramatic miracle, and there is no more to be said."[3]

The sensitivity and eloquence of these critics, together with the unquestionable presence of something mysterious about the play's evil, are almost enough to make us assent to "there is no more to be said." But although most of my concern will be with ascertaining what kind of evil Shakespeare made palpable, I cannot ignore what I consider to be some of the more explainable features of the less palpable evil and the techniques by which it is made mysterious.

II

The atmosphere of *Macbeth* is indeed that of a nightmare world in which the greatest vigilance seems necessary but in which it is nearly impossible to keep that vigilance. Banquo

---

[2] *Shakespearean Tragedy* (New York, 1949; first published 1904), p. 338.

[3] Harley Granville-Barker, *On Dramatic Method* (New York, 1956), pp. 115–116. One wishes that Granville-Barker had extended his *Prefaces* to include *Macbeth*.

makes an important statement about the kind of evil which the major participants in the play must face:

> A heavy summons lies like lead upon me,
> And yet I would not sleep: merciful Powers!
> Restrain in me the cursed thought that nature
> Gives way to in repose!
>
> *(II.i.6–9)*

These cursed thought are unquestionably mysterious and dark. They may be related to that fundamental evil in man's imagination which William Perkins had described. But they here have also a more tangible, though still mysterious, origin. Banquo had "dreamt last night of the three Weird Sisters" (II.i.20), and it is doubtless the impact of that evil dream, lingering in a dimly remembered nightmare, that excites his apprehension. One authority on demonology had written:

> Therefore they bring that misfortune upon themselves, who give themselves to sleep without having first prayed and besought Almighty God for His help; since . . . that is their safest shield and protection against all the wiles of the Prince of Darkness. But the minds of men who are about to sleep too often wander into evil imaginings. . . .[4]

The Powers to whom Banquo prays are appropriately the order of angels appointed by God to guard against and restrain demons.[5] The evil here is certainly that of the diabolical, acting through the Witches. The mysteriousness of the phenomena is enhanced, however, by Shakespeare's vagueness in identifying the agents and workings of the diabolical. The real nature of the Witches is never clearly identified, and such terms as "instruments of Darkness" conduce to a feeling of vague terror more than of comprehension. We shall see presently how the very namelessness of evil contributes to its horror, just as the Witches are often referred to as "these" and "they." But we may first note that not only Banquo testifies to the ways in which evil forces assail the imperfectly guarded mind in repose. Macbeth

---

[4] Nicolas Remy, *Demonolatry*, trans. by E. A. Ashwin; ed. by Rev. Montague Summers (London, 1930), p. 108.
[5] Walter Clyde Curry, *Shakespeare's Philosophical Patterns* (Baton Rouge, La., 1959; first published 1937), p. 81.

knows that in this world "wicked dreams abuse / The curtain'd sleep" (II.i.50–51), and the perils of losing moral vigilance are clear from his lines,

> Good things of Day begin to droop and drowse,
> Whiles Night's black agents to their preys do rouse.
> *(III.ii.52–53)*

Although the sinister quality of the hovering evil, ever ready to attack, is enhanced by the vagueness of "Night's black agents," there should be no question but that the meaning of these agents is intended to be demonic.

The ambiguous role of Nature in the play also contributes to the sense of undefined evil. Nature can be regarded as a force of moral control, as in "Now o'er the one half-world / Nature seems dead" (II.i.49–50), and we shall see that the breach of the natural order is one of the clearly stated themes of evil in the play. But Banquo's uneasy reference to "the cursed thoughts that nature / Gives way to in repose" suggests that not all of Nature in the play is benign. Nature is, rather, similar to the imagination in its post-Lapsarian corruption. As in *King Lear*, it can all too readily revert, especially n the form of human or animal nature, into the evil of wild nature, untouched by the civilizing grace of God or man. This kind of reversion actually happens when Duncan's horses, "Beauteous and swift, the minions of their race, / Turn'd wild in nature" (II.iv.15–16). Other references to Nature bear out this meaning. The bleeding Captain refers to

> the merciless Macdonwald
> (Worthy to be a rebel, for to that
> The multiplying villainies of nature
> Do swarm upon him) . . . .
> *(I.ii.9–12)*

Nature is here seen as spawning unnumbered evils, and notable among them is the first of the evils defined in the play, rebellion, though this evil is later seen to be contrary to the better sort of Nature. But the passage in which Nature appears in most sinister form is Lady Macbeth's speech summoning the "murd'ring ministers" that "wait on Nature's mischief" (I.v.48–50). Admittedly this could mean mischief done upon Nature, but more likely it is similar in meaning to "the multiplying villainies of nature." The demonic ministers are pictured as alert to assail those who are vulnerable because of evil in Nature, as Lady Macbeth wills herself to be. Nature, with its mischief and its villainies, is responsive to humanly solicited evil. But of course this aspect of Nature in the play, though thus explained, still retains much of the unnamed mystery of Bradley's "secret forces lurking below."

Another cause of the mysterious guise of evil in the play is that, as L. C. Knights has noted, there is a pervasive reversal of values.[6] In this respect, as in so many others, the vocabulary of the Witches, depending upon whether we take these strange beings to be originators or merely responsive aspects of evil, either prompts or reflects the vocabulary or thoughts of the human actors. It is well known that the Witches' "Fair is foul and foul is fair" (I.i.11) is echoed in Macbeth's "So foul and fair a day I have not seen" (I.iii.38). But to my knowledge it has not been adequately noticed that every appearance of *fair* in the play must, according to the Witches' equation, in a darker sense be also read as *foul*. It must certainly be read so in Banquo's question,

> Good Sir, why do you start, and seem to fear
> Things that do sound so fair?
>
> *(I.iii.51–52)*

And so read, there is painful irony, forever damning Lady Macbeth, in Duncan's words to her,

> Fair and noble hostess,
> We are your guest to-night.
>
> *(I.vi.24–25)*

Even without the vocabulary, the equation is important in the play. Not only does Lady Macbeth seem fair, but there are two seemingly fair Thanes of Cawdor in whom Duncan places an absolute trust.

[6] *Explorations* (New York, 1947), pp. 15–54.

Perhaps, however, the confusion that thus ensues works more toward the mystification of the characters than of the audience, and this is as it should be in a tragedy that is taut with irony. Duncan is simply fooled by false appearances. Macbeth is tormented by them, trying to tell which is right and which is wrong. One of his most agonizing asides is that beginning:

> This supernatural soliciting
> Cannot be ill; cannot be good.
> *(I.iii.310–131)*

It is this dilemna, an intellectual as well as a moral one for him, which is powerful enough to shake his single state of man and reduce him—so obscure are right and wrong at this point—to the hopeless conclusion that "nothing is, but what is not." Besides Duncan and Macbeth, other characters are confused by an inability to decide which is foul and which is fair. Malcolm and Donalbain distrust everyone; Malcolm requires almost the whole of a very long scene before he can accept the fairness of Macduff; and Lady Macduff cannot trust the rectitude of her own husband. Rosse speaks eloquently for all of the "fair" characters of a world in which no one really knows anyone else or, even more fundamentally, what it is in the evil world that he fears:

> But cruel are the times, when we are traitors,
> And do not know ourselves; when we hold rumour
> From what we fear, yet know not what we fear,
> But float upon a wild and violent sea
> Each way and move—[7]
> *(IV.ii.18–22)*

Macbeth may have some reasonable grievance at the very beginning of the play about the difficulty of differentiating foul and fair. The foul Witches do give him fair prophecies, and one of these is promptly verified by honorable means. But both he

---

[7] D. A. Traversi would trace uncertainty to psychological depths: "The essence of evil, which communicates itself from the usurper to his whole realm, lies in uncertainty, in ignorance of one's impulses, of the true causes of one's own actions." *An Approach to Shakespeare* (New York, 1956), p. 175. I would not agree that this is the essential evil of the play. It contributes, rather, to a moral confusion.

and his Lady can hardly be excused for their own willful contribution to the blurring of evil. This particular kind of blurring has a basis in language, and I think that the latter, more than the often-celebrated "murkiness" of the play, at least in the opening scenes, is responsible for making the evil seem mysterious. But though the linguistic artistry of Shakespeare deserves credit for its sensational effectiveness, the dramatist has so meaningfully related it to character that it is primarily a commentary upon the willfulness of the two protagonists and hence serves as a link between the merely mysterious nature of the evil and the more clearly defined sort.

The blurring of evil to which I refer is due to the reluctance of the two protagonists to name it, and the blurring is so influential because it is through their language that we are for the first part of the play told about the evil. They speak of it mutedly, obliquely, with euphemism, and with extensive reliance upon *it* and other pronouns without antecedents; of this last practice alone I have counted fifteen instances.[8] The literary basis for this kind of linguistic reticence is to be found in rhetorical theory. Abraham Fraunce describes the technique as follows: "*Aposiopesis, Reticentia*, concealing, is when the course of a speech begun is in such sort staid, that some part thereof not uttred, is nevertheles perceived."[9] Shakespeare was probably aware of the obliquely suggestive effectiveness of this literary device, but he gave it a firm grounding in human nature. In one of the most important speeches in the play, one which we shall again find central in the next chapter, Macbeth commits himself, by invocation, to an imperfect vision of his evil:

> Stars, hide your fires!
> Let not light see my black and deep desires;
> The eye wink at the hand; yet let that be,
> Which the eye fears, when it is done, to see.
>
> *(I.iv.50–53)*

---

[8] I discuss this linguistic trait in "A Deed Without a Name," *Pacific Coast Studies in Shakespeare*, ed. by Waldo F. McNeir and Thelma N. Greenfield (Eugene, Oregon, 1966), pp. 190-198. In the present study I give it a different emphasis.

[9] *The Arcadian Rhetorike* (1588), ed. by Ethel Seaton (Oxford, 1950), p. 80.

The "black and deep desires"—an expression which by its vagueness enhances the terrible sense of obscure evil—are not to be exposed to the light of moral vocabulary. And here he begins the use of the pronoun without antecedent: "yet let *that* be," followed by *it*.

In her first speech Lady Macbeth shows that she shares her husband's disinclination to mention precisely what she is about:

> Glamis thu art, and Cawdor; and shalt be
> What thou art promis'd.
> *(I.v.16–17)*

"King" was to have been the climactic world, but she shies away from it. She comes closer to the actual evil, but still evades it by pronouns, in what follows:

> thou'dst have, great Glamis,
> *That* which cries, "*Thus* thou must do," if thou have *it*;
> And *that* which rather thou dost fear to do,
> Than wishest should be undone.
> *(I.v.22–25)*

The first conversation which we witness between husband and wife is a model of circumspect diction, despite the fierce energy of the wife's purpose. There may be eloquence rather than merely caution in her first words—"Great Glamis! worthy Cawdor! / Greater than both, by the all-hail hereafter!" (I.v. 55–56)—in her failure once more, that is, to name the ultimate goal. But what follows is doubtless the most expert querying by indirection that one can find in Shakespeare. Alfred Harbage has briefly noticed this element: "As the two face each other and refer obliquely to what is in their minds, we seem to be watching something like the embarrassment of a nuptial."[10] This is well put, but not, I think, the full truth. What we see is not embarrassment so much as a refusal to face a deed that neither of the two has named even to himself. Lady Macbeth finds a happy euphemism for it—"This night's great *business*" (I.v.69)—a euphemism which Macbeth gratefully borrows for his own use on four later occasions (I.vii.31; II.i.23; III.i.104,

---

[10] *William Shakespeare: A Reader's Guide* (New York, 1964), p. 377.

125). In addition there appear other euphemisms or circumlocutions. The murder itself is "this terrible feat" (I.vii.80), "his taking-off" (I.vii.20), or, perhaps the best of all, "enterprise" (I.vii.48). And instead of "murder," the words "do" and "deed" are so frequent and connotative that they can scarcely be used without arousing sinister reactions.

In assessing the importance of the nameless deed in *Macbeth*, and the apprehension of obscure evil it gives to an audience, we should keep in mind that for the Renaissance the naming of something had a tangible and religious implication. "Names," Miss Mahood has written, "seemed true to most people in the sixteenth century because they thought of them as at most images of things and at least the shadows of things, and where there was a shadow there must be a body to cast it." She also describes a play on the Creation acted at Florence early in the seventeenth century: "... Adam takes a very long time to name the property trees, stars, and the like. It is tedious for the modern reader, but clearly it was exciting for the contemporary spectators when they heard Adam guess all the names right."[11] The age was sensitive to names—and to the absence of names.[12] A deed that is unnamed is not simply too horrible to be named; naming of the deed would merely decrease its horror.

Indeed *Macbeth* is notable for a sensational artistry of language which represents Shakespeare's most mature achievement in expressing the horrible, just as the play as a whole, by no accident, represents his most mature vision of evil. Earlier he had indulged in hyperbole and exclamation. I have always felt, for example, that Hamlet's outcry against his mother's corruption represents one of Shakespeare's most earnest attempts to convey something supremely distasteful:

> Such an act
> That blurs the grace and blush of modesty,
> Calls virtue hypocrite, takes off the rose
> From the fair forehead of an innocent love
> And sets a blister there, makes marriage-vows

---

[11] *Shakespeare's Wordplay* (London, 1957), pp. 169-170.
[12] For the seriousness of being without a name see *Richard II* IV.i.255-259; *Coriolanus* V.i.9-15.

> As false as dicers' oaths; O, such a deed
> As from the body of contraction plucks
> The very soul, and sweet religion makes
> A rhapsody of words.
>
> *(II.iv.40–48)*

Nevertheless, this itself is little more than a "rhapsody of words." The language grows shrill, the evil merely ornate. Perhaps Shakespeare recognized this danger when he had Gertrude ask what the act is that "roars so loud and thunders in the index."

There is of course in *Macbeth* much language that roars and thunders at the evil. Macduff exclaims:

> O horror! horror! horror!
> Tongue nor heart cannot conceive, nor name thee!
>
> . . . . .
>
> Confusion now hath made his masterpiece!
> Most sacrilegious Murder hath broke ope
> The Lord's anointed Temple, and stole thence
> The life o' th' building!
>
> *(II.iii.64–70)*

But the language represents a recoil to the world of daylight and open truth after the sinister and muted evil evoked for us by the language of the two criminals. Its hysterical force is justified for the audience, who have moved too long and too apprehensively in the murky namelessness of the evil and who are grateful to have the horror howled out and named, though imperfectly. It is named repeatedly as "murder" by Macduff and others after the deed, but this is only a superficial and partial word for the evil.

I would, finally, relate this linguistic trait of imperfect naming in *Macbeth* not only to the linguistic artistry of Shakespeare, or even to the willful blinding of their moral natures by Macbeth and his Lady. It must be related fundamentally to the most obvious agents of evil in the play, the Witches, and to the diabolical master whom they either serve or impersonate. When Macbeth asks the Witches what covertly evil and ugly business they are about, they reply in unison, "A deed without a name"

(IV.i.49). Lacking as they do the moral vocabulary of daylight, it is these instruments of Darkness to whom Macbeth is attuned, by his own deliberate choice. In the process of assenting to their evil early in the play, he adopts the namelessness of it. It is with good reason that he exclaims in an anguish of fuller recognition, "To know my deed, 'twere best not know myself" (II.ii.72).

III

The mysteriousness of the evil is important to the play, not only for the sensation it supplies, but for the way the technique of the sensationalism is related to the character of the protagonists. Even more, it gives a sense, noted by the critics, of an inscrutable evil in the universe. Shakespeare did well to leave this evil mysterious for more than artistic reasons, since his knowledge of it was necessarily limited.

But there was a sense in which Shakespeare could not afford to leave the evil impressive in its vagueness. He was writing a Renaissance tragedy, and as he understood tragedy, the hero must be adequately aware of what his moral choice involves so that he can be responsible for it.

Although, therefore, Macbeth and his Lady try to keep the evil nameless, not only early in the play but throughout it,[13] there are a few frightening moments when the evil surfaces to the full consciousness of Macbeth. Lady Macbeth, on the contrary, seems not to see its moral meaning early in the play, concentrating rather upon her "fell purpose" and especially upon the means whereby she will be spared "the compunctious visitings of nature." Both of them, however, are surely aware, though only Macbeth voices it as an evil, of one of the most heinous aspects of their crime: betrayal. Both eloquently express, with conscious hypocrisy, the reasons why they owe Duncan their loyal service—Macbeth once (I.iv.22–27) and his Lady twice (I.vi.14–18; I.vii.25–28). At the end of her second protestation of loyalty and devotion, Duncan makes a statement

[13] Robert B. Heilman has rightly arued that Macbeth's self-knowledge, which would be mainly knowledge of his evil, decreases throughout the play. See " 'Twere Best not Know Myself," *Shakespeare 400*, ed. by James G. McManaway (New York, 1964), pp. 89-98.

and a gesture that give symbolic and ritual meaning to the betrayal that will occur:

> Give me your hand;
> Conduct me to mine host: we love him highly,
> And shall continue our graces towards him.
> *(1.vi.28–30)*

The crime of betrayal and sacrilege against the "Lord's anointed Temple" will bring the loss of the Lord's grace for both of the criminals.

Macbeth alone, however, most directly describes the full horror of the deed, and significantly he pictures it rather than names it. His imagination may not be, as Bradley thinks it is, the best part of him, but it is assuredly the part of his mind which he is least able to silence. In a remarkable soliloquy, Macbeth is compelled not only by his dramatist creator, but by his conscience speaking through his imagination, to recite virtually every heinous feature of the evil toward which he is moving. I know of no other play in which the crime is so nakedly exposed, and I must dwell upon this speech because it has the crucial force we should expect in a drama of crime and punishment and, especially, because without it the punishment and, hence, the sensational artistry of the play would be meaningless.

Although Macbeth almost never speaks without emotion, and although the emotion is almost always given a sense of greater urgency and less control through figurative language, this speech begins with what for Macbeth is relatively literal, logical, and controlled argument. The degree of control is shown by the manner in which he distances himself from the horrible prospect by trying to maintain the namelessness of the deed.

> If it were done, when 'tis done, then 'twere well
> It were done quickly: if th' assassination
> Could trammel up the consequence, and catch
> With his surcease success. . . .
> *(1.vii.1–4)*

He is still, as in his talk with Lady Macbeth, relying upon shrinking words like *it* (four uses) and *do* (three uses). Even here, however, there is a picture-making; and as he proceeds in the speech, even though the careful logic persists for quite a few lines and is never entirely lost,[14] the increasing violence of the imagery attests to the way in which logical comprehension is yielding to emotional apprehension. The very vehemence and painfulness of his imagination during most of the soliloquy are largely due to the horror of what he is picturing; and this picturing in itself becomes a part, in anticipation, of the punishment which he will receive. He will be appropriately, according to the theory of condign punishment explained in the preceding chapter, punished through his imagination. He has already had "horrible imaginings" upon his first contemplating the possibility of becoming King, and now he has them in profusion and in a more specifically instructive and penal way than before.

Recognizing that he will have "judgment here," he sees, as the first action of the judgment, the

> Bloody instructions, which, being taught, return
> To plague th' inventor.

The murder is the most overt and spectacular aspect of the evil, and the blood resulting from the murder will accurately, being taught, return to punish him. He next refers to "this evenhanded Justice" which "Commends th' ingredience of our poison'd chalice / To our own lips." This quality of Justice is at the heart of the play. But the imagery of the poisoned chalice would seem, in terms of sensational punishment, disappointingly unironic here, as it would not have been in *Hamlet*. It does, however, have a possible symbolic reference to the fullest meaning of the crime. Roy Walker sees the chalice as the Eucharist cup, and Macbeth as Judas. "Duncan has almost supped when Macbeth deliberates

> If it were done when 'tis done, then 'twere well
> It were done quickly."

In John's gospel, Walker points out, "it is during the last supper

---

[14] C. C. Clarke, however, makes a good case for the general failure of Macbeth's reason, with its disastrous result. Clarke would even attribute to darkened reason the way in which evil principally manifests itself. See "Darkened Reason in *Macbeth*," *The Durham University Journal*, New Series, XXII (1960), 11-18.

that Jesus says to Judas *That thou doest, do quickly*" (John 13:27).[15] The archetype, then, is that of the worst betrayal Shakespeare knows, and the poisoned chalice will appropriately return to Macbeth's own life in the form of the most excruciating mental torment known to man, despair.[16] Such an interpretation runs the calculated risk of further proliferation of Christ figures in Shakespeare. But in view of the Christlike qualities of Duncan to be noted later, and with the understanding that Duncan resembles rather than is Christ, I present this interpretation impenitently. Critics have become needlessly inhibited since the appearance of Roland Mushat Frye's *Shakespeare and Christian Doctrine* (Princeton, 1963). Although Frye's thesis is that critics have read too much Christian symbolism into Shakespeare, his book actually serves the more valuable purpose of pointing out and clarifying the extensive amount of Christian doctrine in the plays which lends itself to symbolic interpretation. Shakespeare's contemporaries indulged guiltlessly in this activity as they did in Biblical allegory, converting history into poetry in Sidneyan fashion; and the Geneva Bible that Shakespeare used was full of marginal notes explaining what a particular Scriptural statement or episode stood for. What the critics must now do is make Christian interpretation as accurate as they can (wherever possible giving Renaissance commentary) and try to demonstrate that the interpretation lends itself to the central dramatic purpose of the play.

As Macbeth proceeds in his vision of the evil, he recognizes its unnaturalness in that Duncan is

> here in double trust:
> First, as I am his kinsman and his subject,
> Strong both against the deed; then, as his host,
> Who should against his murderer shut the door,
> Not bear the knife myself.

---

[15] *The Time Is Free. A Study of Macbeth* (London, 1949), pp. 53-54. But Walker had been anticipated by Richmond Noble in finding the parallel in John. Noble is, however, somewhat skeptical. See *Shakespeare's Biblical Knowledge* (London, 1935), p. 233.

[16] So Clifford Davidson suggests in "Full of Scorpions Is My Mind" (Letter to the Editor), *The Times Literary Supplement*, Nov. 4, 1965, p. 988.

The Evil · 55

The betrayal is thus made to include that of host to guest and, more important, the killing of kin. The Biblical archetype of killing a kinsman is Cain's murder of Abel, and once again a theological meaning is not only tempting but necessary. Only by associating Macbeth's crime with that of Cain can we, with the help of Renaissance commentary on Genesis, adequately account for much of the subsequent torture of Macbeth, notably the kind of fear that precedes his despair. To the killing of kin is here added that politically supreme form of evil in the Renaissance, the killing of a king; Shakespeare, in earlier plays, had benefited from the fullest kinds of experience in depicting this evil and the impressively condign sort of punishment that awaits the murderer once he is himself king.

In the next portion of the soliloquy, Macbeth contemplates Duncan's innocence, and in doing this his mind is so racked with both pity and horror that imagery takes over almost completely from abstract formulation:

>   Besides, this Duncan
> Hath borne his faculties so meek, hath been
> So clear in his great office, that his virtues
> Will plead like angels, trumpet-tongu'd, against
> The deep damnation of his taking-off;
> And Pity, like a naked new-born babe,
> Striding the blast, or heaven's Cherubins, hors'd
> Upon the sightless couriers of the air,
> Shall blow the horrid deed in every eye,
> That tears shall drown the wind.

In their violence of imagery and of feeling, these are the most genuinely sensational lines in the play; and they represent Macbeth suffering in his most characteristic manner. It is his conscience, his Good Angel, crying out with almost its last trumpet-tongued plea. And this outrage against Innocence, as Macbeth correctly foresees, will be avenged by the essential faculty of Innocence itself: Pity. Macbeth even foresees, though not so completely as to rule out irony, that the eye will be a primary victim of the punishment. There is no question but that he fully grasps the ultimate punishment: deep damnation.

And his vision of the supernatural violence of reaction against this damnation, and against the unnaturalness of the deed, anticipates its macrocosmic amplification in agitated Nature which will accompany the murder and echo long afterward.

Finally, after a pause of exhaustion from the horrible sensation, he perceives the futility of the deed:

> I have no spur
> To prick the sides of my intent, but only
> Vaulting ambition, which o'erleaps itself
> And falls on th' other—

The inadequacy of his motive is a part of his torment. And in his emotionally drained state, he is able to feel in advance the penalty of ambition, the labor of a nightmare in which one repeatedly leaps only to fall again. This will be the source of much of his physical stress. Ambition, moreover, is later seen as "thriftless" and as "'Gainst nature" (II.iv.27–28).

Macbeth's evil is now vividly clear, though of course it will attach to itself the darkly mysterious features of the demonic. It is the worst evil that Shakespeare could imagine. One recent critic even thinks it represents the influence of the worst evil that Dante, the medieval specialist in the abhorrent, could portray and in the order that Dante portrays the separate offences in the ninth circle: against kinsman (Cáina), subject (Antenora), guest (Ptolomaea), and lord (Judecca).[17] Whatever the possible influence of Dante, the only adequate punishment for such an evil requires the most lively features of hell—short of flames—known to Shakespeare.

And Macbeth, to solemnize the espousal of evil, is almost as specific as Lady Macbeth in her conjurations of murdering ministers and the dunnest smoke of hell. After he has yielded to her temptation, Macbeth commits himself, in fullest degree, to the evil which he is compelled to see more clearly than anyone else in the play. This commitment, virtually a pact, comes emphatically at the very end of the first act:

---

[17] Harry Morris, "*Macbeth*, Dante, and the Greatest Evil," *Tennessee Studies in Literature*, XII (1967), p. 26. But Morris admits that the direct influence of Dante cannot be proved. Roy Walker had also called attention to the parallel with Dante in the abhorrence of traitors (*The Time Is Free*, p. 54).

> I am settled, and bend up
> Each corporal agent to this terrible feat.
> Away, and mock the time with fairest show:
> False face must hide what the false heart doth know.
> *(I.vii. 80–83)*

The full meaning intended by Macbeth in thus dedicating his body to evil is to be found in these admonitions by St. Paul:

> Nether give ye your membres as weapons of unrighteousnes unto sinne; but give your selves unto God, as they that are alive from the dead, and give your membres as weapons of righteousnes unto God. Knowe ye not, that to whomsoever ye give your selves as servants to obey, his servantes ye are to whome ye obey, whether it be of sinne unto death, or of obedience unto righteousnes.
> *(Romans 6:13,16)*

Nicholas Ridley seems to be commenting upon these verses when he writes:

> Thy body, O man, is God's, and all the parts thereof, even as thy soul is; . . . and darest thou suffer any parts of either of them to do service to Satan? Surely in so doing, thou committest sacrilege and dost rob God; thou defilest the lively temple of the living God, if thou suffer thy body to do Satan service.[18]

By thus committing himself in body to Satan (as he could do only more luridly, like Faustus, if he were to write in blood), Macbeth becomes the servant of Satan and subject to the temporal advantages and infinite disadvantages which such service entails. In turning from God, he will be eligible for pain of loss; and in choosing instead a lesser good (worldly advancement), he will be eligible, especially since he has so dedicated his body, for the pain of sense.

IV

Most of the remaining chapters will each be devoted to one of the principal kinds or aspects of sensationalism in the play,

---

[18] *A Piteous Lamentation of the Miserable Estate of the Church in England* (1555), in *The Works of Nicholas Ridley, D. D.*, ed. by Rev. Henry Christmas (Parker Society), (Cambridge, 1843), pp. 68–69.

particularly as these derive from the evil that Macbeth has espoused and the crime he commits. Thus there will be chapters upon the bloody instructions, upon the torment and ultimate triumph of Innocence, upon the unnatural ramification of the unnatural evil, upon futile labor and stress, upon tormented senses, and finally upon the torture of the mind, resulting in despair and the end of sensation. These chapters will not, however, attempt to trace all sensational phenomena of the play precisely to the evil which Macbeth and his Lady espouse. To do so would give to the play a symmetry and a literal message which it does not have. But it does have a greater symmetry than has been recognized and a moral message that rises above literal significance to a figurative working out of justice which Dante might have respected.

But before we reach these chapters which show the full consequences in body, in Nature, and in soul of the evil, there is one aspect of the subject, more a part of the evil than a result of it, that invites treatment. This is Shakespeare's artistry in the depiction of the most tangible form the evil takes: murder. And although the next chapter is not predominantly about the punishment of evil, the very act of murder itself is so dolorous to the criminals, so full of unexpected horror and disillusionment, that subsequent punishment can hardly be worse.

Chapter IV

He Is About It

The murder of Duncan is surely the most superbly depicted act of its kind in Elizabethan drama. Only the murder of Marlowe's Edward II can come remotely near it in covertly suggested violence and horror. With a few exceptions, most non-Shakespearean murders, and even most of those in Shakespeare, had consisted of rather perfunctory, sudden stabbings or bludgeonings, and most were onstage, with no artifice of hidden outrage. The sinister artistry of Italianate murders did not make its way to the major English plays before *Macbeth*, except of course for *Edward II*. The murder of Duncan excites the most exquisite horror in the minds of the murderers and of the audience, and it is significant that it is this murder which attracted the appreciation of Thomas De Quincey, that sensitive connoisseur of the art.

In this chapter I would examine with special care and admiration the main features of the artistry with which the preparation for the killing of Duncan and the actual murder are depicted. First of all, it should be noted that by keeping us always at some distance from the scene of violence, Shakespeare depended upon language for his hold upon us, and particularly upon a kind of stylized, often ritualistic use of language. Hamlet's favorite dramatic speech, one which he has substantially memorized, is Aeneas's tale to Dido, "and thereabout of it especially where he speaks of Priam's slaughter" (II.ii.468–469). Critics have not shared Hamlet's "love" for this declamation. It is overstated, lurid in blood, heavy with adjectives, and turgidly rhetorical in movement. Though Shakespeare certainly wrote it, it is a misguided imitation of the epic manner, with an immediate indebtedness to Marlowe's *The Tragedy of Dido Queen of Carthage*. One can see that it might have appealed to Shakespeare, even though mainly as a nostalgic memory, for in its ornate and exaggerated style are to be found the features that persevered in his murders. There is, for example, the juxtaposition of "dread and black complexion" with "smear'd / With heraldy more dismal" which gives, as in *Macbeth*, "a tyrannous and damned light" to the blackness. And "the milky head / Of reverend Priam" calls to mind the meek and gracious Duncan, "his silver skin lac'd with his golden blood." The rhetorical creation of atmosphere, which can give the impression of an impeded or trancelike movement, is especially important and is achieved in the following lines:

> Then senseless Ilium,
> Seeming to feel his blow, with flaming top
> Stoops to his base, and with a hideous crash
> Takes prisoner Pyrrhus' ear; for, lo! his sword,
> Which was declining on the milky head
> Of reverend Priam, seem'd i' th' air to stick.
> So, as a painted tyrant, Pyrrhus stood
> And, like a neutral to his will and matter,
> Did nothing.
> *(II.ii.496–504)*

There is a sense of ritual also in another passage which is "artificial" because it is obviously inserted from an earlier mode; this is Lucianus's conjuration before the murder in the play within a play:

> Thoughts black, hands apt, drugs fit, and time agreeing;
> Confederate season, else no creature seeing.
> Thou mixture rank, of midnight weeds collected,
> With Hecate's ban thrice blasted, thrice infected,
> Thy natural magic and dire property
> On wholesome life usurp immediately.
> *(III.ii.266–271)*

The ritualistic manner of these speeches comes mainly from Seneca. It is especially heavy and sinister in Atreus's careful, priestlike preparation for the murder of Thyestes's children (*Thyestes*, Act IV). The incantatory possibilities of this technique are evident in an English murder tragedy in which there is a symbolical banquet,

> Where Ebon tapers are brought up from hel,
> To leade blacke murther to this damned deed,
> The ugly Screechowle, and the night Raven,
> With flaggy wings and hideous croking noise,
> Do beate the casements of this fatal house,
> Whilst I do bring my dreadful furies forth,
> To spread the table to this bloudy feast.[1]

One is reminded of the bloody dagger which, in *Macbeth*, leads "blacke murther to this damned deed." But even closer to Shakespeare is the way in which language suggests both ritual and nightmarish compulsion.

Shakespeare was, however, even from his first tragedy significantly different from his fellow dramatists in the artistry with which he dignifies murder through ritual. Titus Andronicus acts in an Atreus-like manner in the consummation of his revenge; and even in the slaughter of Tamora's son Alarbus, he proceeds "religiously" and views the deed as a "sacrifice." The language here, however, is not sufficiently measured and evocative to convey a feeling of priestlike movement as in Seneca. The same is true in *Julius Caesar* where, as Brents Stirling has demonstrated,[2] Brutus tries to dignify murder by treating it as ceremony. There are simply no incantatory speeches. It is in *Othello* that we encounter both the ritual and the appropriate kind of language. Othello moves toward his purpose almost hypnotically, gives to the murder a priestly sense of sacrifice, and speaks a poetry that suggests raptness, even a kind of moral anesthesia. This poetry is dark, repetitive, ceremonial; it is not rational or morally alert. This manner and this verse make

[1] *A Warning for Faire Women* (ca. 1599), sig. C 4ᵛ.
[2] "Or else Were This a Savage Spectacle," *Unity in Shakespearian Tragedy* (New York, 1956), pp. 40–54. Later in this chapter I find myself in especial accord with Professor Stirling in his fine essay, "Look, How Our Partner's Rapt," pp. 139–156.

Othello more frightening to the audience and even more so to the just awakening Desdemona, for there is no reasoning with the Moor in his trancelike state. But the manner also creates a kind of dread atmosphere to heighten the horror of the murder, and also—such is the almost unique distinction of *Othello*—the pity of it.

It is in *Macbeth*, however, that Shakespeare made consummate use of ritual in murder. In so doing he depended upon the resonant, adjective-heavy language loved by Hamlet but gave it a much greater restraint and ominous suggestiveness. One haunting speech as Macbeth prepares to kill Duncan will illustrate the improvement in artistry that does not sacrifice the more primitive virtues of the Aeneas speech:

> Now o'er the one half-world
> Nature seems dead, and wicked dreams abuse
> The curtain'd sleep: Witchcraft celebrates
> Pale Hecate's off'rings; and wither'd Murder,
> Alarum'd by his sentinel, the wolf,
> Whose howl's his watch, thus with his stealthy pace,
> With Tarquin's ravishing strides, towards his design
> Moves like a ghost. —Thou sure and firm-set earth,
> Hear not my steps, which way they walk, for fear
> Thy very stones prate of my where-about,
> And take the present horror from the time
> Which now suits with it.
>
> *(II.i.49–60)*

If we consider first Shakespeare's, rather than merely Macbeth's, purpose in this speech, we must be aware that primarily it has the atmospheric value of Aeneas's elocution. Its verse provides verbal orchestration, a muted background music, to send chills down the spines of the spectators and make them feel "the present horror" of the time which so powerfully "suits with it." Shakespeare is making the murder as horrible as possible, and he chooses wisely to do so through language. This language is especially strong in music. It is heard in the howl of the wolf; but more subtly and deeply it is heard in the hushed but insistent sound and pace of the verse as Murder moves toward his design. We notice, for example, the feeling of hesitant but compulsive and cumulative movement forward conveyed by the pace and rhythm of these lines:

> and wither'd Murder,
> Alarum'd by his sentinel, the wolf,
> Whose howl's his watch, thus with his stealthy pace,
> With Tarquin's ravishing strides, towards his design
> Moves like a ghost.

Besides the rhythm of these lines, words like *stealthy* and, especially, the muted *moves*, suggest the sinister. And "Moves like a ghost" calls to mind the stalking of the Ghost in *Hamlet*. Actually, the purport of the speech is to silence the progress toward murder, and hence the words do not howl out the horror but keep it in a kind of horrified whisper. Beneath the whisper, however, the rhythm, the inevitable movement forward, is powerfully felt.

The speech is also, however, what it is for more than atmospheric reasons. It is put in the mouth of Macbeth, and it tells us something about the speaker. Macbeth is moving, not fiercely or passionately but in a kind of painful trance, toward his design. He does so for more than one reason, I think. First of all, at least since his encounter with the Witches, he has been subject to "raptness," a condition referred to three times. But more important, we have *seen* him rapt, for the long asides after he has heard the prophecies would be unworthy of Shakespeare's dramatic art if they did not serve some purpose other than exposition of what is in Macbeth's mind. Perhaps by nature he is given to periods of abstraction; his Lady later complains of his remaining alone and keeping secret, and he has other eccentricities of behavior which make it almost impossible for him to make his face "vizard" to his heart or hide what "the false heart doth know." The shock of the Witches' prophecy would be enough to make even a normally secretive individual lapse, when in company, into only too conspicuous withdrawal; and in his letter to his Lady, Macbeth ascribes his strange behavior as follows: "Whiles I stood rapt in the wonder of it" (I.v.7). He is also picturing murder during one of these withdrawals, and he explains the result of so doing in "function is smother'd in surmise" (I.iii.141). The "function" doubtless refers to his mind.

The picturing of murder, even at this remoteness in time from the deed, is so immediate that his wakeful faculties become rapt. This, I think, is a satisfactory explanation for much of his raptness before and during the murder (though I shall have more to say about this quality in Chapter X).

But there is another possibility, one which perhaps gives more deserved influence to the mysterious kind of compulsion that moves him, though hesitantly, forward like a ghost. He may conceivably be under the spell of the Witches, may even be possessed. He repeats, in his first line, almost their very words, and in the same kind of rhythm that the Witches have used. Later in the play, when the Witches show him the Apparitions, he "Stands ... amazedly" (IV.i.126). "Rapt," moreover, probably has the sense of *extra se raptus*, meaning carried outside or apart from oneself. It was a word of violence, and was sometimes applied to the act of Elizabethan witches in taking possession of their victim.[3] I think, however, that too early a control by the Witches would deprive Macbeth of the moral choice that this play demands. Nevertheless, I think also that Macbeth's incantatory speeches, notably the later "Come, seeling Night" (III.ii.46), have the function almost of conjuration; and in imitating partly the rhythm, with some of the ritual, of the Witches, they serve to commit Macbeth to the evil. As I shall reveal presently, I suspect that Macbeth may be, at least during the murder, not merely possessed by the Witches but, more appallingly, in the service and under the control of a demon.[4] He becomes thus possessed, not as the usual innocent victims of witches were possessed, but by the almost formal commitment of each corporal agent to the horrible feat. In this commitment he is not, as one might loosely read the passage, alerting each member of his body to the acting of the murder. Instead, he is consecrating it, almost ritualistically, to the service of Satan,

---

[3] See, for example, G. B., *A Most Wicked Worke of a Wretched Witch* (1592), p. 4.

[4] Whether or not he is formally possessed by demons or by witches is indeterminable and, according to King James's theory of demonology, not crucial. James wrote that he would deal jointly with the spirit "that outwardlie troubles and followes some persones" and that which "inwardlie possesses them." *Daemonologie* (1597), p. 62.

who will guide him, involuntarily and as in a trance, through the necessary motions.

Indeed, the first clearly demonic response to his commitment is apparent in the bloody dagger. This he correctly sees as a "fatal vision" but is mistaken in also diagnosing it as merely something proceeding from heat-oppressed brain. He is, however, unable to miss the obvious purpose of the dagger:

> Thou marshall'st me the way that I was going;
> And such an instrument I was to use.
>
> *(II.i.42–43)*

It, and its controlling demons, will marshall him, as he moves in rapt manner, through the murder.

This supernatural explanation is supported by another speech, one that is in effect a conjuration:

> Stars, hide your fires!
> Let not light see my black and deep desires;
> The eye wink at the hand; yet let that be,
> Which the eye fears, when it is done, to see.
>
> *(I.iv.50–53)*

The desire is basically the same one as that which prompts him not to name the evil. But the degree of commitment to evil is more serious, and resembles the obviously formal prayer of Lady Macbeth to make both Heaven and herself blind to the murder ("Come, thick Night, / And pall thee in the dunnest smoke of Hell"). It is clearly more significant than simply, as Kenneth Muir calls it, "an image of the deed too terrible to look at" which "requires no interpretation."[5] Macbeth is asking for what the demons are only too willing to give him, temporarily: a moral anesthesia for the murder, so that the eye does not know what the hand or body is doing.

The stars which are to hide their fires are symbolically important in the play. They do go out during the night of the murder, and their dimming is achieved by demonic powers answering

---

[5] Introduction to his new Arden edition of *Macbeth* (New York, 1964), p. 1.

Macbeth's prayer. But the eye is even more symbolically important. And the Bible and Biblical commentary are here our best guide to the symbolism. A wicked man "shutteth his eyes to devise wickednes" (Proverbs 16:30). Of an erring people it is written that "with their eyes they have winked, lest they shulde se with their eyes" (Matthew 13:15). The significance of the eye which "winks," or closes itself, in its effect upon the whole body is well expressed in one of the passages most often commented upon in Biblical exegesis:

> The light of the bodie is the eye: if then thine eye be single, thy whole bodie shal be light.
>
> But if thine eye be wicked, then all thy bodie shalbe darke. Wherefore if the light that is in thee, be darkenes, how great is that darkenes!
>
> *(Matthew 6:22-23)*

In another famous passage discussing the relationship of the various parts of the body, St. Paul writes: "And the eye can not say unto the hand, I have no nede of thee" (1 Corinthians 12:21). Renaissance comments upon such passages demonstrate (even as they illustrate the imaginativeness of the prevailing anagogical exegesis) that Macbeth's closing of his eye means much more than stopping physical sight. Commenting upon the verses from Matthew, Thomas Becon writes:

> What is the eye of man? It is reason, or the wisdom of the flesh. A single eye is reason instructed with the word of God. A wicked eye is reason depraved and corrupt, and envy engendered against their neighbour for the gifts of God. Otherwhiles the eye, hand, right foot, &c. betoken our kinsmen and best beloved friends.[6]

Resisting the temptation to make much out of "kinsmen," we may still accept the significance of the blinded eye as blinded

---

[6] "The Demands of Holy Scripture," in *Prayers and Other Pieces of Thomas Becon, S.T.P.,* ed. by Rev. John Ayre (Parker Society), (Cambridge, 1844), p. 609. For another comment upon this passage, see William Tyndale, "An Exposition uppon the V. VI. VII. Chapters of Matthew," in *Expositions and Notes on Sundry Portions of the Holy Scriptures,* ed. by Rev. Henry Waller (Parker Society), (Cambridge, 1849), p. 102.

reason. Macbeth is deliberately abjuring his highest faculty as he gives himself unto the powers of evil. His prayer is answered during the murder, for he is not aware of seeing; but, as he has also asked, after the murder there will be, only too vividly, that "which the eye fears . . . to see."

During the murder, Macbeth is in effect possessed, as he had prayed to be. His raptness is due not to his fear but to the agency of the demons who have obligingly responded to his dedication of his body to them. When someone laughed in his sleep and one cried "Murder!" Macbeth merely "stood and heard them" (II.ii.23). But they, unlike Macbeth, were able to say their prayers and go promptly again to sleep. Before they did so, they said "Amen." Macbeth, "List'ning their fear," could not say "Amen" when "they did say, 'God bless us'." He had "most need of blessing, and 'Amen' / Stuck in my throat" (II.ii.31–32). He cannot say "Amen" because he is in the service of the Devil, because he has closed the eye of his body and of his soul to light, and, now most of all, because he has done the horrid deed. His trancelike state continues as he emerges from the murder chamber, absently carrying the bloody daggers and, as his wife complains, "lost / So poorly in your thoughts" (II.ii.70–71). His reply to her marks the hideous beginning of his return to consciousness: "To know my deed, 'twere best not know myself."

Besides its terrible meaning for the state of Macbeth's soul, the possessed manner in which he commits the deed powerfully evokes horror in the spectator. It has some of the quality of Othello's "sacrifice" of Desdemona, but it is the more frightening in one's awareness that within Macbeth's body demonic forces are at work. He is no longer a human being—the sentient, conscience-tormented, reasoning man of "If it were done"—but a Frankenstein instrument of murder.

The scene is also painful in the way it separates husband and wife. Crime had at first brought them closely and eagerly together, but now they discover how the execution of the crime separates them. Lady Macbeth receives here the first intimation that her husband is rapt far from her. In fact, after the murder they can speak only in short sentences, not communicating or even answering questions. During the murder we see them only apart, first the Lady and then Macbeth. Each has visited the chamber alone.

There were fine dramatic assets for Shakespeare in what was basically a moral design to show how murder separates, for Lady Macbeth is left onstage to report what is happening. And this reminds us of what is too often overlooked, that the murder is the more horrible for being offstage. Most murders in Elizabethan drama were increasingly enacted onstage. Shakespeare here reverted to an earlier technique dependent on language and suggestiveness, the technique found in Aeneas's speech, to have the murder described and not directly seen. Actually the method can hardly be called a description, for it consists of brief, incoherent fragments of what happened and of emotional response.

The aesthetics of the offstage murder need, at any rate, to be analyzed. Sometimes it is helpful in such an analysis to try to imagine the effect upon us if Shakespeare had radically changed the outcome or the technique. We can appreciate Shakespeare's artistry the better if we ask what our reaction would be, to Hamlet and the play as a whole, if Hamlet had killed Claudius at his prayer. There is equal insight into Shakespeare's artistic judgment if we try to guess the effect upon us if we were to see Macbeth at work killing Duncan. The effect would probably be one only of brutality and physical horror. It would be quickly over, except for the shock that violence gives. Offstage, on the other hand, the murder is infinitely more connotative. Lady Macbeth's "He is about it" (II.ii.4), apparently one of the simplest lines in the play,[7] conjures up the most sinister picture of what Macbeth is "performing" upon the "unguarded Duncan." And if, as is most likely, our identification is at this point

[7] J. H. Siddons describes the powerful effect of this line in Mrs. Siddons's interpretation: "The whispered words, 'he is about it,' drew my attention to the half-opened door. . . . Mrs. Siddons was bending towards the door in the act of listening—her ear so close that I could absolutely feel her breath. The words, I have said, were whispered—but what a whisper was hers! Distinctly audible in every part of the house, it served the purpose of the loudest tones. . . ." *Memoirs of a Journalist* (1873), p. 17; quoted in Dennis Bartholomeusz, *Macbeth and the Players* (Cambridge, 1969), pp. 111–112.

mainly with the murderers,[8] we listen anxiously, helplessly, with Lady Macbeth for word from a scene which we cannot see. We are alert with her to noises, to the possibility that "th' attempt and not the deed / Confounds us" (II.ii.10–11).

Finally, we benefit from experiencing the murder not directly through our own senses but through the tormented, and beautifully expressive, senses of the participants. And this is a lingering experience that extends from Macbeth's "Here lay Duncan, / His silver skin lac'd with his golden blood" through to Lady Macbeth's replaying of the murder in her sleepwalking scene. This sensory experience, informed always by an awareness of the spiritual torment and defeat beneath it, provides some of the finest and most organic sensationalism in the play.

But the deed is not done when 'tis done, and in no way is this tormenting extension of the deed better dramatized than in the nightmare of endless blood, carrying out the bloody instructions which Macbeth himself had taught. We must now, like the murderers, confront, smell, and feel blood.

---

[8] The psychology of this identification, and its subsequent recoil, has been classically analyzed by Thomas De Quincey. A sympathy of comprehension must be with the murderer, "a sympathy by which we enter into his feelings, and are made to understand them,—not a sympathy of pity or approbation." I do not, however, agree that "in the murderer, such a murderer as a poet will condescend to, there must be raging some great storm of passion,—jealousy, ambition, vengeance, hatred. . . ." Macbeth, as I have described him, does not murder with passion. "On the Knocking at the Gate in *Macbeth*," *The Works of Thomas De Quincey: Literary Criticism* (Cambridge, Mass., 1876), IV, 536, 537.

Chapter V

Bloody Instructions

The physical essence of sensational drama, just as it is the essential human horror, is blood; it has even given its name, unflatteringly, to the kind of drama usually stigmatized as the tragedy of blood. The age indisputably was attracted to, was fascinated by, the fact of blood—in rhetoric and onstage.[1] Books and plays were advertised for their bloodiness. The second part of Marlowe's most gory play was printed as *The Bloody Conquests of Mighty Tamburlaine*. Murder tracts bore such titles as *The Most Cruell and Bloody Murther* (1606), *Two Most Unnaturall and Bloodie Murthers* (1605), and *A Horrible Cruel and Bloudy Murther* (1614). The physical presence of blood onstage was a supreme satisfaction. According to Thomas Heywood, writing in defense of actors, a description is only a shadow. "But to see a souldier shap'd like a souldier, walke, speake, act like a souldier: to see a Hector all besmered in blood"—this was a sight "to make an Alexander."[2] And blood was more than a physical horror. "Bloud be the theame whereon our time shall tread," says the bloody Moor in *The Battle of Alcazar* (ca. 1589),[3] and blood did indeed be-

---

[1] For the prevalence and aesthetics of onstage blood, constituting a part of "visual stagecraft," see Leo Kirschbaum, "Shakespeare's Stage Blood," *PMLA*, LXIV (1949), 517–529.

[2] *An Apology for Actors* (1612), sigs. B 3ʳ, B 4ʳ.

[3] Ed. by John Yoklavich, in *The Dramatic Works of George Peele* (New Haven, 1961), I.ii.242.

come a theme of tragedy, and an indispensable property and symbol of the tragedy of crime and punishment.

In *Macbeth* the word *blood* and its synonyms like *gore* appear approximately fifty times, and the prevalence of blood in the imagery has been celebrated by Bradley and by Caroline Spurgeon. But the thematic use of blood, with its origin and meaning, has not, I believe, been explored. Whatever may have been said about it, it requires a careful placement in the present study.

In Holinshed's account blood is not pervasive. It does, however, have a vividness in one passage that surely impressed itself upon Shakespeare's imagination. Donwald sees to it that the body of the slain Duff is conveyed away and buried, "for that the bodie should not be found, & by bleeding (when Donwald should be present) declare him to be guiltie of the murther. For such an opinion men have, that the dead corps of anie man being slaine, will bleed abundantlie if the murtherer be present."[4] This folklore, written about also by King James, is not specifically alluded to in *Macbeth* (possibly because Shakespeare had artistic reasons for never showing the corpse of Duncan), but the concept behind it of blood returning upon the murderer certainly is. A little farther in the same passage, however, Holinshed describes the blood compellingly:

> But in the morning when the noise was raised in the kings chamber how the king was slaine, his bodie conveied awaie, and the bed all beraied with bloud; he with the watch ran thither, as though he had knowne nothing of the matter, and breaking into the chamber, and finding cakes of bloud in the bed, and on the floore about the sides of it, he foorthwith slue the chamberleins, as guiltie of that heinous murther.

The passage, although Shakespeare artistically transmuted "cakes of bloud" into skin "lac'd with his golden blood" (II.iii. 112), must have impressed him with the sheer physical horror of the abundance of blood, even as it will impress Lady Macbeth.

---

[4] *The First and Second Volumes of Chronicles* (1587), II, "Historie of Scotland," p. 150.

II

But for the connotative role he gave to blood, and for much of the blood imagery, Shakespeare depended upon a vast body of writings which had tended to establish immediately recognizable contexts. For the lurid, exaggerated, stylized uses of blood, for example, the kind that is prevalent in the bleeding Captain's speech, Shakespeare drew more or less consciously upon Seneca and especially upon the English classical dramatists who imitated Seneca. Seneca was himself, however, incomparable. In a passage from his *Hippolytus*, which contains the obviously influential but critically unnoticed line, "From rived Grine to th' Navel stead within his wombe it raught," appears the following violent blood image:

> They thumping with their horny Hooves agaynst his Belly kick,
> From bursten Paunch on heapes his blouddy bowells jumble thick:
> The scraiting Bryers on the Brakes with needle poynted pricks
> His gory Carkas all to race with spelles of thorny sticks....[5]

In the Elizabethan classical play that most nearly approximates the profuse sensationalism and moist bloodiness of Seneca, *Gismond of Salerne* (ca. 1566), there is an unripping of the naked belly so that the bowels gush forth, another crude precursor of the unseaming in *Macbeth*; and in the same passage "lumpes of gore" are "sprent" on the innocent victim's "paled face," a memorable image that may have suggested the far more beautiful, and less repulsive, image of Duncan's "silver skin."[6] The most celebrated of these classical plays, *Gorboduc* (1562), has

---

[5] *Seneca His Tenne Tragedies Translated into English*, ed. by Thomas Newton, trans. by John Studley (1581), (London, 1927), I, Act. IV, p. 176. Although Shakespeare may well have used also the Latin original, I have preferred here the sixteenth-century translation as showing how Seneca was rhetorically amplified and made cruder in the Renaissance.
Cunliffe.
[6] In *Early English Classical Tragedies*, ed. by John W. Cunliffe (Oxford, 1912), V.i.178–186. This volume will henceforth be cited as

images of hands stained "with giltlesse blood" and kinsman's blood.⁷ The plays generally have many picturesque images of "wallowing" and "tumbling" in gore⁸ and of "drowning in theyr blood."⁹ Wading in blood is also clearly an image derived from these plays. Balthezer, in *The First Part of Hieronimo* (ca. 1604), would "wade up to the knees in bloud."¹⁰ Blood combined with water makes, in fact, the most common image. In *Caesar's Revenge*, Caesar will "die their rivers with vermilion red" (II.iv.1437). The most Senecan of the plays, *The Misfortunes of Arthur* (1588), is especially rich in imagery of this kind. Mordred threatens:

> E'r Arthur land, the Sea shall blush with blood,
> And all the Stronds with smoaking slaughters reeke.¹¹

In addition the play has "swim in streames of bloud" (III.iii. 126) and, suggestively close to *Macbeth*, two instances of "bathing" in blood (II.i.25; II.ii.6).

If we add to these the well-known instances from Seneca of making the sea red, we can account in these English plays for most of the images in *Macbeth* of smoking and reeking blood, of wading and bathing in blood, and of staining water with blood. What is lacking in most of them, however, is any dramatic reward for the unpleasantness of the images. They are either hyperbolic threats or classically heightened battle descriptions. As such, they are on the same "primitive" level as the bleeding Captain's discourse, but without the irony that sophisticates his speech. They are generally, in these plays, little more than lurid images of one piece and texture with the monotonously heightened language of the plays as a whole. Shakespeare, likewise, does not confine them to safe limits within the Captain's speech; but though they appear in the most decorous

---

⁷ *The Tragedy of Ferrex and Porrex* (1562), in Cunliffe, *Chorus*, III.i.14; IV.ii.15–26.

⁸ *Jocasta* (1566), in Cunliffe, V.ii.123–124.

⁹ Thomas Kyd, *Cornelia*, in *The Works of Thomas Kyd*, ed. by Frederick S. Boas (Oxford, 1901), V; 1. 250.

¹⁰ *The Works of Thomas Kyd*, ed. by Boas, II.i.60. See also *The Tragedie of Caesar and Pompey, or Caesars Revenge* (ca. 1595), Malone Society Reprints (1911), I.iii.249; also 2 *Tamburlaine* I.iv.

¹¹ Thomas Hughes, *The Misfortunes of Arthur* (1588), in Cunliffe, I.iv. 129–130.

74 · OUR NAKED FRAILTIES

parts of the play, even in the banquet, they are distinctly and purposefully used.

As their titles advertise, there is much blood in the popular murder tracts and plays based upon contemporary murders. Much of the bloodiness is for shock appeal only. A husband, led to the deed by the Devil, cuts his wife's throat and leaves "her weltring in her owne goare."[12] But unlike the English classical drama, these humble contemporary accounts, especially the plays, sometimes aim at a retributive or moral purpose in the bloodiness. The murderer in *A Warning for Faire Women* (ca. 1599) sees in the murdered man's son "his Fathers wounds / Fresh bleeding in my sight" (sig. F 4^v), and as he views the body, the wounds plead against him: "In ev'ry wound there is a bloudy tongue, / Which will all speake" (sig. H 1^v). There are also effectively anxious scenes of murderers trying to clean up the blood, as in Robert Yarington's *Two Lamentable Tragedies* (ca. 1594), sig. E 2^r. And in the sometimes powerful *Arden of Feversham* (ca. 1591) there is a frightening moment in which the guilty woman, who has been plagued by the blood of her murdered husband, tries to clean away the blood from the floor. Water will not wash it away. She becomes hysterical:

> But with my nailes ile scrape away the blood,
> The more I strive the more the blood appeares.[13]

III

Shakespeare could also benefit from another "source," his own earlier experiments with the imagery and symbolism of blood. These were at first neither strenuously rhetorical like the English classical tragedies nor instructively frightening like the popular murder plays. There is, to be sure, a most untypically realistic and retributively haunting description of the dead Humphrey, Duke of Gloucester, in *2 Henry VI*. His "face is black and full of blood" (III.ii.168), and "on the sheets his hair, you see, is sticking" (l. 174). And pathetic use is made in the early history plays of the handkerchief dipped in young Rut-

[12] *A Most Horrible & Detestable Murther* (1595), sig. A 3^r.
[13] Malone Society Reprints (1940), V.i.2280–2281.

land's blood. But the theme of divine justice that pursues the guilty is not given symbolic expression through blood. In *Titus Andronicus*, which in its mutilations and killings is predictably a very sanguinary play, both the imagery and the symbolism are disappointing in what they might augur for the future. Blood here is "sweet" (III.i.15), betokening probably the murder of innocents, and it falls very much like tears, expressing the dominance of pity over terror. Bassianus's innocent blood appears appropriately upon harsh briars,

> Upon whose leaves are drops of new-shed blood
> As fresh as morning dew distill'd on flowers;
>
> *(II.iii.200–201)*

and he is likened to

> a slaughtered lamb,
> In this detested, dark, blood-drinking pit
>
> *(II.iii.223–224)*

The earnestly attempted pathos in this play is to be found in the bleeding of the mutilated Lavinia; but the picturesqueness of the imagery calls self-conscious attention to itself:

> Alas, a crimson river of warm blood,
> Like to a bubbling fountain stirr'd with wind,
> Doth rise and fall between thy rosed lips. . . .
>
> *(II.iv.22–24)*

The symbolism is satisfactory for this artful play, but it does not lead Shakespeare to anything tragically deep; the artificial does not produce terror.

In *King John* and *Richard III* there is little blood, but abstract commentary in these plays shows that Shakespeare is becoming aware of a meaning that will help him when he comes to plays in which the blood is more adequate and real. King John, for example, moralizes that "There is no sure foundation set on blood" (IV.ii.104); and Richard, in a passage already cited, recognizes that he is in "So far in blood that sin will pluck on sin" (IV.ii.65)—which is, incidentally, an image difficult to picture.

In *Richard II* the blood is still only an abstraction in the dialogue, but it is used as in no preceding play to suggest the chain of retributive justice to follow. When Bolingbroke accepts the crown, the Bishop of Carlisle predicts:

> And if you crown him, let me prophesy,
> The blood of English shall manure the ground,
> And future ages groan for this foul act.
>
> *(IV.i.136–138)*

The manure image may seem to be not a particularly happy one, but it fits into the garden motif of the play and is given unmistakable intention in Bolingbroke's last lines:

> Lords, I protest, my soul is full of woe
> That blood should sprinkle me to make me grow.
>
> *(V.vi.45–46)*

That, however, which particularly distinguishes blood allusions in this play is the emphatic beginning of Shakespeare's associating of blood with Cain's murder of Abel. In the very first scene the symbolism is voiced by Bolingbroke, who, accusing Mowbray of Gloucester's death, says that he

> Sluic'd out his innocent soul through streams of blood;
> Which blood, like sacrificing Abel's, cries,
> Even from the tongueless caverns of the earth,
> To me for justice and rough chastisement....
>
> *(I.i.103–106)*

And this symbolism is brought ironically close to Bolingbroke's own subsequent history, though he accuses someone else of the murder, when he instructs Exton:

> With Cain go wander through the shades of night,
> And never show thy head by day nor light,
>
> *(V.vi.43–44)*

followed by the lines about blood sprinkling to make him grow. But though retribution hounds Bolingbroke and his family, it does not do so through the symbolism of blood.

In *3 Henry VI* Queen Margaret, lamenting the death of young Rutland, exclaims:

> They that stabb'd Caesar shed no blood at all,
> Did not offend, nor were not worthy blame,
> If this foul deed were by to equal it.
>
> *(V.v.53–55)*

Even near the beginning of his career, Shakespeare had associated Caesar with blood, and this association was to come to full expression in *Julius Caesar*, the play deepest in stage blood. But blood here is, almost as much as in *Titus Andronicus*, disappointing in both imagery and symbolism. In imagery we find not sweet but "costly blood" (III.i.258). And wounds "like dumb mouths, do ope their ruby lips" (III.i.260). The imagery is clever rather than frightening or moving. When Brutus plucked away his dagger,

> Mark how the blood of Caesar followed it,
> As rushing out of doors to be resolv'd
> If Brutus so unkindly knock'd or no.
>
> *(III.ii.182–184)*

One cannot object to "whilst your purpled hands do reek and smoke" (III.i.158) unless one objects to the manner of *Macbeth*. Moreover, it is not so much the feeble prettiness of the blood imagery which is so disappointing in the play as it is the lack of irony in the meaning of blood. There is, to be sure, a dramatic contrast between Brutus's "in the spirit of men there is no blood" (II.i.167) and the profusion of blood which results from the murder of Caesar. But Brutus gladly makes ceremonious use of this blood; he is not pursued or horrified by it. Even the Ghost is not apparently bloody. Only Antony perceives the disparity between Brutus's pious intentions of sacrifice and the bloody butchery that results. There is therefore no irony that leads, in the Aristotelian ideal, to recognition.

Hamlet, *Othello*, and *King Lear* are virtually bloodless tragedies. A sword smokes in *King Lear*, and Edmund scratches himself, but that is about all. Othello is careful to shed no blood in strangling Desdemona. In *Hamlet* the blood is almost entirely restricted to the Player's speech, with its hectic language reminiscent of English classical tragedy and meant to be deliberately apart from the style of the play as a whole. Poison and not blood is the spreading and retributive agent in *Hamlet*. But there is one line, inappropriate to a poisoner, which shows that Shakespeare had continued to associate Cain with blood. Claudius asks:

> What if this cursed hand
> Were thicker than itself with brother's blood,
> Is there not rain enough in the sweet heavens
> To wash it white as snow?
>
> (*III.iii.43–46*)

The image, moreover, is not ornate but simple and powerful. The blood is not given an adjective; it more disturbingly swells the guilty hand. And Shakespeare will make good use of the bloody hand which needs to be purified; Brutus's did not.

What this survey of Shakespeare's apprenticeship to blood imagery and symbolism shows is that, except for a tentative sense of a spreading blood in *Richard II*, he had not really used it as a punishment for murder. It is seldom horrible, never something that appalls by spreading uncontrollably; it never returns to plague the inventor. *Macbeth* is probably the one major play in Elizabethan drama in which blood is used for this purpose, intentionally and powerfully. It is so used, not simply because Shakespeare was artistically ready for it, but also because the subject of the play was a murder which required a kind of punishment such as only the full impact of blood, rendered with relentless artistry, could supply.

IV

It took, however, more than a sense of the heinousness of the murder for Shakespeare to make blood so meaningful in *Macbeth*, and more than a mature artistry. He seems to have benefited from much reading, and hearing, about bloody instructions returning to plague the inventor. Beard's *The Theatre of Gods Judgements* (1597) is rich in sanguinary stories illustrating exactly what Macbeth partially foresees. Cyrus of Persia was so cruel that "it was necessary that he should tast some fruits of his insatiable and bloodthirstie desire"; after his defeat and death, a woman "threw his head into a sacke full of blood, with these tearmes, *Now glut thy selfe with blood which thou hast thirsted after so long time*" (p. 241). One German earl who had sworn to ride up to the spurs in the blood of Lutherans was on the same night struck so "that he was strangled and choked with his owne blood: and so he rode not, but bathed himselfe, not up to the spurres, but up to the throat, not in the blood of the Lutherans, but in his owne blood before he died" (p. 46). One slayer of his brother was so afflicted that "his brothers blood was scarse washed of the ground" before he vomited blood "at his mouth & nosthrils to be mingled with his brothers." He then "fell down starke dead, not without horrible tokens of trembling and despaire" (p. 273). Shakespeare might have read of similar bloody punishments in Dante's *Inferno*, where the malefactor has his blood returning on him to befoul his own face or where tyrants suffer in "the red boiling [river of blood]."[14]

But Shakespeare need have read neither Beard nor Dante. He knew, as shown in *Richard II*, that God had asked Cain, "What hast thou done? the voyce of thy brothers blood cryeth unto me from the grounde" (Genesis 4:10). And on the next verse, reporting the earth's receiving of Abel's blood, Calvin comments "but the brute and senselesse earth it selfe shall require punishment. And this maketh for the inlarging of the hainousnes of the facte, as though a certeine contagion thereof came even to the earth, to whome the execution of the punishment is committed."[15] Renaissance literature and Biblical commentary are full of references to the horrible sound of Abel's blood crying and also of the earth writhing from the reception of the blood. This latter aspect, "the inlarging of the hainousnes of the facte," through its ramification on earth, is of special interest to the function of bloodshed in *Macbeth*. God had warned, Calvin notes, "that the killing even of one man is a defiling of the whole country."[16] And he asks, in the same sermon on Deuteronomy: "Shal not the Sunne, and the Moone, and all the starres of the

[14] *The Divine Comedy of Dante Alighieri*, trans. by John D. Sinclair (London, 1948), Cantos XXVIII, 11. 102–104; XII, 11. 100–105.

[15] *A Commentarie upon Genesis*, trans. by Thomas Tymme (1578), p. 142.

[16] *The Sermons of John Calvin upon the Fifth Booke of Moses Called Deuteronomie*, trans. by Arthur Golding (1583), 120th Sermon, on 21:1–9, p. 736a.

skye cry out for vengeance to God? Shal not the largenesse of the earth frame an inditement as though it were written in paper or parchment?" (p. 739b). The enlargement of the heinousness of the fact takes even cosmic form. But on this earth the murderers themselves must suffer through the enlargement of the deed, for, one minister preached, "murders procure and mark the committers thereof with endless spots of reproachful infamy."[17] "Endless spots" gives, as Shakespeare knew, a perfect statement to one of the major forms that the enlarging of crime through blood would take.

The Book of Revelation was also a prime source for the theme of uncontrollably expanding blood. Certainly it might have influenced Shakespeare's imagery. In the apocalyptic visions blood almost covers the earth, the sea, and the sky. We read of "haile & fyre, mingled with blood" (8:7) and of the third part of the sea becoming blood (8:8) The Renaissance interpreted, correctly it would seem, these sanguinary phenomena as divine punishment. When the blood is described as coming "out of the wine presse, unto the horse bridles by the space of a thousand and sixe hundreth furlongs" (14:20), the Geneva commentator remarks: "By this similitude he declareth the horrible confusion of the tyrants and infideles, which delite in nothing but warres, slaughters, persecutions and effusion of blood."[18] For Macbeth, a tyrant bloody-sceptred, the retribution by "bloody instructions" will take a form far worse than he had imagined. It will return, in terrible abundance, to convey the sense of the enlarging of the heinous fact.

V

There are, in a sense of which Macbeth is unaware, two not so happy prologues to the swelling act of the imperial theme. The first is the appearance of the Witches in scene one. The

---

[17] *The Decades of Henry Bullinger:* "Of the Second Precept of the Second Table, Which Is in Order the Sixth of the Ten Commandments, Thou Shalt not Kill," ed. by Rev. Thomas Harding (Parker Society), (Cambridge, 1849), p. 307.

[18] Cf. Revelation 16:6: "For they shed the blood of the Saintes, and Prophets, and therefore hast thou given them blood to drinke: for they are worthie."

second is the sustained appearance and narration of the bleeding Captain in scene two. It is the Captain's role which, in apparent innocence, introduces the theme of blood in the play. To be sure, the Captain's narration is in itself one of the most violently sanguinary passages in the entire play. Macbeth "carv'd out his passage" (1. 19) and "unseam'd" the traitor (1. 22). His sword "smok'd with bloody execution" (1. 18), and Macbeth himself "meant to bathe in reeking wounds" (1. 39). But the Macbeth whom the Captain describes is bloody in a just cause. Still, there are ominous, ironic aspects to the Captain's role. Duncan's first words upon seeing him are:

> What bloody man is that? He can report,
> As seemeth by his plight, of the revolt
> The newest state.
>
> *(1.ii.1–3)*

Duncan will of course himself shortly be the bloody man; and throughout the play bloody men will report "of the revolt / The newest state." The Captain may himself even be an image of revolt or rebellion.[19] There is also ominous irony in the Captain's emphatic, but at first glance only informative, words addressed directly to Duncan:

> As whence the sun 'gins his reflection,
> Shipwracking storms and direful thunders break,
> So from that spring, whence comfort seem'd to come,
> Discomfort swells. Mark, King of Scotland, mark....
>
> *(1.ii.25–28)*

Duncan would indeed do well to mark the seeming comfort of the good news. And we would do well to mark the Captain. For a long and crucial period he dominates the stage, and with details that are not apparently crucial to the tragedy. He could have told the political background without blood; and most important he need not himself have been bleeding, keeping the fact of blood constantly before the audience. He can be explained

---

[19] John Holloway so interprets him in *The Story of Night* (London, 1961), p. 58. Holloway is perceptive in considering that "*Macbeth* is a more than realistic, a truly poetic play" (p. 57).

only as an ominous prologue symbolizing the role that rebellious blood will play in the tragedy.[20]

Many such prologues, in the form of dumb shows, presenters' speeches, and other kinds of induction, would have prepared the audience for ominous symbolism.[21] In *Gorboduc* (1562) there is a dumb show in which three furies, "clad in black garmentes sprinkled with bloud and flames," move thrice about the stage; "hereby was signified the unnaturall murders to follow."[22] Peele's *The Battle of Alcazar* begins with a bloody man who is described, as though he were part of a symbolic dumb show, by the Presenter. The figure is pictured as

> Blacke in his looks, and bloudie in his deeds,
> And in his shirt staind with a cloud of gore. . . .
>
> *(II. 1–20)*

Bloody symbolic figures were not limited to prologues. They appear as actual, though often personified, forms. In *A Warning for Faire Women* (ca. 1599), a character called Murther, described by Tragedy as a kind of presenter, enters with a bowl of blood with which she "doth possesse" the characters who are to be murderers. There is a very suggestive stage direction: "Murther settes downe her blood, and rubbes their hands" (sig. D 1ᵛ). There ensues a kind of bloody banquet. In Thomas Preston's *Cambises* (ca. 1561), Murder enters with bloody hands.[23] In Yarington's *Two Lamentable Tragedies* (ca. 1594), Murder is replaced by Homicide, who melodramatically announces his own bloody role:

> I cannot glut my blood delighted eye;
> With mangled bodies which do gaspe and grone,

---

[20] For the authenticity of the scene in which he appears, see J. M. Nosworthy, "The Bleeding Captain Scene in 'Macbeth'," *Review of English Studies*, XXII (1946), 126–130.

[21] Dieter Mehl writes briefly about the "Show of Kings" in *Macbeth* in *The Elizabethan Dumb Show: The History of a Dramatic Convention* (London, 1965), pp. 120–121. He does not take up the bleeding Captain scene.

[22] "The order and signification of the domme shew before the fourth act," in Cunliffe, 11. 1–11.

[23] In *Specimens of the Pre-Shaksperean Drama*, ed. by John Matthews Manly (Boston, 1897), II, 190.

> Readie to passe to faire Elizium,
> Nor bath my greedie handes in reeking blood....
>
> *(Sig. A 2ʳ)*

Homicide's looks are described as "like thy selfe," and he will "wade up to the chin in gore" (sig. C 3ʳ). Again there is banqueting blood symbolism. Homicide will "quaffe thy health in bowles of blood"; and, of his victim-murderers:

> Then blood on blood, shall overtake them all,
> And we will make a bloodie feastivall.
>
> *(Sig. A 2ᵛ)*

In *Caesar's Revenge* there is portended a similar kind of rioting in blood. Discord, the presenter, announces:

> The furies have proclaym'd a festivall:
> And meane to day to banquet with thy bloud....
>
> *(V.i.2133–2134)*

The profusion of bloody figures, human or personified abstractions, entering to symbolize subsequent bloodshed and often involving a banquet,[24] is surely indicative of a meaningfully ominous function for the bleeding Captain. He is more than a real character, even as he is less than one. His artificial language helps to call attention to his symbolic role in the play. He stands for Murder, Homicide, Rebellion, or anything violent and bloody. He has a fatal message for Duncan; and for the spectators he would "signify," as *Gorboduc* has it, both "the unnaturall murders to follow" and the bloody banquet prepared for the murderer.

After the "induction" to the play, the first reference to blood is by Lady Macbeth, and this is not to external blood. She asks the spirits to "make thick my blood" (I.v.43). Paul H. Kocher describes her purpose here as follows: "Thick melancholic blood, reinforced by fresh supplies of melancholy from the spleen, will flow towards the heart and there be made yet heavier and colder. It will stop up the avenues to conscience." He thinks that the spirits invoked are bodily fluids and not demonic

---

[24] A "bloudie blanket" is also announced by a presenter in *The Battle of Alcazar*, ed. cit., IV, 1. 983.

agents.[25] The explanation of melancholy is good, for Kocher finds in it a satisfying irony, appropriate to this play, in that her thickened blood cannot stop the conscience. But clearly "the spirits / That tend on mortal thoughts" are demons, and these have control over much of the external blood in the play. It may be of minor significance, but *thick* is one of the Witches' words in "Make the gruel thick and slab" (IV.i.32). There is an irony, not needing Kocher's explanation, in the way blood, Duncan's blood, will become "thick" for Lady Macbeth and her husband. It will "stick" so that water cannot wash it off.

In planning the murder, it is Macbeth who first recognizes that there will be blood. He foresees the "bloody instructions," but in discussing the strategy with his Lady, he unwittingly, and without revulsion, inaugurates the action that will spread the blood. The two of them, he plans, will "mark" with blood the two grooms of the chamber and thus place the guilt on them. "Mark" is a tidy, controlled word which will prove sadly inadequate for the splash and spread of blood. Here he has obviously not *pictured* the blood. He does so, through the terrible force of his demonically instructed imagination, in the dagger soliloquy.[26] On the blade and dudgeon appear "gouts of blood, / Which was not so before" (II.i.46–47). This is his first felt realization that blood can be horrible; he had not, in the service of the King, been frightened by the "strange images of death" which he made. Blood becomes for him now a symbol of evil and guilt. We may ask why the demons, who are eager to lead him to crime, would seem to warn him of the consequences so painfully. We need, however, only remember that they never lie to him, any more than Mephostophilis lies to Doctor Faustus. They simply show him, now that he has bent up each corporal agent in their service, what is required. And their function is punitive as well as tempting. Moreover, they are not now so much tempting as guiding him.

---

[25] "Lady Macbeth and the Doctor," *Shakespeare Quarterly*, V (1954), p. 347.

[26] Garrick recognized this *seeing* function of the speech. "The horror and vivid sense of *seeing*, marked in his wonderful face, perfectly conveyed the meaning of the whole situation." Percy Fitzgerald, *The Life of David Garrick; From Original Family Papers, and Numerous Published and Unpublished Sources* (London, 1868), II, 70.

It is in the scene after the murder that the copiously widening stain of the blood, the more than natural amount involved, becomes tangible to Macbeth. This scene is noteworthy for the emphasis on tainted hands. Macbeth deplores "these hangman's hands" (II.ii.27). His hands "pluck out" his eyes (II.ii.58). And in the most anguished and powerful image of blood in Shakespeare, he recognizes that not only will not "all great Neptune's ocean wash this blood" clean from his hand, but that the hand will the "multitudinous seas incarnadine" (II.ii.59–61).[27] Lady Macbeth, in contrast, seems to be merely impatient with his infirmity of purpose. Her hands are of his color, but her heart is not so white. Her solution to their problem seems to show no painful awareness:

> A little water clears us of this deed:
> How easy is it then!
>
> *(II.ii.66–67)*

But there may be a hint of awareness in her use of "deed" for "blood." She may know that the blood is the whole appalling deed, and that the deed is bloody. Or, perhaps, "deed" may merely be a substitute for a word she has avoided using during the scene: *blood*. We cannot be certain. But there is a dramatic loss in underrating Lady Macbeth's shock during this episode. Her feminine distaste for the messy blood is perfectly expressed by the word *filthy* in "wash this filthy witness from your hand" (II.ii.46) and in her preference for "witness" over the offensive "blood." There may be more than impatient purposefulness in her

> If he do bleed,
> I'll gild the faces of the grooms withal,
> For it must seem their guilt.
>
> *(II.ii.54–56)*

The pun may be savage, but savagery may be hysteria. Puns in Shakespeare, as Laertes demonstrates (*Hamlet IV*.vii.186), may be expressions of hysteria. Lady Macbeth's sleepwalking

---

[27] The stylistic power of these lines has been explained by John Crowe Ransom, as a mingling of Anglo-Saxon and Latin words. "On Shakespeare's Language," *Poems and Essays* (New York, 1955), pp. 118–120.

scene cannot be satisfactorily explained unless we see it as the surfacing, in a replay, of the horror that she is now feeling. It is unlikely that she is later feeling it for the first time.

What torments her ultimately and her husband immediately is the inability to cleanse the hands. One of the spectators at a 1611 performance of *Macbeth* recalls particularly that "when Mackbeth had murdred the kinge, the blod on his hands could not be washed of by Any means, nor from his wives handes, which handled the bloddi daggers in hiding them, By which means they became moch amazed and Affronted."[28] This episode, if it ever existed, is no longer in the text of the play, but its action still may seem to many readers as having taken place, so strong is the theme of futile handwashing. This theme, found also in Spenser, that master of the nightmarishly futile compulsion (*The Faerie Queene* II.ii.3–4), and more influentially in Seneca,[29] would nevertheless have been most symbolically known to Shakespeare in the Bible. The Lord's displeasure at the bloody hands is expressed in Isaiah 59:2–3:

> But your iniquities have separated betwene you and your God, and your sinnes have hid his face from you, that he wil not heare.
>
> For your hands are defiled with blood, and your fingers with iniquitie. . . .

Here is good reason why Macbeth, his hands defiled with blood, could not say "Amen" to a God who has hidden his face from him. But for the futility of the handwashing, the inevitable archetype is Pilate. That futility is implicit in the Biblical version, but it is made explicit in Calvin's comment upon it:

> What gayned Pilate by washing of his handes? Was hee cleared from the death of Jesus Christ? No, that washing of his was a token of his defiling. Wherefore washed he his handes, but because hee knewe himselfe guiltie of the death of Jesus Christ?

---

[28] Simon Forman, *The Bocke of Plaies and Notes therof per Formans for for Common Pollicie* (Ashmolean MS. 208), as quoted in Kenneth Muir, new Arden *Macbeth* (New York, 1964), p. xiv.

[29] See Francis R. Johnson, "Shakespearian Imagery and Senecan Imitation," *Joseph Quincy Adams Memorial Studies* (Washington, D. C., 1948), pp. 33–53. Johnson cites *Hippolytus*, ll. 715–718, and *Hercules Furens*, 1325–1329, as sources for *Macbeth* II.ii.58–60.

Whereof hee thought to cleere himselfe by a drop of water: and that was too great a dalying with God. And that is the cause why I sayd that his washing ingraved his sinne the deeper before GOD, and made him the more unexcusable.[30]

There is a tantalizing similarity between Calvin's "thought to cleere himselfe by a drop of water" and Lady Macbeth's "A little water clears us of this deed." But the idea and perhaps even the phrasing are archetypal. What matters is that the futile effort of the two criminals to rid themselves of guilt takes the powerful, sensory form of one of the oldest compulsive symbols known to mankind.

After the murder is discovered, blood is the major symbol of the discovery, of blowing the horrid deed in every eye, just as it had first been the "bloody business" which "informed" thus to Macbeth's own eye. In a sense that can describe the action of the rest of the play, all the surviving participants will "question this most bloody piece of work, / To know it further" (II.iii. 128–129). The first public disclosures have a figurative, hyperbolic language, befitting the horror of discovery. Duncan's grooms were "badg'd with blood" (II.iii.102). "Badg'd" is a strange word, suggesting honored or specially marked. And Duncan in death becomes almost a thing of beauty, but one visited by violence, contrasted with the gory ugliness of the daggers:

> Here lay Duncan,
> His silver skin lac'd with his golden blood;
> And his gash'd stabs look'd like a breach in nature
> For ruin's wasteful entrance: there, the murderers,
> Steep'd in the colours of their trade, their daggers
> Unmannerly breech'd with gore.
>
> *(II.iii.111–116)*

The lines are ornate, as are many of Shakespeare's early experiments in blood imagery. But their ornateness is more beautiful than pretty (as contrasted with *Titus Andronicus*), is powerful rather than primarily decorative, and is dramatic in the contrast between the silver skin laced with golden blood and the repulsive gore of the "murderers." And the "golden blood"

---

[30] *Sermons . . . upon . . . Deuteronomie*, 21:1–9, p. 741a.

may have more than a picturesque significance. It reflects the angelic status of Duncan in heaven. It is Duncan's saintly nature perfected and manifest.[31] Moreover, these lines are spoken by Macbeth. Their hyperbole reflects upon the speaker as well as upon the horror of the spectacle. Macbeth is of course trying to make the others aware of his horror, but as in other passages he is also involuntarily expressing what is in his tormented imagination. He is by now learning to speak eloquently about blood. And he is aware as never before of how it is expanding on him. The "gash'd stabs look'd like a breach in nature" to him because that has been the macrocosmic significance of the bloody deed. This enlargement of the blood guilt is implicit in Rosse's generalization upon Nature's agitation the night of the murder: "Thou seest the heavens, as troubled with man's act, / Threatens his bloody stage" (II.iv.5–6).

It is becoming increasingly a bloody stage. Macbeth, who had originally contemplated only one murder, has already, at the very outset, committed three. Sin is being punished by sin. And Macbeth's first sin will be punished by a series of subsequent murders, which will torment him with what he can no longer bear to look upon, blood.

When he moves compulsively to the murder of Banquo, he conjures Night to do his business with a hand bloody—for he knows there will be blood—*but* invisible (III.ii.46–50). To keep blood safely remote, he has suborned two murderers to do the deed at a distance. But the murderers bring Banquo's blood back with them and make his banquet a bloody one. Just as he is prepared to "drink a measure / The table round," one of the assassins appears at the door. Macbeth draws back with revulsion: "There's blood upon thy face" (III.iv.11–13). And he learns, and will be repeatedly reminded, that Banquo's being "safe" means that he has "twenty trenched gashes on his head" (III.iv.24–26). The least of these would have been "a death to

---

[31] So argues W. A. Murray in "Why was Duncan's Blood Golden?" *Shakespeare Survey 19* (1966), pp. 34–43. Although Murray's interpretation may be unduly influenced by alchemy, he errs in the right direction in finding symbolism in the blood. I do not share Richard D. Altick's conviction that in *Macbeth* blood "has but one significance—the literal one." "Symphonic Imagery in *Richard II*," *PMLA*, LXII (1947), 345.

nature"; the savage excess will also fully return to plague him. The bloody banquet is made complete with the invited, but not expected, appearance of Banquo himself. The feature of the guilt which especially unmans Macbeth is the blood. Banquo's locks are "gory" (III.iv.50), "twenty mortal murders" are on his crown (III.iv.80), and his "blood is cold" (III.iv.93). Macbeth, who knew it only in theory before, knows now in practice that it will not be done when 'tis done and that bloody instructions will return. "Blood hath been shed ere now, i' th' olden time" and murders performed "Too terrible for the ear," but now, he remarks ruefully and almost with indignation, they rise again twentyfold (III.iv.74–80).

His now hopeless recognition of nightmarishly expanding blood takes the form temporarily of the futility of trying to conceal murder, because blood engenders blood, and all of Nature reports the deed and enlarges its horror:

> It will have blood, they say: blood will have blood:
> Stones have been known to move, and trees to speak;
> Augures, and understood relations, have
> By magot-pies, and choughs, and rooks, brought forth
> The secret'st man of blood.
>
> *(III.iv.121–125)*

Macbeth's recognition may be horrible to him partly as a sheer recoil from the sensory fact of blood. But there is a moral message beneath the physical horror, and this converts physical dismay to the spiritual anguish of despair. The quoted lines are almost entirely Biblical, though only the first line seems to have been identified by scholars. This line, as Kenneth Muir notes in his edition of the play, is probably based upon Genesis 9:6.

> Whoso shedeth mans blood, by man shal his
> blood be shed: for in the image of God hathe he made man.

But an at least equally tempting source, and one which prepares for the defiling of the land of Scotland, is Numbers 35:33: "for blood defileth the land: and the land can not be clensed of the blood that is shed therein, but by the blood of him that shed it." This has the Genevan commentary that God "maketh his dumme creatures to demand vengeance thereof." Stones *mov-*

ing to disclose the "secret'st man of blood" are not from the Bible, but the betraying eloquence of stones and of birds is:

> Thou hast consulted shame to thine owne house, by destroying manie people, and hast sinned against thine owne soule.
>
> For the stone shal crye out of the wall, and the beame out of the timber shal answer it.
>
> Wo unto him that buyldeth a towne with blood, and erecteth a citie by iniquitie.
>
> *(Habakkuk 2:10–12)*

On the reference to the stone, the Geneva Bible comments: "The stones of the house shal crye, and say that they are buylt of blood...."[32] Drawing partly upon this passage, but extending it as Macbeth does to include fowls, the contemporary murder tract, *A most Horrible and Destestable Murther* (1595), comes closer to the play than any other possible source I know:

> Thus God revealeth the wicked practises of men, who though the act bee kept never so secrete, to their great rebuke he discovereth: especiall notes in scriptures, and many examples we have, how the Fowles of the ayre, yea the stones in the wall shall declare such horrible sinnes, that the punishment due for the same may be worthely rewarded, as we see by this and many others.
>
> *(Sig. A 4ᵛ)*

Macbeth cannot stanch the flow of blood and he cannot conceal it. Desperation is the only recourse, a desperation which will require still more blood and a hardened acquiescence in a life of blood:

>   For mine own good,
> All causes shall give way: I am in blood
> Stepp'd in so far, that, should I wade no more,
> Returning were as tedious as go o'er.
>
> *(III.iv.134–137)*

Wading in blood is an image normally used by bloody tyrants on the Elizabethan stage. Its connotation was one of savage,

---

[32] See also Joshua 24:27 for another stone which "shalbe therefore a witnes against you," with Genevan marginal comment, "the dumme creatures shal crye for vengeance."

brutal purpose. Macbeth is at this point a tyrant. Macduff will shortly refer to him as "an untitled tyrant bloody-scepter'd" (IV.iii.104). But the speech departs effectively from a tradition that it does not altogether abandon. The lines connote still a bloody tyrant, but he is a uniquely disillusioned one. The impression is poignant with great weariness and loss of purpose. Just as in the murder scene he had acted involuntarily because of his commitment to the demons, so here his despair deprives him of human volition. It is noteworthy that the Witches, in preparing for their next meeting with him, use the word *blood* twice. "Baboon's blood" (IV.i.37) and "sow's blood" (IV.i.64) are ingredients in their gruel. And the Second Apparition now advises Macbeth to be "bloody" (IV.i.79). In willfully changing blood from something that merely sticks on his hand to the very element he moves in, he has invited the kind of bloody charm which the Witches prepare for him and which will lead him to his most inhuman murder of all—that of Macduff's entire family.

Though it may not appear at first to be a part of his torment, the land itself is now shown to be bleeding. It has, after all, in Biblical terms had to receive the blood he has shed. Macduff cries, "Bleed, bleed, poor country!" (IV.iii.31) and Malcolm says:

> It weeps, it bleeds; and each new day a gash
> Is added to her wounds.
> *(IV.iii.40–41)*

But also, in Biblical terms, this tyrant bloody-sceptered will have to give his own blood to cleanse the land he has defiled.

Meanwhile we are shown Lady Macbeth in her lonely agony of dealing with the "spot." A little water was to have cleared her of the deed. Her obsession, unlike her husband's, is uncleanliness. He has had to reckon with a sea of blood, and has desperately chosen to wade through it. The contrast is dramatically powerful. Blood had been her undoing. Though she had steeled herself to speak contemptuously of it to her husband, it was doubtless his graphic recall of it on the morning after the murder, when she was weak and tired, that caused her to faint. For her the blood has also been expanding. She has seen her husband turn into a bloody tyrant who tries to keep her "innocent" of the knowledge but who actually leads her to the hopeless realization that she has put a man, now strange to her, into maniacal motion. Her dull, hopeless "What's to be done?" (III.ii.44) is the clue to her collapse.

However, it is the first murder that haunts her in her sleepwalking; and what has obsessed her in madness is the incredible spread of the blood—not the seas of Macbeth's imaginings, but the spots and the unclean hands that would worry a woman. And she is never more the woman, which she had resolved not to be, than in her

> Here's the smell of the blood still: all the perfumes of Arabia will not sweeten this little hand. Oh! oh! oh!
>
> *(V.i.48–50)*

or in her unexpected feeling for the Thane of Fife's wife, a feeling which is on her own hands now. But she speaks for both her husband and herself in "Yet who would have thought the old man to have had so much blood in him?" (V.i.38–39). Almost pathetically, she finally imagines a union with her long estranged husband in the joining of their bloody hands (V.i.64). Throughout the episode, the blood is made sensory as never before. Mrs. Siddons's performance shows that it can be so from the stage. Edwin Forrest asked Sheridan Knowles about the impression she made:

> "I have read all the high flown descriptions of the critics, and they fall short. I want you to tell me in a plain blunt phrase just what impression she produced on you." Knowles replied with a sort of shudder. . . . "Well, sir, I smelt blood! I swear that I smelt blood!"[33]

The blood theme returns to Macbeth with Angus's accurate description:

> Now does he feel
> His secret murders sticking on his hands.
>
> *(V.ii.17–18)*

---

[33] W. A. Alger, *The Life of Edwin Forest* (1877), II, 545, as quoted in Arthur Colby Sprague, *Shakespearian Players and Performances* (Cambridge, Mass., 1953), p. 67.

The hands are still very important, for both husband and wife, and the sticking quality of the blood is for him as terrible as the spots and smell are for her. But just as Lady Macbeth has a surprising awareness of the slain Lady Macduff, so does her husband. He tells Macduff:

> Of all men else I have avoided thee:
> But get thee back, my soul is too much charg'd
> With blood of thine already.
> *(V.viii.4–6)*

This is not real compassion, however. It is more the desperate outcry of a man sated with blood who must now meet the fatal man of blood—for so Macduff was shown to be in the Apparition of the bloody babe.

That bloody babe, and all the innocence and the retribution that he stands for in the play, will be the subject of the next chapter. Macbeth's bloody instructions do not return fully until the bleeding innocents he has killed come back in surprising form. But in concluding the present chapter, we may note that Macbeth was wrong when he complained that the fatal vision of a bloody dagger was not sensible to feeling as to sight. The feeling was slow in coming, but it came.

Chapter VI

Babes Savagely Slaughtered

In Holinshed King Kenneth hears a voice crying after he has murdered Malcolme Duffe: "Thinke not Kenneth that the wicked slaughter of Malcolme Duffe by thee contrived, is kept secret from the knowledge of the eternall God: thou art he that didst conspire the innocents death. . . ."[1] The phrase "innocents death" does not represent an emphatic part of Holinshed's whole story, but related as it is to the memorable voice, it may have served as a catalyst for Shakespeare's remarkable development of the theme of violated or outraged Innocence in the play. If Shakespeare achieves terror for his play through the fact and symbolism of blood, he achieves pity by giving poignant emphasis to the innocence of the victims, and even of the protagonists themselves. Duncan, for example, becomes not the contemptibly weak king of Holinshed but a much older man, a "sainted" sovereign who is meek and clear in his great office, who trusts everyone, who weeps out of goodness of heart—who is hardly, indeed, little more than Innocence personified. The idea of Innocence as victim is so insistent in Shakespeare's concept of the action that it gets into the most intuitive part of the play, the imagery. And the imagery, as well as the action, is full of that most universally appealing symbol of Innocence, babies.

Perhaps the most deeply felt part of Macbeth's vision of re-

---

[1] *The First and Second Volumes of Chronicles*, II, "Historie of Scotland," p. 158.

tributive justice is in the lines expressing his reaction to destroying so meek and clear a king:

> And Pity, like a naked new-born babe,
> Striding the blast, or heaven's Cherubins, hors'd
> Upon the sightless couriers of the air,
> Shall blow the horrid deed in every eye,
> That tears shall drown the wind.
> *(I.vii.21–25)*

Pity here takes the form of a babe who is seemingly helpless and yet powerful to blow the horrid deed in every eye. Cleanth Brooks, in a widely known essay, has discussed this passage at length, with considerable emphasis upon babies. There is the irony, which we should expect Brooks to find, in the surprising power of the helpless babe. "For the babe signifies the future which Macbeth would control and cannot control." It signifies

> not only the future; it symbolizes all those enlarging purposes which make life meaningful, and it symbolizes, furthermore, all those emotional and—to Lady Macbeth—irrational ties which make man more than a machine—which render him human. It signifies preeminently the pity which Macbeth, under Lady Macbeth's tutelage, would wean himself of as something "unmanly." [2]

Helen Gardner, studying the connotation of cherubim, takes issue with Brooks's view of the baby as avenger, particularly in the form of Macduff:

> It is the judgement of the human heart that Macbeth fears here, and the punishment which the speech foreshadows is not that he will be cut down by Macduff, but that having murdered his own humanity he will enter into a world of appalling loneliness, of meaningless activity, unloved himself, and unable to love.[3]

Although this is beautifully put and worthy of the pity which

---

[2] "The Naked Babe and the Cloak of Manliness," *The Well Wrought Urn* (New York), 1947), pp. 45–46.

[3] *The Business of Criticism* (Oxford, 1959), p. 61. For further comment on Brooks's article and on the babe, see Kenneth Muir, "Image and Symbol in 'Macbeth'," *Shakespeare Survey 9* (Cambridge, 1966), 45–54; Grover Smith, "The Naked New-born Babe in *Macbeth*: Some Iconographical Evidence," *Renaissance Papers* (1964), pp. 21–27.

we should find in Macbeth's own plight, and although the cherubim may not be correctly seen by Brooks as avengers, we cannot so easily dismiss his paradoxical view of the babe as both helpless pity and as an agent of retribution. Against the formidable learning of Helen Gardner's study, Brooks can offer only his impression about the play's structure, and this impression seems, especially in its notorious dependence upon the "unmannerly breech'd with gore" image, to be ingenious. I do not believe that the babe symbolizes primarily the future or all the other things that Brooks intuits, but I also do not believe that Pity is quite so harmless as Dame Helen would have it. We would do well to see how the Renaissance viewed, not Dame Helen's cherubim, but the far more pervasive babe, recognizing that *babe* for the Elizabethans could mean not only newborn infants (as in Macbeth's speech) but young children as well.

Only by doing so, I believe, can we appreciate the full force of Shakespeare's artistry in the depiction of Innocence in a play of singular violence. For the sensational artistry of *Macbeth* depends to a large extent upon the utter innocence of the victims. We would know this, partly, from our uninstructed response as human beings today. But we would not know it fully. It has apparently occurred to no critic to make a study of the theme of violated Innocence in the play. Structural concerns would impel him, as they have impelled Cleanth Brooks, to see the babe symbolism. But for the full meaning which Shakespeare must have attached to the slaughter of babies and innocents, we must see how powerful and traditional a theme this was in the writings popular in the Renaissance.

II

For this theme, as for many others, Shakespeare would have found a suggestive model in Seneca, notably in translation. Seneca was especially prone to enhance horror by a strenuously sought pity. Jasper Heywood, one of his most active English translators, demonstrated an accurate awareness of Seneca's technique by one of the "sundrye additions" which he inserted in "The Argument" to *Troas*:

> Not I with spere who pearced was in fielde,
> Whose throate there cutte, or head ycorved was
> Ne bloudshed blowes, that rent both targe and shield
> Shal I resight, all that I overpasse.
> The worke I wryght more woeful is alas,
> For I the mothers teares must here complayne,
> And bloud of babes, that giltles have bene slayne.
>
> And such as yet could never weapon wreast,
> But on the lap are wont to dandled bee,
> Ne yet forgotten had the mothers breast,
> How Greekes them slew (alas) here shall ye see
> To make report therof ay woe is mee,
> My song is mischiefe, murder, misery,
> And hereof speakes this doleful tragedy.[4]

The episodes exemplifying this announced tragic purpose are legion. The violent death of Astynax, "little sone of Hector and Andromache," is piteously reported (p. 50), as are Hercules's killing of his sons and Atreus's sacrifice of the "babes" of Thyestes (p. 80). Heywood's *babes* here (from *capita devota* in the original) is a rather common change for the Elizabethan translator. John Studley makes a similar change (*victimas* to *Babes*) in describing Medea's plan for revenge on Jason by sacrificing their children:

> Then at the Aulters of the Gods my chyldren shalbe slayne,
> With crimsen colourde bloud of Babes their Aulters will I stayne....
>
> *(Medea*, vol. II, p. 57)

The heart-hardening preparation of Medea for the sacrifice may have influenced Lady Macbeth's unsexing passage in which she would take the babe from her breast and dash it to the ground. Studley is solely responsible in this passage for the reference to "dugges" and to "tender Children" with their mutilated bodies:

---

[4] *Seneca His Tenne Tragedies Translated into English*, ed. by Thomas Newton (1581), (London, 1927), II, 7.

With naked breast and dugges layde out Ile pricke with
   sacred blade
Myne arme, that for the bubling bloude and issue may bee
   made,
With trilling streames my purple bloude let drop on Th'
   aulter stones.
My tender Childrens crusshed fleshe, and broken broosed
   bones
Lerne how to brooke with hardned heart.
                                        (P. 90)

Again the Elizabethan translator contributes to the Senecan original the term of "babes" and their innocence:

            holde, holde, my babes they be
God wot, most harmelesse lambes they are, no crime nor
   fault have they:
Alas they bee mere innocents, I doe not this denay.
                                        (P. 95)

Among the classical sources best known to Shakespeare, Ovid also provided a model for Lady Macbeth's fierce determination in Procne's murder of her son. She is likened, in Golding's translation, to a tiger dragging away "a little Calfe that suckes upon a Hynde."[5] When Procne strikes him with the sword, the child is described as

         holding up his handes, and crying, mother, mother,
And flying to her necke: even where the brest and side doe
   bounde,
And never turnde away hir face.
                                (Pp. 134-135, II. 810-812)

The pitiable murder of babies is found throughout non-Shakespearean literature of the Renaissance. In Thomas Preston's *Cambises* a young boy, referred to as "O blisful babe," is cruelly murdered by the tyrant, to the accompaniment of senti-

---

[5] *Metamorphoses*, trans. by Arthur Golding, Book 6, p. 134, 1. 806, in *Shakespeare's Ovid*, ed. by W. H. D. Rouse (New York, 1961).

Babes Savagely Slaughtered · 99

mental laments by the mother.[6] Faustus promises to build an altar and a church to Beelzebub "and offer lukewarm blood of newborn babes,"[7] a line that may give more sinister meaning to Lady Macbeth's proffered sacrifice of her baby. In Foxe's *Book of Martyrs* innocent babies as victims appear. One of the most striking woodcuts is entitled "A Lamentable Spectacle of three women, with a sely infant brasting out of the Mothers wombe, being first taken out of the fire, and cast in agayne, and so all burned together in the Isle of Garnesey. 1556. July 18."[8] In the woodcut three women are tied to a stake surrounded by flames. The center woman's stomach is torn open, and a child is seen flying out. There is in this illustration a possibly significant departure from the uniformly pathetic fate of slaughtered babies. The child flying out may suggest victory coming from the ordeal, much as the naked newborn babe strides the blast in *Macbeth*. We should, at any rate, turn to evidence that apparently helpless Innocence, especially in the form of babies, had a tradition of triumphing over violence.

III

From the Bible, Shakespeare would have known repeated references to God's abhorrence of the shedding of innocent blood. Among the six or seven things that the Lord hates, Proverbs mentions "the hands that shede innocent blood" (6:17). What is more, God will not pardon it (2 Kings 24:4). For those who "wait for blood, & lie privelie for the innocent without a cause," "feare cometh like sudden desolation, and your destruction shal come, like a whirle winde" (Proverbs 1:11, 27). Only the expiation prescribed by the Lord can "take away the crye of innocent blood from thee" (Deuteronomy 21:9).

One of the most popular subjects in the medieval cycles, still played in Shakespeare's youth, was the massacre of the innocents by Herod. Herod is typically shown after the slaughter as

[6] *Specimens of the Pre-Shaksperean Drama*, ed. by John Matthews Manly (Boston, 1897), II, 185–186.
[7] *Doctor Faustus*, ed. by John D. Jump (The Revels Plays), (London, 1962), scene V, ll. 13–14.
[8] *Actes and Monuments* (1583), p. 1944.

quaking for fear because of the child he cannot kill: "yit I am in no certeyn of that young child."⁹ Jesus is of course the major example of Innocence perennially rising triumphant, and I need not argue the archetypal importance of this example for a play in which the babe is associated with "heaven's cherubins." But the later image of the bloody baby which appears to Macbeth is startlingly suggested by an episode in another cycle play. In *The Play of the Sacrament,* Jonathan and others have "done tormentery" to the Eucharist. They are themselves tormented by the spectacle of

> A chyld apperyng with wondys blody:
> A swemfulle syght yt ys to looke upon.¹⁰

In Elizabethan England the tradition of the baby who arises triumphantly, sometimes retributively, from violence took most sensational form in the genre which especially catered to popular taste—that of the murder pamphlets. Two of these tell a current story that appealed so much to the public. The sister of a boy who was murdered had her tongue cut out so that she could not reveal the crime. She for "foure yeeres remayned dumme and speechlesse, and now perfectly speaketh, revealing the Murther, having no tongue to be seen." The girl is presented as an "innocent."¹¹ One of the most memorable details which excite the tearful pity of even some of the culprits is that in which the murderess kills a pregnant woman: "shee ript her up the belly, making herselfe a tragicall midwife, or truly a mur-

---

⁹ "Candelmas Day & the Killynge of the Children of Israell" [1512], in *The Digby Plays,* ed. by F. J. Furnivall (Early English Text Society), (London, 1896), pp. 15–16. The slaughter is also found in the Towneley and York cycles. Herod is briefly mentioned in connection with *Macbeth* in Roy W. Battenhouse, *Shakespearean Tragedy. Its Art and Its Christian Premises* (Bloomington, Ind., 1969); p. 72. Professor Battenhouse's book, which did not appear until I had completed this study, is, like Roland Mushat Frye's, the work of a learned theologian as well as literary scholar and it serves as a massive counterbalance to Frye's book, which is perhaps too much limited to the Reformers. Battenhouse makes only occasional references to *Macbeth.*

¹⁰ *Specimens of the Pre-Shaksperean Drama,* I, 269.

¹¹ *The Most Cruell and Bloody Murther Committed by an Inkeepers Wife* (1606), title page and sig. A 4ʳ. Also, *The Horrible Murther of a Young Boy of Three Yeres of Age* (1606).

theresse, that brought an abortive babe to the world" (sig. A 3ᵛ). The babe does not arise victorious except through the miraculous agency of the little girl who regains her speech. Another pamphlet tells of *A Most Horrible and Destestable Murther Committed by a Bloudie Man upon His Owne Wife: and Most Strangely Revealed by His Childe that Was under Five Yeares of Age* (1595). And another pamphlet, though not dealing with a murder, celebrates the mysterious force of babies through the story of one who was heard to cry in the mother's womb before birth. The moral appended to the story expresses the proverbial wisdom which must underly all these events: "Gods might and power is disclosed by the mouthes of sucking Babes."[12]

IV

In determining Shakespeare's attitude toward babies and other symbols of Innocence in *Macbeth*, the best background material must, of course, be his practice in earlier plays. These works, especially the history plays, almost invariably exploit to the fullest the innocence of the victims. In fact, murder in the histories for Shakespeare seemed to involve in its very concept a victim who is very young and who might in Elizabethan parlance be called a babe. But Shakespeare does not always explicitly, as do the murder pamphlets, point out any triumph for the innocent victims. He prefers to leave this message to the more forceful commentary of the stories themselves. The babes eventually rise again, they inevitably rise again, but in different form, to avenge the murders. Shakespeare concentrates his art and language upon making the murder of Innocence as heart-rending as possible. He makes us feel the very quality of Pity like a naked new-born babe.

One of the first and most influential murders in Shakespeare's histories is that of young Rutland in *3 Henry VI*. Though a boy, he is given many qualities which Shakespeare associated with the babe: "this innocent child" (I.iii.8) and "sweet Rutland"

[12] *A Strange and Miraculous Accident Happened in the Cittie of Purmerent, on New-yeeres Even Last Past, 1599* (1599), p. 7.

(I.iv.147). In *Richard III* his innocence is expressed as "the faultless blood of pretty Rutland" (I.iii.178), and he himself is called "the innocent" and "that babe" (I.iii.182,183). No murder in Shakespeare's early plays makes a deeper impression. "Tyrants themselves wept when it was reported" (*Richard III* I.iii.185). Tears do, in fact, lead to the inevitable retribution that overtakes Margaret and her allies. York speaks prophetically:

> These tears are my sweet Rutland's obsequies;
> And every drop cries vengeance for his death. . . .
> *(3 Henry VI I.iv.147–148)*

One thinks of Macbeth's vision of tears drowning the wind. Pity swells to such proportions (even Northumberland weeps) that, we are almost made to feel, it brings about the overthrow of the Lancastrians. At any rate, the triumph of the "babe" is made clear in *Richard III* when Elizabeth declares for all parties present: "So just is God, to right the innocent" (I.iii.182).

Another long chain of retribution, resulting partly from Rutland's death, is begun in *3 Henry VI* with the killing of Margaret's own son Edward, who is, "in respect, a child" (V.v.56), a "sweet young prince" (V.v.67). Obvious force is given to Margaret's protest, anticipatory of *Macbeth*:

> You have no children, butchers! if you had,
> The thought of them would have stirr'd up remorse;
> But if you ever chance to have a child,
> Look in his youth to have him so cut off. . . .
> *(V.v.63–66)*

The curse does take effect in *Richard III*. Thus two innocent children in *3 Henry VI* are instrumental in rising again to provide the tragedies in *Richard III*.

Queen Margaret's curse will, of course, be fulfilled in the most atrocious murder in these early plays, that of the two young princes in *Richard III*. Even the guilty Tyrrel calls it

> The most arch deed of piteous massacre
> That ever yet this land was guilty of.
> *(IV.iii.2–3)*

And the two murderers, "flesh'd villains, bloody dogs, ... Wept like two children in their death's sad story" (IV.iii.6–8). Their sad story takes the most emotional of the conventional forms, with the young children given the more pathetic name of "babes":

> "O, thus," quoth Dighton, "lay the gentle babes";
> "Thus, thus," quoth Forrest, "girdling one another
> Within their alabaster innocent arms.
> Their lips were four red roses on a stalk,
> Which in their summer beauty kiss'd each other."
>
> *(IV.iii.9–13)*

But tears drown the wind, in more than a pretty, sentimental sense, within the play. This heinous act is the beginning of the disastrous separation of Richard and Buckingham; and a babe does return to discomfit Richard the night before his fatal battle.

One could extend this survey further, through Arthur in *King John*, for instance; the death of this "pretty child" (IV.i.130) is instrumental in John's downfall. The lords turn against him, for this is "The height, the crest, or crest unto the crest, / Of murder's arms" (IV.iii.45–46). But the point has been sufficiently made that Shakespeare, even in his earliest plays, conceived of the supreme form of violence as that against Innocence and, at the same time, showed that Innocence is anything but helpless in the working out of providence. Macbeth knew this part of his fate in the "If it were done" soliloquy, but like other parts of his fate, he did not know its frightful power.

V

In this soliloquy Macbeth pictures Pity as "a naked new-born babe." He could image nothing more vulnerable, more sensitive. The "naked" adds what "new-born" really does not need, the essence of exposure. But feeling in this play takes the form of nakedness. When, for instance, all the thanes are gathered after Duncan's murder is known and Lady Macbeth has just fainted, Banquo suggests:

> And when we have our naked frailties hid,
> That suffer in exposure, let us meet,
> And question this most bloody piece of work,
> To know it further.
>
> *(II.iii.126–129)*

On a literal level Banquo may mean only, since those present are hastily clad, that they should meet after getting dressed. But the "naked frailties" well expresses the exposed feelings of all present, even of Lady Macbeth; and we shall see that in a play unparalleled in sensation, the naked frailties of almost all the actors are of major importance—those who clearly represent Pity and those who, like Macbeth and his Lady, have the horrid deed blown in their eye. And we should look ahead here by noting a feature of the soliloquy which will occupy our attention later: the eye, of all parts of the body, is the most helpless, the most sensitive; and a major part of Macbeth's punishment from Pity will be through the eye.

There are other emphatic examples of helpless babies in the play. Lady Macbeth requires an allusion to a baby in order to give the utmost force to her resolution:

> I have given suck, and know
> How tender 'tis to love the babe that milks me:
> I would, while it was smiling in my face,
> Have pluck'd my nipple from his boneless gums,
> And dash'd the brains out, had I so sworn
> As you have done to this.
>
> *(I.vii.64–59)*

It would be difficult to exceed this speech in the combination of innocence and violence. There are words of great softness of feeling; *tender, love, milks, smiling, nipple,* and *boneless gums.* Against these are matched the ferocity of *pluck'd* and *dash'd the brains out.* No speech better illustrates the basis on which sensationalism is built in much of the play: naked frailties violated by brutal evil. And we should not fail to note that the naked frailties exposed here are those of Lady Macbeth. She knows "How tender 'tis to love the babe that milks me"; she has seen the infant smiling in her face. If she were without nakedness, we should not feel the full horror of her demonic resolution and commitment. That she is here attuning herself to the Witches is suggested by the lines of one of them:

> Finger of birth-strangled babe,
> Ditch-deliver'd by a drab. . . .
>
> *(IV.i.30–31)*

The Witches, too, sacrifice a babe for their brew, and this particular brew differs from Lady Macbeth's sacrifice only in being deliberately prepared for Macbeth's ruin. It will be, like the naked feelings Lady Macbeth sacrifices in the imagined form of a baby, an agent of retribution.

Except for the Apparitions, the other babe figures are less symbolic. The suffering of Scotland under Macbeth as tyrant is expressed by the crying of orphans (IV.iii.5). Macduff's penalty for helping to save his country is to have his "babes, / Savagely slaughter'd" (IV.iii.204–205). The scenes of the slaughter and the reception of it by Macduff are made much of, doubtless to enhance the strong strain of Pity suffering under tyranny and the necessary, but temporal, sacrifice of Innocence in the ultimate triumph. This purpose is found in another form in the scene of Macduff's grief—Malcolm's testing of Macduff. This scene is often criticized as a lengthy distraction, but we should remember that it contains, besides the report of Macduff's children slaughtered, another theme of Innocence: that of the innocent Malcolm who will soon be victorious. Shakespeare takes great pains to point out not simply the virtue of Malcolm but also his almost babelike innocence. He protests to Macduff:

> I am young; but something
> You may deserve of him through me, and wisdom
> To offer up a weak, poor, innocent lamb,
> T' appease an angry god.
>
> *(IV.iii.14–17)*

In the earnestness of his dramatic message, Shakespeare almost overstates the theme of Innocence violated. We have not just "lamb"—adequate in itself—but "weak, poor, innocent lamb."

Malcolm further protests that he is unknown to women, has never told a lie or broken faith (IV.iii.125–131). At the risk of making his savior of Scotland Innocence personified rather than a real character, Shakespeare lays on the childlike qualities relentlessly.

The ultimate triumph of babes, including young Malcolm, is figured forth in the Apparitions shown to Macbeth as his destiny. The First Apparition is an armed head, representing probably not Macduff, as some critics think, nor Macbeth's own head, but the armed head of the rebellion that will unseat the tyrant. The Second Apparition, "a bloody child," is almost certainly the baby who was untimely ripped from his mother's womb—Macduff. Significantly, a Witch describes him as "more potent than the first" (IV.i.76). The symbolism is perfect for the theme of Innocence ultimately triumphant, for the babe is shown to be more awful to Macbeth than the armed head. It is, moreover, this Apparition who by his message helps to lead Macbeth, through willful blindness, to destruction. The Third Apparition is another babe figure: "a child crowned with a tree in his hand," obviously Malcolm. He too is of terrible consequence, for he "wears upon his baby brow the round / And top of sovereignty" (IV.i.88–89).

Allied to the babe motif in suggestion of Innocence is that of milk. Malcolm, to express the worst possible horror that he would allegedly perpetrate as King, puts it in terms of desecrated milk:

> Nay, had I power, I should
> Pour the sweet milk of concord into Hell,
> Uproar the universal peace, confound
> All unity on earth.
>
> *(IV.iii.97–100)*

Milk is the ideal substance to betoken concord, that which brings men together in fundamental compassion. Such meaning is hinted at by Lady Macbeth in the first reference to milk in the play. She describes her absent husband as "too full o' the milk of human kindness, / To catch the nearest way" (I.v.17–18). Her misgiving is justified, for it is an important part of his tragedy that he can feel for humankind. Without this quality in him the sensationalism of the play would be expended purely from without, upon the observers and victims. Macbeth, as his beautiful description of Duncan shows, has within himself the innocence, the nakedness of feeling, that makes him at first the principal sufferer from the horrid deed. So, to a lesser extent, does Lady Macbeth herself. The most appropriate symbol of the innocence that she is trying to give up is her milk, which she offers in exchange for gall to the murdering ministers (I.v.47–49). Indeed, one of the most shocking instances of Innocence violated is her prayer for unsexing.

To exactly what degree she succeeds in destroying her own milk of human kindness, we shall never know. She does faint. She must secretly, nightly, relive the murder until her desperate death. She remains innocent of murder after the first horrible crime. Unlike her husband, she never hardens into further brutality. There is even a pathetic solicitude, a desire to keep his wife innocent, in Macbeth's affectionate concern for her as he plans the murder of Banquo. Her frightened, hopeless "What's to be done?" draws his reassurance, "Be innocent of the knowledge, dearest chuck, / Till thou applaud the deed" (III.ii.44–46). And there is a pathetic quality even in the bloody Macbeth after Banquo's murder when he sees his hallucination as "the initiate fear, that wants hard use: / We are yet but young in deed" (III.iv.142–143). One never completely loses sight of the pity, in both of them, that is being hardened. But tears do not, for either of them, really drown the wind. The Pity that defeats them is that babelike Innocence that rises triumphant, not within themselves, but in others.

However, one aspect of violated Innocence does arise, within Macbeth himself, to torment him. This is sleep. Macbeth's first reference to sleep as victim shows that he is aware of its vulnerability:

> Now o'er the one half-world
> Nature seems dead, and wicked dreams abuse
> The curtain'd sleep.
>
> *(II.i.49–51)*

The image is a very good one. It may mean that wicked dreams attack, or deceive, the helpless sleep beneath the closed eyelids, the vulnerable place. Or it may suggest the picture of a bed of state, curtained like Duncan's, behind which protection the insidious intruder may slip in. Lady Macbeth has a skeptical, perhaps resolutely skeptical, idea of both the sleeping and the dead (II.ii.42–54). But Macbeth receives horror from the act of murdering the sleeping Duncan. This act enlarges for him the voice which cries:

> "Sleep no more!
> Macbeth does murder Sleep,"—the innocent Sleep. . . .

He will be able to sleep no more, perhaps unto eternity. And it is worth noting that once again Shakespeare makes the victim specifically innocent, and yet potentially terrible.

Innocence may rise victorious in many instances, but its victory is made the more important by the pervasiveness with which it is buffeted and outraged in scattered images throughout the play. Darkness *entombs* the face of the earth when living light should kiss it (II.iv.9–10). *Entomb* is a particularly strong verb to apply to *face*, and it achieves strengh by contrast with a word of love, *kiss*, singularly rare in *Macbeth*. Dark night also *strangles* the symbol of goodness, the *travelling lamp* (II.iv.6). While the face of earth is entombed, "new sorrows / Strike heaven on the face" so that it yells out in dolor (IV.iii.5–8). Heaven struck on the face is certainly the supreme symbol of Innocence violated. And we may note that Heaven "felt with Scotland." Innocence is not quiescent. Another disturbing instance of darkness as a threat to Innocence comes from Macbeth's observation before the murder of Banquo:

> Good things of Day begin to droop and drowse,
> Whiles Night's black agents to their preys do rouse.
>
> *(III.ii.52–53)*

Under Macbeth's tyranny, the good things of day generally suffer. Macduff cries out at the apparent powerlessness of good:

> Bleed, bleed, poor country!
> Great tyranny, lay thou thy basis sure,
> For goodness dare not check thee!
>
> *(IV.iii.31–33)*

And of his wife and children he asks, "The tyrant has not batter'd at their peace?" (IV.iii.178). But Macbeth, ironically, has more than battered at the innocent peace of others. He has "Put rancours in the vessel" of his own "peace" (III.i.66). And not only for others but for himself and his Lady, he violated one of those great symbols of humankindness, human fellowship, when he "broke the good meeting / With most admir'd disorder" (III.iv.108–109).

Unlike his contemporaries, therefore, Shakespeare extends the horror and pity of outraged Innocence to more than the fact of murder, and to more than babies. He includes the innocence of the mild Duncan, of the good people of daylight, of Heaven, and even—to a limited but moving degree—of Macbeth and Lady Macbeth, who are, in a terrible manner neither of them fully knows, still very young in deed.

Chapter VII

More Strange
Than Such a Murder Is

Uncontrolled, expanding blood and the outrage committed upon Innocence constitute two of the most strongly sensational aspects of violence in *Macbeth*. But the play's disturbing power sometimes enlarges from deed and tangible horror to macrocosmically atmospheric repercussions, from the natural to the supernatural, from merely human violence to the agitation of the country, mankind, and the universe. These enlarging, atmospheric effects, found more densely in *Macbeth* than in any other Shakespearean play, help to characterize its sensational distinction. And if we seek a generic term for them, we may well use the word that appears so frequently (eighteen times) in the play, *strange*.

When Macbeth sees one of the dead rising again with twenty mortal murders on his crown, he speaks for the play as a whole in declaring the phenomenon "more strange / Than such a murder is" (III.iv.81–82). Strangeness enhances the feeling of alarm, transmutes brutal violence and ugliness into mystery and the awesomeness of evil. It adds tension and ineffable fear to the play. The meaning of *strange* covers most of the unusual, unnatural, or supernatural phenomena. The word is first used to convey the excitement of the unknown and to prepare us for strangeness of event when Rosse enters with news of the rebellion. Lennox comments:

What a haste looks through his eyes! So should he look
That seems to speak things strange.

(I.ii.47–48)

Almost all reports in the play, including that of the bleeding Captain, of Seyton, who reports the death of Lady Macbeth, and of the Messenger who tells of the moving woods, have this strange quality. The Witches bring Macbeth "strange intelligence" (I.iii.76), and Banquo refers to their appearance and message as "strange" (I.iii.122). When Duncan's horses eat each other, it is reported as "a thing most strange" (II.iv.14). The eerie, unfamiliar, undefined quality of the strange is felt in the "strange screams of death" which are heard on the night of Duncan's murder (II.iii.57). The word tends during the course of the play to take on more and more the connotation of its Latin original, *extraneus*, something outside and not related to oneself, and hence unknown. The new honors come upon Macbeth like "strange garments" (I.iii.145). He refers to seeing Banquo's Ghost as his "strange and self-abuse" (III.iv.141). And he comes to feel strange even to himself. When others do not share his horrifying vision, he protests:

> You make me strange
> Even to the disposition that I owe,
> When now I think you can behold such sights,
> And keep the natural ruby of your cheeks,
> When mine is blanch'd with fear.
>
> *(III.iv.111–115)*

He develops "strange things" in his head (III.iv.138). He knows himself less and less. And other characters in the play almost similarly separate into *strangers*, the word that effectively develops from *strange*. Malcolm does not at first recognize his countryman Rosse in the separation caused by Macbeth's evil, and he prays, "Good God, betimes remove / The means that makes us strangers!" (IV.iii.162–163). Scotland is a country that is "Almost afraid to know itself" (IV.iii.165).

For the present purpose, however, the most important connotation of *strange* is that of disturbingly ominous events, for these precede, accompany, and follow the crucial murder and give to the play most of its mystery. Two references in the play underscore this primary meaning by suggesting a possible source for many of the strange happenings. Lady Macbeth warns her husband during his premurder terror:

> Your face, my Thane, is as a book, where men
> May read strange matters.
>
> *(I.v.62–63)*

From Chapter II we know what kind of book the Lady is referring to. There were, we recall, many books dealing with unnatural events, almost all of which books had *strange* in the title. Macbeth's face is like such a book in registering his impression from the Witches, from the "horrible imaginings," and from the "horrid image" of the murdered Duncan. These books contained also unnatural births, unnatural darkness, portents, with frequent references to Doomsday, and other "strange" events—virtually all the phenomena dramatized in *Macbeth*. They are even now, in the first act, at least a dim threat in Macbeth's mind. And it is noteworthy that their effect is noticeable in Macbeth's face. He will be throughout the play the principal registrar for all that is horrible. However, there is another, though brief, chronicler of the strange. This is the Old Man, who, like the character of the same name in *Doctor Faustus*, is meant to be both less and more than a human being. He is an abstraction, a voice almost outside the play, who can comment with the authority of one who has experienced almost everything, worldly and unworldly. He has witnessed nothing like the events on the night of the murder:

> Threescore and ten I can remember well;
> Within the volume of which time I have seen
> Hours dreadful, and things strange, but this sore night
> Hath trifled former knowings.
>
> *(II.iv.1–4)*

Again there is the reference to the book of "things strange." Their dreadful news characterizes the sought-for effect of the "strange" tradition, but these treatises are nothing in effect as compared with the horrors in the play and the artistry with which they are presented. But though the sensational treatises were usually crude in artistry, they did have, as we have noticed, a meaningful design, and this design may have helped to make the strange effects of *Macbeth* more than merely thrilling in horror. Moreover, many of their details, notably of witches, seem to have found their way into *Macbeth*. It is also startling to find in one of them—more literary, to be sure, than the typical pamphlets—Thomas Deloney's *Strange Histories, of Kings, Princes, Dukes, Earles, Lords, Ladies, Knights, and Gentlemen* (1602), an account of the woods moving, exactly as they do in *Macbeth*, to amaze and discomfit an army (sig. A 2^v). Even more, perhaps, the popularity of this kind of book may have influenced Shakespeare in his remarkable amplification of the prodigies that he read of in Holinshed.[1]

II

In Chapter V we observed how the bleeding Captain serves as one of two not so happy prologues to the swelling act of the imperial theme. The other prologue, occurring at the very beginning of the play, consists of the three Witches and the tumult in nature which accompanies them. To understand their strange, ominous role, so emphatically placed, we should again do well to look first at similar kinds of portentous, unnatural figures in earlier plays.

Like *Macbeth*, *Caesar's Revenge* (ca. 1595) opens with no human figures but rather with a personification named Discord. She is announced with an alarum and with "flames of fire," and the scene is one of darkness because of terrible events to ensue. Caesar is currently enjoying military victory like that of Macbeth as described by the bleeding Captain:

---

[1] Another possible reference in the play to the "strange" books is Macbeth's statement:

> The time has been, my senses would have cool'd
> To hear a night-shriek; and my fell of hair
> Would at a dismal treatise rouse, and stir,
> As life were in 't.
>
> (V.v.10–13)

> Caesars keene Falchion, through the Adverse rankes,
> For his sterne Master hewes a passage out,
> Through troupes & troonkes, & steele, & standing blood.[2]

It is Discord's business both to prophesy and to abet the ruin of this hero and his state. She calls upon both the heavens and the furies to carry out the destruction as a kind of punishment:

> You gentle Heavens. O execute your wrath
> On vile mortality, that hath scornd your powers.
> You night borne Sisters to whose haires are ty'd
> In Adamantine Chaines both Gods and Men
> Winde on your webbe of mischiefe and of plague....
> *(11. 25–29)*

These "night borne Sisters" are suggestive of the Witches. Why they are linked with the "Heavens" is not clear in this play, except that both have a chastising function. Discord herself seems merely to revel in the condition that her name signifies. She appears as an introduction to each act of the play, much as the Witches make periodic appearances as the condition of Macbeth's career and soul warrants. At the beginning of Act V, as we have earlier noted, Discord announced that "The furies have proclaym'd a festivall" for Brutus and mean to banquet with his blood (11. 2133–2134). She invokes the sun to hide itself: "Let no light shine" (1. 2143). Further,

> Furies, and Ghosts, with your blue-burning lampes,
> In mazing terror ride through Roman rankes:
> With dread affrighting those stout Champions hearts,
> All stygian fiendes now leave whereas you dwell:
> And come into the world and make it hell.
> *(11. 2145–2149)*

She produces, or at least superintends, as an infernal "presenter" of the play, the hell on earth, with its fiends and ghosts and furies.

If this play were unique, we should be tempted to overvalue

---

[2] *The Tragedy of Caesar and Pompey, or Caesars Revenge* (ca. 1595), Malone Society Reprints (1911), Chorus I, 11. 17–19.

it as an influence on *Macbeth*, for it contains many of the strange phenomena of *Macbeth*, and these are presided over by a spirit, Discord, who in turn directs the "night borne Sisters." But similar spirits exist in other plays, also with a "presenting" function. In *Locrine* (ca. 1591), Discord is replaced by Ate. At the beginning of each act there is a dumb show in which she appears "with thunder and lightning all in black, with a burning torch in one hand and a bloodie sword in the other hand." [3] She symbolizes the punishment and destruction that are to come, and there is a ghost who comments upon the dumb show. After the thunder and lightning, the Ghost of Corineus describes the lurid fire, the trembling of the earth, the birds of darkness, the "hellish night"—all " Foretelling some unwonted miserie" (V.iv.1–13). In *The Battle of Alcazar* (ca. 1589), Nemesis is the Presenter of a dumb show, and three ghosts and three furies carry out the mission of Nemesis. In *Gismond of Salerne* (ca. 1566), Megaera is the spirit who arises from hell to bring discord. Examples might be added, notably Revenge in *The Spanish Tragedy*, to these merely suggestive ones.

What they all tend to show is that spirits at the beginning of a play, whether they are in a dumb show or are presenters of the action, would have connoted for Elizabethan audiences strange and baleful events to follow. They would not necessarily control the action, but they would certainly preside over it. They would be either furies or closely associated with ministers of retribution. They are not morally responsible agents, but, like Discord, seem to be gloating participants in whatever temptation or punishment the Heavens have ordained for man's evil. In *Macbeth*, by preceding the narration of Macbeth's military victory, the spirits would have cast a pall over the whole narration, giving a sinister light to the bloody conquest and alerting the audience for irony. But the Witches in *Macbeth* are something special, too—not merely conventionally ominous prologues; and we must look more closely at the sensational artistry in this most remarkable of Elizabethan strange phenomena.

---

[3] So she is described in the first act. Thereafter, every appearance has "Enter Ate as before." References are to the edition in *The Shakespeare Apocrypha*, ed. by C. F. Tucker Brooke (Oxford, 1929).

III

Shakespeare's Witches, or Weird Sisters, are the more remarkable in that before *Macbeth*, as Miss Bradbrook reminds us, witches had primarily "appeared on the stage only in such harmless forms as Mother Bombie or the Wise Woman of Hogsdon.... *Macbeth* was the first play to introduce to the stage in a serious manner the rites and practices of contemporary witchcraft." [4] Why it was the first to do so we can only speculate. Shakespeare had made drab use of witches and witchcraft in the *Henry VI* plays, but these did not in any way prepare for the powerfully disturbing and central role they would have in *Macbeth*. He was, to be sure, becoming more interested in the supernatural, as shown by *Julius Caesar* and *Hamlet*, and by the demidiabolic in *Othello*. He may also have been slightly influenced by King James's interest in witches. I would certainly not underrate the appropriateness of these creatures in a play which is almost unique for a tragedy in the number of "strange" ingredients. But Shakespeare did not set out to write a "strange" play, despite the increasing Jacobean taste for the baroque and for spectacle. Rather, in *King Lear*, generally conceded to be his preceding tragedy, he had demonstrated a supreme artistic involvement with the evil and its ramification in the world of nature. And so, more concentratedly, he was to do in *Macbeth*. Evil in this play is so great, so mysterious, that it cannot be confined to human character any more than it can be confined to natural phenomena.

But like the major aspect of evil described in Chapter II, the Witches have a specific, a defined, as well as a larger, more mysterious nature. Robert H. West, an able authority on Elizabethan pneumatology, has good grounds when he concludes that there is no tight demonology in *Macbeth*, that Shakespeare

> treats both Macbeth's fall and the Weird Sisters' part in it as awesome mysteries which we may feel and in part observe, but for which we have no sort of formula. Shakespeare does not look behind these mysteries, and he does not suggest that we

[4] M. C. Bradbrook, "The Sources of *Macbeth*," *Shakespeare Survey 4* (Cambridge, 1951), p. 41.

may do so. Rather he looks *into* them, shows us the phenomena in a piercing way that conveys a sense of their ghastly significance without bringing us much the nearer to a rational account of them or of it.[5]

This vaguely awesome concept of the Witches makes for as moving a sense of mystery as does the kindred treatment of evil in general. And it has certain advantages over trying to identify the Sisters more precisely. My attempt here is not to deprive the Witches of that quality of mystery to which, even as imperfect women, they may make some fundamentally feminine claim but to describe some of the features that made them most conspicuously sensational embodiments of evil. I shall later, however, suggest some moderately specific traits that their meaning for the play seems to dictate.

Shakespeare may have deliberately, as West suggests, made them difficult to define in order to enhance their impressiveness as "awesome mysteries." But a part of the confusion comes simply from Shakespeare's combining Holinshed's account (which in itself was conflicting) with what he had heard and read of contemporary witches. Holinshed describes them primarily in the "awesome" manner that would make their role close to ministers of fate. In his narration they appear to Macbeth and Banquo as "a strange and uncouth wonder." They are "three women in strange and wild apparell, resembling creatures of elder world." At first they were reputed as "but some vaine fantasticall illusion by Mackbeth and Banquho. . . . But afterwards the common opinion was, that these women were either the weird sisters, that is (as ye would say) the goddesses of destinie, or else some nymphs or feiries, indued with knowledge of prophesie by their necromanticall science, bicause everie thing came to passe as they had spoken." [6] Shakespeare keeps their "strange" appearance, but he cheapens it, as we shall see. They possibly retain some association with destiny, though they have "masters" and seem to work more by charms than as "goddesses of destinie." They do, however, keep a remark-

[5] "Night's Black Agents in *Macbeth*," *Renaissance Papers* (1956), p. 24.
[6] *The First and Second Volumes of Chronicles* (1587), II, "Historie of Scotland," p. 170.

able "knowledge of prophecie." They are not inappropriately referred to as "Weird Sisters" in the text; so Macbeth himself prefers at first to call them, for he wishes to give them the best of auspices.

In the stage directions, however, the Sisters are called "Witches," and most of their *appearance* in the play bears out this designation. Shakespeare wanted these agents of evil to be foul in looks as they are fair in promise. He found the repulsiveness not in Holinshed but unforgettably detailed in stories about witches which he had either heard about or read, as we must today, in popular tracts on witches or in more learned books, such as those on the Continent or by King James, on demonology. The main tangible impression that he would have gotten from most of the books was that witches were ugly and filthy. It is the ugly and filthy quality, according so well with their primary motto about foulness, that Shakespeare used to major advantage in *Macbeth*.

Witches were generally old women, but they had more than the usual indignities of female age. Samuel Harsnet, in a book that Shakespeare used for *King Lear*, describes one as

> an olde weather-beaten Croane, having her chinne & her knees meeting for age, walking like a bow, leaning on a shaft, hollow-eyed, untoothed, furrowed on her face, having her lips trembling with the palsie, going mumbling in the streetes....[7]

The skeptic Reginald Scot describes the popular impression as that of "women which be commonly old, lame, blearie-eied, pale, fowle, and full of wrinkles; . . . They are leane and deformed, shewing melancholie in their faces, to the horror of all that see them."[8]

Their filth takes various forms. A witch may be referred to simply as "the olde filth."[9] Remy argues that they are filthy because the Devil, whose element is vile, chooses for servants "filthy old hags whose age and poverty serve but to enhance their foulness; and these, as being of a vitiated nature most apt

---

[7] *A Declaration of Egregious Popish Impostures* (1603), p. 136.

[8] *The Discoverie of Witchcraft* (1584), with an introduction by Rev. Montague Summers ([London], 1930), p. 4.

[9] George Gifford, *A Dialogue Concerning Witches and Witchcraftes* (1593), sig. B 2ʳ.

to his purpose, he instructs in all impurity and uncleanness." They are not, for example, to wash their hands.[10] Women are the most likely persons to become witches because of their lust, the "evill humors, that out go their venemous exhalations, ... increased by meanes of their pernicious excrements," and their being "monethlie filled full of superfluous humors." These features make them more infectious and potent to bewitch.[11] Their filthiness is aggravated by their ceremonial anointing of themselves with "the bowels and members of children." They seethe these and other loathsome ingredients in a cauldron, and of the thickest parts of the stew they make ointments.[12] When a group of six witches were ordered searched by officers, "they founde hidden under every one of their cloathes next to their skinnes, a bagge of Swines dounge: which being taken away, stounke so fylthely, that no man could indure the smell."[13] Their favorite familiars, indeed the only kind they could have, were the most repulsive animals, such as toads. In mind they were as filthy as in body, being able both to excite and to frustrate lust. Under the Devil's tutelage, they "fall a dansing and singing of bawdie songs, wherein he leadeth the danse himselfe."[14] The air about them, which they can control, corresponds to their own foulness in the sudden and localized storms they can raise and the thickness and infection of the air.[15]

The Witches in *Macbeth* are typically loathsome in appearance, but with many individualizing features. Banquo describes them (referring to them with the distantly distasteful "these") as

> So wither'd and so wild in their attire,
> That look not like th' inhabitants o' th' earth,
> And yet are on't.
>
> *(I.iii.40–42)*

---

[10] Nicolas Remy, *Demonolatry*, trans. by E. A. Ashwin; ed. by Rev. Montague Summers (London, 1930), p. 38.
[11] Scot, *The Discoverie of Witchcraft*, p. 158.
[12] Ibid., p. 23.
[13] *A Strange Report of Sixe ... Witches* (1601), sig. A 3^r.
[14] Scot, p. 25.
[15] For the storms and atmospheric effects, see King James, *Daemonologie* (1597), p. 46; *Newes from Scotland* (ca. 1591), pp. 16–17; Francesco Maria Guazzo, *Compendium Maleficarum* [1608], trans. by E. A. Ashwin; ed. by Rev. Montague Summers (London, 1929, pp. 19–20; Henry Holland, *A Treatise against Witchcraft* (1590), sig. G 4^r.

Except for the "wither'd," this description corresponds to Holinshed and suggests the unworldly Weird Sisters. But then Banquo proceeds to the disturbingly ugly features that unmistakably mark human witches, referring to their choppy fingers, their skinny lips, and, most distressing of all, their beards. Macbeth, however, is at first impressed by their more "than mortal knowledge" (I.v.3). But as their fairness of omen turns ugly, so do they physically become odious. They are "secret, black, and midnight hags" (IV.i.48) and "filthy hags" (IV.i.115); and he correctly consigns them to their foul element: "Infected be the air whereon they ride" (IV.i.138). In their incantations they use ingredients that make those of the witch tracts seem savory. Their "hell-broth" comprises, however, all the conventional horrors, including the baby; and, as in the tracts, the gruel is to be "thick and slab" (IV.i.32). Their loathsome sexuality is expressed in their chant:

> But in a sieve I'll thither sail,
> And like a rat without a tail;
> I'll do, I'll do, and I'll do.
>
> *(I.iii.8–10)*

A part of the sexual allusion is innocent. As a woman, the Witch would perforce have nothing to correspond to the rat's tail. But the repeated "I'll do" has never, I think, been appreciated for its lewdness. "Do" had the common bawdy meaning of sexual intercourse, and the repeated emphasis suggests the futility of tailless labor. (Probably there should be a comma rather than a semicolon after "tail.") The atmosphere about the Witches is "fog and filthy air." It is effectively contrasted with the castle at Inverness around which, before the evil forces have congregated there, "heaven's breath / Smells wooingly" (I.vi.5–6). It may be the earthly form of "the dunnest smoke of hell" with which Lady Macbeth would enshroud herself and perhaps is a part of the violent forms of darkness on the night of the murder.

In all, the Witches cast their stench of evil over much of the play. They are not merely agents of evil; they manifest it in all its naked ugliness, like Spenser's Duessa stripped. They make, with their hideous forms and their gruesome brew, the audience almost tangibly feel the unsavoriness of the evil. They are mysterious, and far more than filthy women, but their foulness must be foremost in any sensory apprehension of their meaning.

But to say that the Weird Sisters have, for a very good reason, these witchlike features (and others such as killing swine and possibly inducing fits) is not to say that they signify no more than this in the "strange" metaphysical world of the play. They are also the "instruments of Darkness." Although demons are more conventionally to be found in witches' familiars, in the toad and the cat, and also in the witches' masters, there is always a feeling, which grows as the play advances, that the Witches are demonic manifestations of the dark part of a supernatural world. In one of the most sensible of the pamphlets accepting the reality of witches, George Gifford argues that the real powers behind witches are the "Principalities, and Powers, the Rulers of the darknesse of this world" and that "when they take upon them the shapes of such paltrie vermine, as Cats, Mise, Toads, and Weasils, it is even of subtiltie to cover and hide his mightie tyrannie, and power which he exerciseth over the heartes of the wicked."[16] The Devil would so blind the people that, by concentrating on witches, they lose sight of the demonic power at work. "And hereupon all is on a broyle against old women, which can any wayes be suspected to be witches, as if they were the very plagues of the world" (sig. D 1ʳ). Beneath it all, the powers of Darkness, of which the witches are only mean instruments, are

> occupied about the greatest things, as in stirring up Tyrants and wicked men to persecute . . . , to set division and warres between kingdoms and kings . . . : yea, to set all in a broyle and confusion: they would seeme to be busied about trifles, and about these they busie mens mindes, that they may not observe and take heed of them in those other.
>
> (Sig. C 2ʳ)

This is at least a plausible explanation for *Macbeth*. Demons greater than witches are at work in the thoughts of men, waking and sleeping. They, rather than the Witches, stir up tyrants and punish them, while the Witches merely go through the superficial business of troubling by charms.

[16] *A Dialogue Concerning Witches and Witchcraftes*, sig. C 2ʳ.

But may not the Witches themselves be demons? Walter Clyde Curry thinks so; and Willard Farnham presents extensive evidence for his conclusion that they are "demons of the fairy order such as the Elizabethans also called hags or furies. They are fiends in the shape of old women who do evil wherever and however they can...."[17] That they are demons, Farnham argues, is borne out by what Macbeth finally calls them: "juggling fiends" (V.vii.48).

I would add to his persuasive analysis only that Macbeth also seems to recognize something larger than the Witches, and something singular, behind their evil when he begins "To doubt th' equivocation of the fiend, / That lies like truth" (V.v.43-44). Here the Witches are lost sight of and Macbeth confronts directly his single and ultimate Adversary. For whatever the Witches are—and perhaps West's wariness is still wise—we must not err with Macbeth in excitedly achieving "the perfect'st report" (I.v.2) of the Witches if thereby we forget that they met him in the day of his success and that, in the day of his tragedy, it will be "the common Enemy of man" who is waiting for him.

IV

Although the Witches are altogether strange and bring a "strange intelligence," Banquo's Ghost is, as we have seen, the phenomenon which especially impresses Macbeth as "more strange than such a murder is." The Ghost is not so crucial to the interpretation of the play as are the Witches, and it is far less crucial than the Ghost in *Hamlet*. But to Macbeth it is the most excruciating sight he encounters, and for several good reasons. It is, first of all, one of the most impressive ghosts ever to have appeared on the stage. Its closest rival, that of the elder Hamlet, is formidable in his armor and in the chilling atmosphere surrounding him on the battlements. He stalks and he "wafts" with dignity. But like all the other early ghosts, he talks, and talks too much. True, he talks wth a majestic tone of mystery, but he tells

---

[17] *Shakespeare's Tragic Frontier: The World of His Final Tragedies.* (Berkeley and Los Angeles, 1950), p. 99. Professor Farnham's analysis is much more complex than can be adequately represented here. It is the only thorough semantic study of Shakespeare's Witches that I know.

everything except the secrets of his prison house. He is most impressive when he appears silent before Horatio and the sentries.

Banquo makes a more enigmatic and frightening ghost. His most obvious source of terror is in the vivid way he is described physically, surpassing any earlier ghost. Only Seneca could have provided a helpful model in Creon's account of his meeting Laius in Hell:

> Til out at length comes Laius with foule and grisly hue:
> Uncomly drest in wretched plight with fylth all overgrowne:
> All perst with wounds, (I loth to speake) with bloud quight overflown.[18]

Banquo's bloodiness we have already noted, as well as the coldness of the blood, and also the way in which the "twenty mortal murders" on his head recall to Macbeth the excessive brutality of the deed. Even more terrible than the blood, perhaps, are the features of lifeless animation which make of the Ghost a "horrible shadow! / Unreal mock'ry" (III.iv.106). His bones are marrowless and he has no "speculation," that is to say, sense of life, in the eyes which he "glares" with (III.iv.92–94). Such features as these evoke Macbeth's hysterical challenge to "Take any shape but that" and meet him in natural combat (III.iv.101); then his "firm nerves" would never tremble.

The very silence of this specter is frightening. There would have been some reassurance, some assailable opposition, for Macbeth if Banquo had verbally responded to his hysterical protests and challenges. But Banquo merely nods, shakes his gory locks at him, and, in a later appearance, smiles. There is a sinister knowingness in his manner. This can only remind Macbeth of the fundamental threat that Banquo poses, and knows that he poses, to the insecure, barren tyrant. Banquo may be maimed; but his ultimate victory over Macbeth can never be thwarted by murder, for he will appear again and again, as in the Show of Kings.

This silent knowingness of the Ghost is especially harrowing to Macbeth because it recalls for the bloody king not only Ban-

---

[18] *Oedipus*, trans. by Alexander Nevyle, in *Seneca His Tenne Tragedies*, ed. by Thomas Newton (1581), (London, 1927), I, 212.

quo's superiority in the turn of events and his own fate, but also his ironic composure. For Banquo has always been a master of irony. He had capped Macbeth's probably perfunctory "Good repose, the while!" with the more troublingly aware reply, "Thanks, Sir: the like to you" (II.i.29–30). There is consummate irony in the unwelcome way he responds by his presence to Macbeth's command invitation, "Fail not our feast" (III.i. 27). He appears, a little late to be sure and not perfectly dressed for the occasion, but urbane and assured, to take, symbolically, Macbeth's position at the table. In this appearance what is most noticeable, and shocking, is his combination of gory appearance and polite behavior, entering only when he is bidden and acting always with urbane decorum, even leaving when he is told to do so.

What the Ghost actually is constitutes almost as much of a problem as does the nature of the Ghost in *Hamlet*. He could be merely a feverous hallucination, proceeding from a heat-oppressed brain. He could be a suffering soul returning from Purgatory. He could be the veritable dead body of Banquo raised from the grave by the Devil; this explanation would have had the approval of King James,[19] and Macbeth himself seems to think that "charnel-houses and our graves must send / Those that we bury, back" (III.iv.70–71). But in an important treatise on ghosts that Shakespeare must have read before writing *Hamlet*, Ludwig Lavater finds no basis in Scripture that God would, contrary to his own express commandment, give the Devil "leave to raise dead bodies."[20] Lavater offers an explanation for ghosts who, like Banquo's, appear in their murdered form, an explanation that seems to be more consonant with the other apparitions in *Macbeth*. Demonic spirits, he writes (and Hamlet

[19] *Daemonologie*, p. 59. J. C. Maxwell argues that "what makes the apparition of Banquo so terrible to Macbeth, what makes it so tragically shallow of Lady Macbeth to attribute what he sees to mere imagination, is that it is Banquo in person, the real dead body of the man he had murdered, that has appeared at the table." "The Ghost from the Grave: A Note on Shakespeare's Apparitions," *Durham University Journal*, XVII (1956), 58.

[20] *Of Ghostes and Spirites Walking by Nyght*, Englished by R. H. (1572), ed. by J. Dover Wilson and May Yardley (Oxford, 1929), p. 128.

concurs with him), can "appear in divers shapes, not only of those which are alive, but also of deade menne" (p. 167). What is most noteworthy about Lavater's explanation is that a small part of it comes very close to three of the phenomena that torment Macbeth: the Ghost, the dagger, and the voice. At one time

> hath appeared a man al burning in fire, or berayde with bloud: and somewhile, his bowelles have seemed to traile out, his belly being as it were rypped up. Sometimes a shadowe hath only appeared: sometimes a hand, sometimes an instrument, as a staffe, a sworde, or some such like thing which the spirite helde in his hande. Sometimes he appeared in maner of a bundle of hey, burning on fire: another while onely a hoarse kinde of voyce was heard.
> *(P. 92)*

I would therefore, on the strength of this book, of Hamlet's reference to the Devil's ability to assume a desired form, and of the way in which dagger, Witches, and Ghost are thus linked, assume that it is the Devil or a spirit who appears as Banquo, and that Curry is right in believing that his purpose is to confound Macbeth.[21] But it is equally important to recognize that a major purpose of ghosts, Senecan or Christian, is to punish or revenge. Shakespeare could not possibly have devised a more terrifying torment for Macbeth than the re-emergence of his principal threat, bloody but assured; confidently, maddeningly silent ("If thou canst nod, speak too"); and obviously victorious in his ironic mastery of every situation. The Devil, as God's punitive agent, deserves much of the credit; his role here is not inferior to that of the urbane, ironic Mephostophilis in *Doctor Faustus*.

V

There are many other strange phenomena in *Macbeth*, including that of Duncan's horses eating each other, which Shakespeare took from Holinshed. Most of these portend, accompany, or follow the murder of Duncan and most of them involve an unnatural darkening of the world of nature. But they include

---

[21] Walter Clyde Curry, *Shakespeare's Philosophical Patterns* (Baton Rouge, La., 1959; first published 1937), p. 85.

night itself, which pervades the play more than in any other of Shakespeare's plays. We may group these phenomena, with their sense of a darkened world in agony, under the rubric supplied by Shakespeare: "The night has been unruly" (II.iii.55). Not blood, nor the Witches, nor the Ghost, nor the act of murder casts a more oppressive pall of horror over the audience and characters than does the prolonged exposure to darkness entombing the face of the earth and of night's black agents in gigantic activity. This is a good deal more than, though it includes, the filthy kind of murk first raised by the Witches.

For the agitated darkness, natural and unnatural, in the play there is only a brief hint in Holinshed. Referring to Donwald's murder of King Duff, he writes;

> For the space of six moneths togither, after this heinous murther thus committed, there appeared no sunne by day, nor moone by night in anie part of the realme, but still was the skie covered with continuall clouds, and sometimes such outragious winds arose, with lightenings and tempests, that the people were in great feare of present destruction.
>
> *(P. 31)*

It is not enough for us to say that Shakespeare made this hint into a dominant mood and theme of the play solely because, as with other wondrous phenomena, the unnatural darkness was a prominent part of the "strange" lore which he found suitable to the subject of the play. There are other reasons.

One of the most elementary, but not least important, was the popular and literary convention associating tragedy, and the sinister, with darkness. Thomas Nashe recounts that "When anie Poet would describe a horrible Tragicall accident; to adde the more probabilitie & credence unto it, he dismally beginneth to tell, how it was darke night when it was done, and cheerfull daylight had quite abandoned the firmament."[22] John Marston describes the convention for the Elizabethan stage, though in a manner which applies to more than the physical stage:

---

[22] *The Terrors of the Night Or, A Discourse of Apparitions* (1594), in *The Works of Thomas Nashe*, ed. by Ronald B. McKerrow, with corrections and supplementary notes by F. P. Wilson (Oxford, 1958), I, 386.

> The stage of heav'n, is hung with solemne black,
> A time best fitting, to Act Tragedies.[23]

And Shakespeare associates this tradition more clearly with supernatural happenings in Bedford's speech, at the opening of *1 Henry VI*, pronouncing the disturbance in nature appropriate to the death of Henry V:

> Hung be the heavens with black, yield day to night!
> Comets, importing change of times and states,
> Brandish your crystal tresses in the sky,
> And with them scourge the bad revolting stars
> That have consented unto Henry's death!
>
> *(1.i.1–5)*

For murders the backdrop of portentous darkness was almost wholly conventional. In the Fourth Addition to *The Spanish Tragedy*, Hieronimo instructs the Painter how to paint a scene sufficiently horrible for his son's murder: "Let the clouds scowl, make the moon dark, the stars extinct, the winds blowing, the bells tolling, the owl shrieking, the toads croaking, the minutes jarring, and the clock striking twelve."[24] And doubtless many dramatists had some such pictorial precept in mind as, more or less by rote, they painted their scenes of murder.

Certainly the precept is almost always followed in the popular murder plays. The hired assassins in *Arden of Feversham* (ca. 1591) call upon "Black night" and "sheting darknesse" to hide their deed from the eye of the world.[25] In *A Warning for Faire Women* (ca. 1599), the murderers conjure the equivalent of Macbeth's "seeling night":

> Oh sable night, sit on the eie of heaven,
> That it discerne not this blacke deed of darknesse....
>
> *(Sig. D 2ᵛ)*

In answer to the prayer, the sun does not shine on the day of the

---

[23] *The Insatiate Countess* IV.i. In *The Plays of John Marston*, ed. by H. Harvey Wood (Edinburgh, 1939), III, 65.
[24] *The Spanish Tragedy*, ed. by Philip Edwards (The Revels Plays), (London, 1959), p. 132, ll. 147–151.
[25] In *Malone Society Reprints* (1940), III.ii.1121–1124.

murder. One sees in these plays at least an attempt to make darkness functional in a thematic way. It is requested to hide the murderers from the eye of earth or, of course an impossibility, from the eye of heaven. The further and significant association of night with the powers of Darkness is made in a murder tract, *The most Horrible . . . Murther* (1591). Here the murderer consulted with the

> cursed ruler of darknesse howe hee might worke mischiefe, and yet defende his owne credite from blot of infamie. Well somewhat was devised and concluded upon, as after by his actions might be gathered: for the daie no sooner appered, but as prefiguring some dismall accident, it covered the earth with a lowring countenaunce, and black cloudes in signe of ensuing miseries. . . . *(Sig. A 3ʳ)*

Whether or not associated with murder, night when used most significantly came to be associated with evil forces. Nashe so regards it in *The Terrors of the Night* (1594); and I am reasonably confident that Shakespeare read this chilling account of the world of darkness. In a passage relevant to *Macbeth*, Nashe writes that night hinders men from looking to heaven for help from their Redeemer. It is proved "that the divell is a speciall predominant Planet of the night, and that our creator for our punishment hath allotted it to him as his peculiar segniorie and kingdome" (p. 346). Night, then, is not only the Devil's province; it is assigned to him for our punishment. An atmosphere detailing the nightmarish punishments that the evil spirits make possible in night is nowhere better created than in The Wisdom of Solomon. There the unrighteous "were bounde with the bands of darkenes, and long night," hoping thereby "to escape the everlasting providence."

> And while they thought to bee hid in their darke sinnes, they were scattered abroad in the darke covering of forgetfulnesse, fearing horribly and troubled with visions.
> For the denne that hidde them, kept them not from feare; but the sounds that were about them, troubled them, and terrible visions and sorrowfull sightes did appeare.
> . . . . .
> And the illusions of the magicall artes were broght downe. . . .
> *(17:2–7)*

Shakespeare did not come promptly or easily to the dramatic and meaningful use of darkness that is so inseparable from the distinction of *Macbeth* as a tragedy. In his early works night tends to be conventionally decorative as in *1 Henry VI*. In *The Rape of Lucrece,* most memorably a night piece, it is a "Black stage for tragedies and murders fell" (1. 766). It is picturesquely "sable Night, mother of Dread and Fear" (1. 117). More promisingly, it is used with a sinister power, and with symbols that Shakespeare will never altogether abandon, as Tarquin prepares, like Macbeth, for his evil deed. There is an effectively ominous tone, with some of the rhythm of incantation found in *Macbeth*, in this stanza:

> Now stole upon the time the dead of night,
> When heavy sleep had clos'd up mortal eyes.
> No comfortable star did lend his light,
> No noise but owls' and wolves' death-boding cries;
> Now serves the season that they may surprise
>   The silly lambs. Pure thoughts are dead and still,
>   While lust and murder wakes to stain and kill.
>   *(ll. 162–168)*

Here is the starlessness of *Macbeth*, the ominous owls, and the rising of evil thoughts. The last line in particular must have been memorably felt by Shakespeare, for it recurs, in more supernatural form, in "Whiles Night's black agents to their preys do rouse" and, with the earlier wolves, in "Wither'd Murder alarum'd by his sentinel, the wolf." In *2 Henry VI* night is used as mysteriously as Shakespeare then could do so for a scene of conjuration (I.iv.16–43). And in the same play a murderer, without any apparent motive other than setting the scene, describes the "tragic melancholy night" (IV.i.4) as he prepares for the deed. There is a hint of the supernatural, however, in that wolves arouse the "jades"

> Who, with their drowsy, slow, and flagging wings,
> Clip dead men's graves, and from their misty jaws
> Breathe foul contagious darkness in the air.
>   *(IV.i.5–7)*

And it should be noticed that Shakespeare, although the mood of night is not sustained, was occasionally concerned with omens and sorcery in this play. In *Titus Andronicus*, Aaron's gloating identification with "Acts of black nght" (V.i.64) does not pervade the play, nor does his villainy succeed in descending to infernal meanings.

It is not until *Julius Caesar* that the depiction of night becomes dramatically, and not merely scenically, meaningful. Scenes depicting the night before Caesar's assassination are designed to be tumultuously portentous. It is a "perilous night" (I.iii.47), a "dreadful night" (I.iii.73), and a "fearful night" (I.iii.126, 137). The disturbances are clearly meant to be more than natural. They are explained by the Epicurean Cassius as merely a suitable setting for the bloody business:

> And the complexion of the element
> In favour's like the work we have in hand,
> Most bloody, fiery, and most terrible.
>
> *(I.iii.128–130)*

But Casca sees the disturbances as supernatural:

> Either there is a civil strife in heaven,
> Or else the world, too saucy with the gods,
> Incenses them to send destruction.
>
> *(I.iii.11–13)*

Calpurnia, too, in her vivid recounting of the night sees the events as portentous, and so they are recalled in *Hamlet*. But although they mainly surround and trouble the conspirators, they do not create a sense of supernatural evil. There is much upheaval but little feeling of the murky pall of dark. The darkness is atmospherically valuable mainly as a backdrop for the fierce color of the fiery warriors, the drizzled blood, and the lightning.

There is a somewhat similar situation in the "wild night" (II.iv.311) that is in travail with the tempest in *King Lear*. Although Shakespeare several times calls passing attention to the night, it is lighted up with "sheets of fire" (III.ii.46), and there is little feeling of mysterious darkness. And despite the preternatural violence of the storm, Shakespeare does not make it unmistakably an action by either the heavens or evil spirits, though there is certainly much human evil that, in Lear's awakening awareness, should "cry / These dreadful summoners grace" (III.ii.58–59). The nocturnal storm in *King Lear* is unquestionably Shakespeare's most awesome one, and we are made to feel it as such. For *Macbeth*, his next tragedy, Shakespeare retained some of the tumult and gave more sustained meaning and mystery to the darkness. *Julius Caesar* and *King Lear* demonstrate that in stagecraft and in poetry Shakespeare could now give more than decorative significance to an unruly night.

Although night in *Macbeth* goes well beyond the conventional scenic qualities prescribed by Nashe to give a somber backdrop for the tragic action, these qualities must not be underestimated. They are better used here than probably in any other English literary work. But to account analytically for the way Shakespeare thus makes us feel the night and the dark is almost impossible. A large part of the secret would lie in the ominous, often hushed music of the verse and in the incantatory rhythms used by both the protagonists in their famous night invocations. For it is in these invocations that the mood of night is principally achieved. Other characters describe it, at a distance, with alien horror. Macbeth and his Lady are almost a part of it; and because they feel it so intimately, and contribute morally to it, we are made to feel it also.

Macbeth is beginning to immerse himself, body and soul, in evil when he approaches the murder of Duncan. He sets the scene powerfully, but he also becomes a part of the evil as much as were the conventional symbols of night:

>   Now o'er the one-half world
> Nature seems dead, and wicked dreams abuse
> The curtain'd sleep: Witchcraft celebrates
> Pale Hecate's off'rings; and wither'd Murder,
> Alarum'd by his sentinel, the wolf,
> Whose howl's his watch, thus with his stealthy pace,
> With Tarquin's ravishing strides, towards his design
> Moves like a ghost.
>   *(II.i.49–56)*

One feels, as he does not in the earlier "scenic" descriptions, the real, latent danger and evil of night. When Nature is dead, the agents of evil such as wicked dreams, witchcraft, animals of prey, and murder, take over half—the dark half—not only of the world but of man's nature. These forces are not static, as in Nashe's hypothetical picture, but very active. Their movement is covert but felt; and their sinister sound is heard not only in the wolf's howl but in the music of the verse. An even better use of sound to convey the drowsiness of night, when to relax one's vigilance is dangerous, occurs in Macbeth's speech which virtually summons night for the murder of Banquo:

> Ere the bat hath flown
> His cloister'd flight; ere to black Hecate's summons
> The shard-born beetle, with his drowsy hums,
> Hath rung Night's yawning peal, there shall be done
> A deed of dreadful note.
>
> *(III.ii.40–44)*

The figurative language is almost too heavy, extending even to a possible pun on "note." Virtually every noun has an adjective, often in the interest of sound, such as "Night's yawning peal." It is onomatopoetic in a way that Spenser might envy.[26] The danger of night is especially felt in the combination of drowsiness and violence in the "Come, seeling Night" invocation. When night "seels" the eye of pitiful day, it will, with its "bloody and invisible hand, / Cancel and tear to pieces" (III.ii. 46–49). While good things of day droop and drowse, "Night's black agents to their preys do rouse" (III.ii.52–53).

---

[26] Spenser's corresponding description of night is, surprisingly, loud with actual sound but not with the appropriate verbal music:

> And all the while she stood upon the ground,
>   The wakefull dogs did never cease to bay,
>   As giving warning of th' unwonted sound,
>   With which her yron wheeles did them affray,
>   And her darke griesly looke them much dismay;
>   The messenger of death, the ghastly Owle
>   With drearie shriekes did also her bewray;
>   And hungry Wolves continually did howle,
>   At her abhorred face, so filthy and so fowle.

The Faerie Queene I.v.30, in *The Poetical Works of Edmund Spenser*, ed. by J. C. Smith and E. De Selincourt (London, 1950).

The conventional birds of night descriptions are given not only sound but a significance. The raven is "hoarse" and "croaks" (I.v.38), but it also announces "the fatal entrance of Duncan" under Lady Macbeth's battlements. The owl "clamors" the entire night (II.iii.61). It "screams" (II.ii.15). It "shrieks" as the "fatal bellman, / Which gives the stern'st goodnight" (II.ii.3–4). The "Scritch-Owle," as Shakespeare might have learned from Pliny, "alwaies betokeneth some heavie newes and is most execrable and accursed, and namely, in the presages of publick affaires.... In summe, he is the very monster of the night."[27] But the owl in *Macbeth* connotes the demonic. It was a demon-familiar Harpier and probably one of the most tangible ways the Devil presided over the "rough night."[28]

The night and darkness in *Macbeth* seem, indeed, to be not only the portentous wonder of *Julius Caesar* but often an unnatural condition, an "unruly" disturbing of nature, caused by the demons who are more or less formally invoked. Banquo correctly sees the Witches as "instruments of Darkness." They both serve the purpose of the greater powers of Darkness and help to bring darkness to this one half-world. Lady Macbeth prays, "Come, thick Night, / And pall thee in the dunnest smoke of Hell" (I.v.50–51). Her prayer is answered, so that she knows, from judgment here, that "Hell is murky." Hell itself becomes almost a part of the play, as the demons riot on earth in their element, the night. The tumult of the fatal night was heard by all characters. Lennox describes it almost as well as Macbeth:

> The night has been unruly: where we lay,
> Our chimneys were blown down; and, as they say,
> Lamentings heard i' th' air; strange screams of death,
> And, prophesying with accents terrible
> Of dire combustion, and confus'd events,

---

[27] *Natural History*, trans. by Philemon Holland (1634), X.xii.276; quoted by Kenneth Muir, note to II.iii.58–60, in the new Arden Edition of *Macbeth* (New York, 1964). In Shakespeare, so far as I have been able to determine, the owl invariably augurs ominous, usually fatal, events, Cf. *The Rape of Lucrece*, 1. 165; 2 *Henry VI* III.ii.327; 3 *Henry VI* II.vi.56–57; V.vi.44.

[28] See Arthur R. McGee, "Macbeth and the Furies," *Shakespeare Survey 19* (Cambridge, 1966), p. 55.

> New hatch'd to th' woeful time, the obscure bird
> Clamour'd the livelong night: some say, the earth
> Was feverous, and did shake.
>
> *(II.iii.55–62)*

But although this may be explained, as Curry explains it, as purely demonic and suggestive of hell, I feel in it a struggle going on between the forces of good and evil. There is terrible suffering. This suffering may of course be hellish, but the lamentings heard in the air suggest the agony of Pity, fighting against the demons. And Pity ultimately drowns the demonic winds. Moreover, the "prophesying with accents terrible" would be appropriate here less to the demons than to the admonitory powers of good. When, furthermore, the Old Man makes his statement that "this sore night / Hath trifled former knowings," Rosse offers an explanation of the night that involves heavenly concern, though it is more punitive than loving:

> Ha, good Father,
> Thou seest the heavens, as troubled with man's act,
> Threatens his bloody stage.
>
> *(II.iv.4–6)*

The darkness of hell, with its rampant demons, may come appropriately for the Macbeths, but all of Scotland seems to be in dark agony during the sore night. The evil, though committed by only two persons, may be so tremendous as to call to mind Doomsday, a possibility which we shall consider later. Whether or not Doomsday is imminent, the threatenings seem to be more prominent in both of these passages than the finality and relative stability of hell would warrant. And threatening, through portents, was of course a major concern of the "strange" literature. Ludvig Lavater, writing of spirits by night, explains the frightening phenomena as having a twofold purpose: "it turneth to good unto the just, & to further damnation to the wicked." To the good, it shows God's concerned warning "with rare and strange apparitions." Furthermore, "albeit it be very likely, that most of these happen by the devils procurement, yet neverthelesse, we heerin perceive Almightie God his fatherly care, love, & preservation of us against the devises of the devil."[29] The nocturnal storm, then, may be diabolical by God's permission. It will be punishment for the criminals and a threat, in the form of a warfare between good and bad, for the other characters. Holinshed—I believe unnoticed by critics—had given Shakespeare the idea that more than two persons were a part of the evil. When Constantine, regarded by Kenneth's son Malcolm as a usurper, was crowned, there were widespread "dreadfull wonders" and "grislie sights and tokens" which "menaced some great mischiefe to fall unto the whole nation." These failed to "withdraw the Scotishmen from their wicked vices, whereunto in those daies they were wholie given" (p. 259). Elizabethans were taught in the Homilies and elsewhere that the emergence of a wicked ruler is due to God's displeasure with the wickedness of the nation. And in *Macbeth* there does seem to be an enlargement of the evil from Macbeth to the whole kingdom. It is very hard to ascertain who is completely untainted; even Banquo, whom Shakespeare has cleaned up considerably from the accomplice in Holinshed, does not decisively enough separate himself from Macbeth's cause. Whatever the explanation—and a totally satisfactory one is difficult—all of Scotland does become involved in what seems to be a macrocosmically symbolic warfare between the forces of night and the good things of day. It will be worth while to look briefly at this symbolic function of darkness in the play.

The demidarkness of the Witches' scene at the beginning of the play is a premonition of the ensuing conflict between a more decisive night and a clear daylight. It foreshadows the way in which a not fully realized human evil can obscure the light of goodness. Real night does not come to the play until Duncan is in Macbeth's castle. As he approaches it, and comments upon its pleasantness, night is just beginning to fall. Night becomes more explicitly a symbol just before the murder when Banquo asks his son, "How goes the night, boy?" (II.i.1). The question might serve as a motto for the role and relative strength of darkness in the play and might be asked at almost any point. At this particular moment, because Duncan has not been killed, there is darkness without tumult: the moon is down and the stars are

---

[29] Lavater, p. 186.

not shining. Then comes the dreadful and tumultuous night, the moral nadir of the play. Following this atrocity, we expect the question about the night to be raised with special anxiety; and so it is, even in daytime. When the Old Man observes, "this sore night / Hath trifled former knowings," Rosse asks:

> Is 't night's predominance, or the day's shame,
> That darkness does the face of earth entomb,
> When living light should kiss it?
>
> *(II.iv.8–10)*

Night is clearly, at this point, predominant over day. Natural night again is returning, but with ominous overtones, as Macbeth prepares for Banquo's murder. On his mysterious ride Banquo may become "a borrower of the night, / For a dark hour, or twain" (III.i.26–27). Morally Banquo may have become a borrower of the night—that is, a passive sharer in the evil fortunes of Macbeth, which are linked by the Witches with his own. His fatal dark hour is now at hand. And in Macbeth's plans, Fleance "must embrace the fate / Of that dark hour" (III.i.136–137). In this murder episode, the night symbolism is especially rich and evident. While the murderers wait for Banquo, "The west yet glimmers with some streaks of day" (III.iii.5), as the "lated traveller" spurs to reach the timely inn. Either this is a hint of the partial good yet remaining in Scotland or, more likely, it merely heightens the suspense of the impending doom for Banquo, whose day on earth is almost over. Banquo's first words, "Give us a light there, ho!" (III.iii.9), are a plea against his coming night. Especially sensitive symbolizers will find meaning in the stage direction, "Enter Banquo, and Fleance, with a torch" (III.iii.14). It will be Fleance who carries light for the two of them, and for Scotland, into the future.

The night of Banquo's murder proves to be the turning point of the play. The Banquet Scene results in Macbeth's worst discomfiture and in sufficient disclosure of his guilt. Following the banquet, Macbeth repeats the motto question in asking his wife, "What is the night?" Her reply connotes much more than clock time: "Almost at odds with morning, which is which" (III.iv.125–126). In the struggle between light and darkness, Scotland now stands at odds, which is which. Thanes like Rosse and Lennox must actively take sides. There can be no more complying attendance at bloody banquets. Moreover, forces of good are rallying, though hesitantly, in England, where Macduff has gone. There will still be another terrible night scene, but it is one in which the demons have no power over the virtuous in Scotland; they have come only to claim their own, the "fiendlike queen." In moving to purge Scotland, Malcolm comments finally upon the state of the night: "The night is long that never finds the day" (IV.iii.240). And in his first pronouncement upon a healed country, he puts into effect what his father had been able only to promise: "signs of nobleness, like stars, shall shine / On all deservers" (I.iv.41–42). When night returns, it will be a natural night in which the stars shine and in which there is not only a freedom from prodigious tumult but a freedom from nightmare and a return of innocent sleep.

VI

One of the constant themes of the "strange" treatises, and of corresponding sermons, is the imminence of Doomsday; and I have already suggested that in the portentous events of the unruly night one of the strongest explanations is that the heavens, troubled with man's act, threaten his bloody stage. Many of the phenomena of the night are to be found in the Biblical works describing the Last Judgment. "The sunne shalbe turned into darkenes . . . before the great and terrible daie of the Lord come" (Joel 2:31). There will be earthquakes and both the sun and the moon shall be dark and the stars shall fall (Mark 13:19, 24, 25). There will be voices, thundering, lightning, and earthquake (Revelation 8:5).[30]

Besides these portents, there is in *Macbeth* some imagery of the ominous trumpet of Revelation. Macbeth predicts that Duncan's virtues will "plead like angels, trumpet-tongu'd, against / The deep damnation of his taking-off" (I.vii.19–20). And so, in almost a literal sense, they do. The alarum bell which sounds

---

[30] See also Zephaniah 1:14–16. Jane H. Jack believes that Shakespeare, for "expression of his imaginative apprehension of overwhelming evil," leaned heavily not only on Revelation but on King James's commentary on it. See "*Macbeth*, King James, and the Bible," *ELH*, XXII (1955), 173–193.

upon the discovery of Duncan's body seems to the guilty Lady Macbeth a trumpet of judgment:

> What's the business,
> That such a hideous trumpet calls to parley
> The sleepers of the house?
>
> *(II.iii.81–83)*

It is perhaps more than a coincidence that in a play on Judgment Day from the York Cycle, a wicked soul cries out:

> Allas! allas! that we were borne,
> So may we synfull kaytiffs say,
> I here wele be this hidous horne
> Itt drawes full nere to domesday.[81]

The plainest image of the Last Judgment comes in Macduff's trumpetlike voice in arousing the sleepers of the house to behold "the great doom's image" in the form of the murdered King:

> up, up, and see
> The great doom's image! Malcolm! Banquo!
> As from your graves rise up, and walk like sprites,
> To countenance this horror!
>
> *(II.iii.78–81)*

Macduff, in "To countenance this horror," seems to know that he is speaking metaphorically, that Doomsday is not a real possibility even in view of the terrible night and the sacrilegious murder. Shakespeare was probably following his successful dramatic precedent in *King Lear*, in which there is a very difficult line of demarcation between the *image* of Doomsday and the real thing. There, when Lear enters with the dead Cordelia in his arms, Kent asks, "Is this the promis'd end?" and Edgar adds, "Or image of that horror?" (V.iii.263–264). So powerfully, in both plays, have the portents of both evil and heavenly displeasure spoken, that Shakespeare, while seemingly content to have used only the imagery of Doomsday, does not rule out the advantage of having sensation translated into idea.

---

[81] *York Plays. The Plays Performed by the Crafts or Mysteries of York on the Day of Corpus Christi in the 14th, 15th and 16th Centuries*, ed. by Lucy Toulmin Smith (New York, 1963), p. 500, ll. 113–116.

And it is roughly the same with hell in *Macbeth*. S. L. Bethell has counted thirty-seven diabolic images in *Macbeth*, in some way "suggesting the notion of hell or damnation."[32] The Porter Scene locates Hell Gate temporarily in Macbeth's castle. And Roland Mushat Frye has pointed out that Macbeth's second meeting with the Witches takes place at the "pit of Acheron," a river in hell, and thus "this assignation may be seen as occurring, symbolically, at the very gates of hell."[33] With such expressions as "the dunnest smoke of hell," "dire combustion," and "Hell is murky," *Macbeth* offers among Shakespeare's plays by far the most tangible *image* of hell. And in no other of his plays is there a comparable commerce between earth and hell. But unlike the portents and the strange phenomena generally, the presence of hell centers mainly around the Macbeths. We feel its presence because they are so large a part of the play. Well above, however, the atmospheric presence of hell in the play, oppressive as this is, must be ranked its function as punishment for Macbeth. Hell is where Macbeth is, not primarily as dire combustion and dunnest smoke, but as a torment to his body and spirit. The next three chapters will consequently show how the crime returns to plague specifically the inventor and not, as with the present chapter, how it terrifies the whole of Scotland.

[32] "Shakespeare's Imagery: The Diabolic Images in *Othello*," *Shakespeare Survey* 5 (1952), p. 68.
[33] "*Macbeth* and the Powers of Darkness," *Emory University Quarterly*, VIII (1952), 169. I am especially pleased to find this imaginative instance of theological symbolizing in a scholar who has taken a severe attitude toward such a practice.

Chapter VIII

The Rest Is Labor

It may seem odd, or misguided, to include a chapter on labor, that most conservatively stolid of man's activities, in a book on sensational art. Moreover, there is singularly little of constructive labor accomplished in *Macbeth*. A hasty impression of the action is that of virtue murdered; of witches arousing and then baffling human endeavor; of a frustrated banquet; of hopeless gestures in sleep walking; and of action smothered in surmise. And yet, somehow, the play leaves the reader and audience exhausted—even more so (though perhaps not for an audience) than *Hamlet*, a play nearly twice as long. Some of the exhaustion doubtless derives from the intensity of the emotion, expressed in heavily charged speeches. And what one goes through in the tension of guilt and apprehension shared with the protagonists leaves one, as it does Macbeth, limp and aweary of the sun.

But most of our fatigue from the play must be credited, I believe, to a special kind of labor, to a labor which is never really accomplished but which entails all the motions of achieved effort. *Macbeth* is singularly tense and alive with images of labored gesture, of stress, climbing, leaping, running, and straining, of the "deed" and the "business," all of which constitute a futile or meaningless kind of labor. The bleeding Captain early in the play exemplifies the futile stress in the imagery when he describes the inconclusive striving of the two warriors:

> Doubtful it stood;
> As two spent swimmers, that do cling together
> And choke their art.
>
> *(I.ii.7–9)*

And Rosse, describing the same battle, tells how Macbeth fought against the traitorous Cawdor "rebellious arm 'gainst arm" (I.ii.51–59). At this point in the play the forces of good and evil are not distinct and the struggle is one of equipoise. Mainly, the "Doubtful it stood" kind of report about Macbeth expresses the condition of his soul before the profound moral struggle. The imagery gives the effect of indecisive, almost immobilized, stress. For the swimmers, the greater the effort the less is their success. And "rebellious arm 'gainst arm"—admittedly a crux—possibly suggests that a present rebel is locked in combat with an enemy who is on his way to becoming a rebel too. The Witches, at the very beginning of the play, announce the theme for much of the furious effort that leads to nothing. They will meet again

> When the hurlyburly's done,
> When the battle's lost and won.
>
> *(I.i.3–4)*

After all the hurlyburly, the outcome will be no better than that of rebellious arm against arm; the battle will be both lost and won—won in a military sense, but lost in a more important way. And nothing—certainly not the hurlyburly—will be "done" when it is done in *Macbeth*. The beginning of the play also suggests the kind of effort that is so futilely applied, the "pains" of endeavor (I.iii.118–151). We do, then, have much of the stress of labor in the play, and it is full of "pains." And this kind of sensation produces, I would suggest, the high level of tension, much as in an imperfect sleep, that accounts for our exhaustion and for whatever acquiescence we finally feel in Macbeth's sense of futility.

Modern psychologists have a term for the images, gestures, and strain of felt or arrested movement: kinaesthesia. The term is occasionally used in poetic critism,[1] but in general the force of this kind of imagery in Shakespeare seems to have been neglected in favor of images of sight and sound. In *Macbeth* this neglect is particularly unfortunate. It is possibly due, quite pardonably, to a devoted attention to Macbeth's visual imagination. But we should remember that even in his finest visual passage he makes us feel the kinaesthetic shock of the baby striding the blast. Macbeth is tormented almost as much by muscular, nervous tension as by what afflicts his mind's eye. We should recall that futile, sometimes compulsive, labor and strain are one of the most common and least felicitous punishments of hell. And it is this frequently punitive kind that characterizes *Macbeth*. We would do well, therefore, while being aware of the psychological and imaginative explanation for the physical sense of exhaustion, to seek a more fundamental reason in the purpose and kind of the labor.

The futility of labor (a term that will be used here to include all effort, strain, and movement) is almost always the result of its association with evil. Hugh Latimer had preached that unless God "bless our labour, no doubt we shall labour all in vain."[2] The text is probably Psalm 127:1: "Except the Lord buylde the house, thei labour in vaine that buylde it: except the Lord kepe the citie, the keeper watcheth in vaine" (an observation that underlies Macbeth's "strongly fortifying" Dunisane, and the futility of doing so). And of course the idea of futile labor is a commonplace of Scripture. Job asks "If I be wicked, why labour I thus in vaine?" (9:29). And Eliphas, the false comforter, adds the imagery of stress to the futility in "The wicked man is continually as one that travelleth of childe, and the number of yeres is hid from the tyrant" (Job 15:20). This observation is

---

[1] See, e.g., René Wellek and Austin Warren, *Theory of Literature* (New York, 1956), p. 176; Kenneth Burke, *The Philosophy of Literary Form* (New York, 1957), pp. 31–32; Jerome Beaty and William H. Matchett, *Poetry from Statement to Meaning* (New York, 1965), pp. 177–178; June E. Downey, *Creative Imagination: Studies in the Psychology of Literature* (New York, 1929), pp. 13, 82, 159. Without using the term, L. C. Knights briefly finds some "images of physical strain and tautness" in *Macbeth*; see "Shakespeare's Imagery," in *The Living Shakespeare* (no. 455), pp. 64–65.

[2] *Sermons and Remains by Hugh Latimer, Sometime Bishop of Worcester, Martyr*, ed. by George E. Corrie (Parker Society), (Cambridge, 1845), p. 39.

especially pertinent to Macbeth, in that he cannot learn the details of his future or of his progeny. And two of Calvin's comments upon the passage are also suggestive. In one of them he remarks that once a man goes astray, "the mischiefe increaseth and groweth dubble,"[3] implying much the sort of cumulative painful effort that we shall find in the Witches. In the second of them he paraphrases the passage from Job to mean that the wicked man "never hath any rest, that hee is in continuall tormente, that hee looketh ever at the sworde, and that he knoweth not the number of his dayes" (p. 276b), which is eloquently expressive of the timorous career of Macbeth as tyrant.

Though the Bible and its commentaries would have been adequate sources for the concept that labor is futile unless it is good labor, the most compelling inspiration for the literary depiction of the concept was surely Edmund Spenser. Spenser's world of *The Faerie Queene* is in theme and story fundamentally a pursuit, usually by imperfect "characters." The pursuit involves battles in which an adversary (essentially an internal one) may be thrown to the ground and then suddenly rise again; so it is with Guyon in his encounter with Malegar:

> Nigh his wits end then woxe th' amazed knight,
> And thought his labour lost and travell vaine....[4]

Guyon's labor is lost because of a fault in himself which makes him choose the wrong way to fight. We encounter also arduous labor, like that of the two spent swimmers in *Macbeth*, in Atin's attempt to save Pyrochles from willful drowning in the "slow and sluggish" waves,

> Whiles thus they strugled in the idle wave,
> And strove in vaine, the one himselfe to drowne
> The other both from drowning for to save....
> *(II.vi.47)*

The pursuit leads the characters into strange and baffling labyrinths, as happened to Una and the drawf en route to Errour's Den (I.i.10). There are especially effective instances of baleful

---
[3] *Sermons of Master John Calvin upon the Book of Job*, trans. by Arthur Golding (1574), p. 278a.
[4] *The Poetical Works of Edmund Spenser*, ed. by J. C. Smith and E. De Selincourt (London, 1950), II.xi.44.

labor in the Garden of Proserpine. The figures are not of Spenser's origin, but they belong with peculiar appropriateness to his nightmare world of compulsive and continually baffled exertion. Tantalus, seeking drink, "wades" in the cold liquor, which recedes from him and "made him vainly swink" (II.vii.58). Pilate compulsively washes his hands,

> Yet nothing cleaner were for such intent,
> But rather fowler seemed to the eye;
> So lost his labour vaine and idle industry.
>
> *(II.vii.61)*

The pursuit; the frantic galloping; the wrestling; the desperate climbing for honor; the proliferation of ordeals—most are symptomatic of a defect in character which leads to a defect in strategy. There is almost no real rest in *The Faerie Queene*.

Although generally Shakespeare, except for *Macbeth*, has few episodes of labor made futile by evil (the comedies are sometimes an exception), there are occasional passages that almost parallel, without the nightmare quality, the *idea* in Spenser. Ulysses describes the baffled movement that results "when degree is suffocate":

> And this neglection of degree is it
> That by a pace goes backward, in a purpose
> It hath to climb.
>
> *(Troilus and Cressida I.iii.127–129)*

And Antony, in a way that recalls Macbeth's brief candle and its futility, declares that

> All length is torture; since the torch is out,
> Lie down, and stray no farther. Now all labour
> Mars what it does; yea, very force entangles
> Itself with strength.
>
> *(Antony and Cleopatra IV.xiv.46–49)*

These sad and beautiful lines have some of the deep fatigue of the later Macbeth, but their message of useless and impeded effort is not so cogently depicted as in the strong images of the earlier play.

II

There are two main influences that shape the kind of labor which Macbeth undergoes. The first is that of the Witches. Renaissance witches, though mainly responsible for toil in others, were themselves subject to the most arduous labor. Whereas other people dance for pleasure, witches dance always in a symbolically futile circle, and their measures "bring them labour and fatigue and the greatest toil."[5] In these dances there is a curious duplication, symbolic of doubled labor, in the accompanying chants: "Har, har, divell divell, danse here, danse here, plaie here, plaie here, *Sabbath, sabbath*."[6] Even in their air-borne rides there is the greatest of exertion; the Devil leaves his disciples after such a trip "far more heavily overcome with weariness than if they had completed a rough journey afoot with the greatest urgency."[7] The very mark of the Devil upon his converts gives such "intollerable dolour" as never "to let them rest."[8] Witches thus have a foretaste of the restless and useless labor that they will have under the Devil in hell.

One of the most characteristic mottoes of the Witches in *Macbeth* occurs in the chant as they dance in a circle around the caldron:

> Double, double toil and trouble:
> Fire, burn; and, cauldron, bubble.
>
> *(IV.i.10–11)*

Here is the duplication of effort noted in Renaissance witches. Perhaps the dance itself should express the drooping fatigue that conventionally troubled witches. More important, since the brew is being prepared for Macbeth's discomfiture, its spell may be an imprecation on Macbeth, helping to bring upon him the weariness of the ensuing scenes; or it may merely reflect the purposeless labor that he has already been suffering under their auspices. Throughout the play the Witches reinforce their kind

---

[5] Francesco Maria Guazzo, *Compendium Maleficarum* [1608], trans. by E. A. Ashwin; ed. by Rev. Montague Summers (London, 1929), p. 37.

[6] Reginald Scot, *The Discoverie of Witchcraft* (1584), p. 24.

[7] Nicolas Remy, *Demonolatry*, trans. by E. A. Ashwin; ed. by Rev. Montague Summers (London, 1930), p. 73.

[8] King James, *Daemonologie* (1597), p. 33.

of futile labor, and the effect it may have on others. There may possibly be some influence of the Witches on the sailor's wife who "mounch'd, and mounch'd, and mounch'd" (I.iii.5). Certainly their influence is felt upon the sailor who is to be tempest-tossed. And we have already noticed the futile effort of the Witch who, to trouble the sailor, will sail in a sieve (itself a symbol of futility) to Aleppo;

> And like a rat without a tail;
> I'll do, I'll do, and I'll do.

Although the Witch cannot destroy the ship, she can cause it a buffeting from winds that constantly frustrate its reaching port (I.iii.11–17).

The doubling of labor, characteristic of the Witches, appears as an image of stress, and possibly superfluous labor, in the Captain's account of Macbeth's and Banquo's service against the rebels:

> If I say sooth, I must report they were
> As cannons overcharg'd with double cracks;
> So they
> Doubly redoubled strokes upon the foe.
> *(I.ii.36–39)*

There may, even thus early in the play, be irony in the exaggerated effort Macbeth applies in the service of the man he will soon kill. There is unquestionable irony in the protestation of double labor for Duncan expressed by Lady Macbeth:

> All our service,
> In every point twice done, and then done double,
> Were poor and single business, to contend
> Against those honours deep and broad, wherewith
> Your Majesty loads our house.
> *(I.vi.14–18)*

And it is of course Lady Macbeth, so close in her redoubled labor to the Witches, who is the second main influence upon Macbeth's labor. The above speech typifies the intensity of her almost every utterance, which, when she is really aroused, can become the valor of her tongue. Her contempt for idleness is shown in her reference to the chamberlains as lying in "swinish sleep" (I.vii.68). It is she, once Macbeth has bent up each corporal agent, who chides him, "You do unbend your noble strength" (II.ii.44). Macbeth may complain that he has no "spur" other than vaulting ambition to prick the sides of his intent. But we learn from Duncan, with a choice of words that may be more than casual, that Macbeth's "great love, sharp as his *spur*, hath help him / To his home before us" (I.vi.23-24). It is the object of this great love who uses one of the most cogent images of stress in spurring him on:

> But screw your courage to the sticking-place
> And we'll not fail.
> *(I.vii.61-62)*

Freudian comparisons may be "odorous" in this somber play, but it is tempting to find an obscene reflection of Lady Macbeth's female-aroused tension in the drunken Porter's description of the effect of drink on lechery:

> ... it makes him, and it mars him; it sets him on, and it takes him off; it persuades him, and disheartens him; makes him stand to, and not stand to. ...
> *(II.iii.32-35)*

This states fairly well Lady Macbeth's influence upon her husband, whom she arouses and torments with taunts about his manliness. Like witches, she can cause both desire and impotence in the man. Her stimulus to labor will be first invigorating and later disheartening; it will make him and it will mar him. She will urge him to put "This night's great business into my dispatch" (I.v.67) and then will collapse at the horror of the blood and the sick realization of futile labor in her

> Nought's had, all's spent,
> Where our desire is got without content. ...
> *(III.ii.4-5)*

The night's great "business" proves, under the Witches' supervision, to be far more arduously busy than she had planned.

And, for Macbeth, proving himself a man proves also, as he foresaw, that he will be less than a man.

III

Although Lady Macbeth suffers grievously from nervous exhaustion, her labor and her suffering are for her husband's career. It is Macbeth whose nervous system is made to register primarily the theme of labor in the play. And the theme is very clearly this: that labor in response to the evil of Lady Macbeth and the Witches is both painful and futile. Macbeth himself, in two speeches, makes the theme emphatic. There is, we recall, much pain related to loyal service early in the play. Duncan, for example, "teaches" (for the play as a whole)

> How you shall bid God 'ild us for your pains,
> And thank us for your trouble,
>
> *(I.vi.13–14)*

thereby anticipating how double toil and trouble should be used. It is in reference to one of these "pains" that Macbeth, who by now knows the meaning of the opposite kind of pain, says, "The labour we delight in physics pain" (II.iii.51). His other thematic statement expresses the effect of the kind of labor that does not physic pain. There is powerful irony, prophetic of much of his future suffering, in his polite protestation to Duncan: "The rest is labour, wihch is not us'd for you" (I.iv.44). Dolorous effort not employed for a good cause will signify the primary meaning of labor for the rest of Macbeth's life. Perhaps the line is more than ironic. It is the manner of this play to have the protagonist will his own doom and pronounce it emphatically, though not with full realization. Macbeth does this elsewhere in the "If it were done" soliloquy and, more clearly, in his deliberate bending up of each corporal agent. If he does so here, he is invoking upon himself a curse leading to the most exquisitely condign of punishments. The line, moreover, is a doubly rich one in that Shakespeare sometimes, as in Hamlet's "The rest is silence," puns upon the word *rest*. The meaning is not only "that which remains," but "repose." Most of the remainder of Macbeth's life will be one of restless ecstasy. He will experience, by his own imprecation and in every sense, the arduousness of "labour, which is not used for you."

Shakespeare underlines, with the irony that informs the "message" of this play, the reason for the laborious punishment that will torture Macbeth. The earlier Thane of Cawdor also had "labour'd in his country's wrack" (I.iii.114), and "under heavy judgment bears that life / Which he deserves to lose" (I.iii.110–111). Macbeth, too, will bear his life under the burden of heavy judgment. And the heaviness is significant, for in this play it represents the burden of evil. Banquo is troubled by the "heavy summons" of the Witches, and this "lies like lead upon me" (II.i.6). The sin of his imagined ingratitude lies "heavy" on Duncan (I.iv.15–16). One would expect that Macbeth would exclaim like Claudius, "O heavy burden!" (*Hamlet* III.i.54), and we do indeed feel some of it in his sense of restriction, in images of function being smothered, of the will being servant to defect, and of generally being cabined, cribbed, and confined. Only once, however, does he use the idea of heaviness in his imagery: when he refers to "The perilous stuff / Which weighs upon the heart" (V.iii.44–45). Mainly his labor takes the form not of bearing but of doing, futile doing, and this leads to his most shattering awareness, that of the futility of being.

A thematically basic form that movement takes in the imagery is leaping. It is predictably so in a play dealing with ambition, and would ordinarily require no discussion. But the leaping is invariably a futile kind, usually characterized by the excessive effort of a nightmare. It is labor not used for the King. Macbeth first pictures himself as leaping when Duncan names Malcolm as his successor:

> The Prince of Cumberland!—That is a step
> On which I must fall down, or else o'erleap,
> For in my way it lies.
>
> *(I.iv.48–50)*

Such is the nature of the obstacle—a moral rather than a physical one—that he can surmount it only by o'erleaping it. How he will do so is not clear at this point; but in view of his inclination to avoid direct confrontation with the "deed," "o'erleaping" may well denote an effort to ignore the moral aspect of what he will do. The other use of "o'erleap" is clearly intended to convey the meaning of leaping too hard and hence profitlessly:

>   I have no spur
> To prick the sides of my intent, but only
> Vaulting ambition, which o'erleaps itself
> And falls on th' other—
>   *(I.vii.52–28)*

"O'erleaps itself" also suggests hopeless contention with oneself, lifting oneself by one's bootstraps, or, as in an earlier image, raising "arm against rebellious arm." There is one other key image of leaping, that in which Macbeth imagines himself on this bank and shoal of time *jumping* the life to come (I.vii.6–7). "Jump" here means "risk," but it had not lost its premetaphoric strength. The "jump" is the most hopeless one in the play, even more onerous and futile than that of ambition o'erleaping itself.

Akin to the images of leaping are those of pursuing, for these, too, suggest the nightmare world of the compulsive but never achieved quest. Although these, unlike the leaping images, are not confined to Macbeth, they serve to reinforce his moral ordeal. For example, the First Murderer describes the ominous scene in which Banquo is trying to reach, but will never reach while alive, the castle of Dunsinane:

> The west yet glimmers with some streaks of day;
> Now spurs the lated traveller apace,
> To gain the timely inn.
>   *(III.iii.5–7)*

Duncan, whose movement is unburdened with evil, can appropriately use the following image:

>   Thou art so far before,
> That swiftest wing of recompense is slow
> To overtake thee.
>   *(I.iv.16–18)*

His image of flying will serve also as a contrast to later images of more difficult movement associated with Macbeth. It is characteristic of Lady Macbeth that her impatience should express itself in an image of a quickly successful pursuit. She deplores

The Rest Is Labor · 151

her husband for being "too full o' th' milk of human kindness, / To catch the nearest way" (I.v.17–18). In this context, fullness with milk is a condition that slows the pursuit of evil. (The image, suggestive of the nursery or dairy, should probably not be too consciously pictured by the reader.) Normally in the play, it is fullness with evil that will slow pursuit. It is also characteristic of Lady Macbeth in the impatience of her pursuit that she should say, "th' attempt and not the deed / Confounds us" (II.ii.10–11). Her husband, for whom the deed is the frightful thing, is less concerned with the attempt—that is to say, the pursuit of the deed.

Only at the first does Macbeth seem to pursue the deed. He does so mainly in his grasping for the dagger which he cannot clutch. In the "If it were done" soliloquy, he recognizes the hopelessness of all pursuit of the deed; the whole speech is, in fact, a series of frustrated gestures toward action, culminating in a fall on the other side of the horse he has overleaped. He images the assassination, dimly personified, as trying vainly to "catch / With his surcease success" (I.vii.3–4). This is related to the equally vain attempt to "trammel up the consequence." Thereafter, we see Macbeth desperately trying to pursue, and confine, the consequences of the deed. In killing Duncan, he has "scorch'd the snake, not kill'd it" (III.ii.12), for Banquo will forever elude him. Then he learns that "the son is fled" (III.iii. 20). After Macduff has eluded him, he grows more desperate and turns again to the deed:

> Time, thou anticipat'st my dread exploits:
> The flighty purpose never is o'ertook,
> Unless the deed go with it.
>
> *(IV.i.144–146)*

Overtaking his own purpose is another kind of self-contesting gesture, and like the others it cannot succeed. The deed, horribly proliferated, will for the rest of the play race after the flighty purpose. But the deed, as Macbeth knew from the beginning, can never really catch success, can never be done even when it is done.

Images of pursuit are often a part of the more general imagery of moving forward, especially by running. Just as there can be exaggerated effort in overleaping, so can there be in running, especially when the cause is hopeless. Francis Fergusson had commented upon this kind of running in a suggestive essay.[9] His thesis is that *Macbeth* is the imitation of action, in the Aristotelian sense, "which may be indicated by the phrase 'to outrun the pauser, reason' " (p. 124). The full sentence is Macbeth's

> Th' expedition of my violent love
> Outrun the pauser, reason;
> *(II.iii.110–111)*

and certainly a large part of Macbeth's trouble—though not, I think, the major part—is due to his passion outrunning his reason. But in the context of the present chapter, the sentence is also pivotal, for it is an expression of the kind of futile labor resulting when one of a person's faculties strives against another one, especially if an inferior faculty does the outrunning. But Shakespeare probably had an irony beneath the hypocrisy in the speech. Outrunning cannot win, any more than overleaping. In *Henry VIII* there is a passage that illuminates the probable meaning of *outrun* in *Macbeth*:

> We may outrun
> By violent swiftness that which we run at,
> And lose by over-running.
> *(I.i.141–143)*

Macbeth's protestation goes one fold deeper than he intends: he will indeed lose by over-running.

Early in the play, just as he leaps and vaults, so he tends to use images of rapid movement; for example, "Time and the hour runs through the roughest day" (I.iii.147). Time moves fast for Macbeth when he says this. It will get him through the most difficult of days, and will even get him through a very "rough night." But later the movement is not agile or swift. His deed cannot overtake the flighty purpose. He is burdened with heavy judgment, and immersed in an element of blood as thick and slab as the Witches' brew. He will now force himself through all obstacles, not run: "For mine own good, / All causes

---

[9] "*Macbeth* as the Imitation of an Action," in *The Human Image in Dramatic Literature* (New York, 1957), pp. 115-125.

shall give way" (III.iv.134–135). He is in blood "stepp'd"—a word denoting slow, tentative movement. Through this blood he then grimly "wades." And returning is as "tedious" as "go o'er." He had, in imagery, once before gone o'er: when he overleaped the horse. But here the image, in its lack of a stated goal, represents the utmost in futile gesture; for he no longer has any idea where labor will lead him.

In the context of slow, labored progress toward a vague "o'er," the famous "To-morrow" speech takes on a new significance. The threefold statement of "to-morrow," slowed down by two uses of "and," gives a potent sense of slow, difficult progress and shows the result of following the Witch's "I'll do, I'll do, and I'll do." Time no longer runs through the day; it creeps in a petty pace. Life itself is a *walking* shadow; and all its strutting and fretting takes it in no direction and with no real movement forward. This, then, is the depressing result of all the hectic stress and strain in the play. And the image of putting out the brief candle is taken appropriately from the Book of Job, which is eloquent concerning the futility of labor by the wicked: "The light shalbe darke in his dwelling, and his candel shalbe put out with him" (18:6). Even the tale told by an idiot is, in Biblical context, suggestive of meaningless repetition: "A man without grace is as a foolish tall [sic] which is oft tolde by the mouthe of the ignorant" (Ecclesiasticus 20:18).

Perhaps the saddest impression which we get from the wasted labor in *Macbeth* is one of sterility. The two lonely protagonists seem, of all Shakespeare's tragic characters, the most barren and ultimately loveless. Their castle had, before the murder, been the "procreant cradle" (I.vi.8) for the breeding martlet. In it, possibly, Lady Macbeth had known the tenderness of nursing a baby. And the profusion of babies in the imagery of the play accentuates the barrenness that Lady Macbeth's resolutely unsexed activity has brought them to. In espousing the demonic, she has sacrificed procreation and friends. "There is," wrote Remy, "war and deathless hatred between the wicked Demon and Nature; for whereas every effort of Nature is directed upon procreation and production, the Demon always strives to spoil and destroy her works."[10] Lady Macbeth is also close to the

---

[10] *Demonolatry*, p. 67.

spirit of the Witches. The worst kinds of witches, those which can raise tempests, are those "that procure barrennesse in man, woman, and beast. These can throwe children into waters, as they walke with their mothers, and not be seene.... These can take awaie mans courage, and the power of generation."[11] In all of her feverous activity there is, despite an intense devotion to her husband's career, little real love. There is absolutely no evidence that she feels love for him rather than for what, under her fell purpose, he can become. This lovelessness is only accentuated by her one intimate cry, "My husband!" (II.ii.13). Her loveless ambition deprives him of the only thing that can meet the challenge symbolized by Banquo—an enduring family.

Labor as expressed in the planting of seeds is a significant part of the play's imagery. It is imaged first in the form of vegetation; but the seeds, explicitly later and implicitly throughout, come to mean the seeds of human reproduction, the seeds that Lady Macbeth will make useless. It is Banquo, who will represent triumphant progeny, who thinks to question the Witches about the ultimately all-important question of fertile seeds:

> If you can look into the seeds of time,
> And say which grain will grow, and which will not,
> Speak then to me, who neither beg, nor fear,
> Your favours nor your hate.
>
> *(I.iii.58–61)*

By not allying himself with the Witches' powers—though he will accept without commitment their prophecy—he avoids their evil, which produces sterility. There is an important episode in which he is matched with Macbeth in terms of potential fertility. Duncan, in whose service labor and planting can prosper, tells Macbeth:

>   Welcome hither:
> I have begun to plant thee, and will labour
> To make thee full of growing.[12]
>
> *(I.iv.27–29)*

---

[11] Scot, p. 6.
[12] The irony of these lines is explained in terms of Jeremiah 12:1–3 by Norman Nathan in "Duncan, Macbeth, and Jeremiah," *Notes and Queries*, New Series, I (1954), 243.

But Macbeth balks at the simultaneous "planting" of the Prince of Cumberland and ironically, as we have seen, pronounces his own sentence of barrenness in "The rest is labour, which is not us'd for you." But when Duncan turns to Banquo with equal proffer of loving auspices of growth, Banquo loyally commits himself to service "us'd for you." If, he says, he grows in Duncan's heart, "the harvest is your own" (I.iv.32–33).

There is something almost pathetic in Macbeth's excited compliment to his wife—the compliment of an ungraced man to an unsexed woman—when she finds a way to the deed:

> Bring forth men-children only!
> For thy undaunted mettle should compose
> Nothing but males.
> *(I.vii.73–75)*

For Banquo's seed will prevail, and Macbeth will suffer one of the worst curses of futile labor made in Scripture: "you shal sowe your sede in vaine: for your enemies shal eat it" (Leviticus 26:16). It is partially this threat that starts Macbeth, after Duncan is slain, on his desperate series of futile murders. He realizes that he wears "a fruitless crown" and wields "a barren sceptre."

> If 't be so,
> For Banquo's issue have I fil'd my mind;
> For them the gracious Duncan have I murder'd;
> Put rancours in the vessel of my peace,
> Only for them; and mine eternal jewel
> Given to the common Enemy of man,
> To make them kings, the seed of Banquo kings!
> *(III.i.63–69)*

This, as he sees it, is the most bitterly ironic aspect of all his striving—of the "deed," of "the enterprise," of the "business." But, though just, it is a judgment not executed without our sense of pity for him. We cannot ignore the mournful eloquence of his hopeless forecast, now that his way of life is fallen into the sere, the yellow leaf:

> And that which should accompany old age,
> As honour, love, obedience, troops of friends,
> I must not look to have.
> *(V.iii.24–26)*

And even for his Queen we feel pity as she goes nightly in her sleepwalking through the hopeless effort of guiding and then controlling her husband in crime. She has forsworn procreative love. There is a pathetic irony as, alone in her nightmare world, she seeks—never to achieve—her husband's hand and tries to lead him "To bed, to bed, to bed."

Chapter IX

Pestered Senses

If *Macbeth* can be said to figure forth an image of the horror of hell, labor without rest or meaning should perhaps be considered part of the punishment called pain of sense. It involves bodily pain and it results from the inordinate pursuit, as Aquinas defined it, of a mutable good. If so, it leads logically to the punishment which is the subject of the present chapter, that which torments specifically the senses. Of this infernal punishment, Ephraim Huit writes that "if the scalding of one finger will cause so much smart, what will not the torture of all the senses, and members?"[1] In *Macbeth*, as I have said, we do not find an exact dramatic embodiment of the schoolmen's doctrine. But we do find, more than in any other of Shakespeare's plays, a concentrated torment of the tragic hero's senses and so great a torment that it has brought the play a unique reputation, usually ascribed to other causes, for its sensory imagery. Much of the poetic quality of the play, and much of the vividly perceived imagery, results, I suspect, not so much from Macbeth's poetic nature as from the fact that his senses, and the imagination that afflicts them, are singularly excited by a specific kind of punishment.

Not all of Macbeth's senses, or those of his Lady, are equally affected. The protagonists are tormented almost entirely

---

[1] *The Anatomy of Conscience* (1626), p. 310.

through the eye and through the ear. There are, to be sure, occasional references to the suffering of other senses. Macbeth does, after all, bend up "*each* corporal agent" to his terrible feat. The poisoned chalice will, figuratively, be commended to Macbeth's own lips, and he later refers not simply to having felt fear but to having *tasted* it (V.v.9). He has "*supp'd* full with horrors" (V.v.13). He feels, according to Angus, his "secret murders *sticking* on his hands" (V.ii.17). Lady Macbeth is especially obsessed by the sticking; and one of Shakespeare's finest touches is her feminine displeasure with "the *smell* of the blood still." Taste, touch, and smell can become a part only of the dialogue—and at best the imagery—of a stage play, whereas sight and sound can be a part of the action. But in a play notable for the way in which sensation is made meaningful, it is tempting to look for a more organic explanation. Shakespeare's poetry can both mean and be. I find one meaning, not to be applied too literally or systematically, in the doctrine of condign punishment. George Gascoigne, translating Pope Innocent III, had written of the punishment of sense, both in future hell and in hell on earth:

> Every member [of the body] for his sinnes shall beare his proper punishment. That it may therewith be punished wherwith it hath sinned. For it is written: by what soever a man sinneth, by the same shall he be punished. So that he which sinned with his tongue, shall be tormented by the tongue.[2]

The eye and the ear are the principal members whereby Macbeth and Lady Macbeth are tempted and offend, and so the two protagonists are appropriately punished through them. They also, especially Macbeth, offend through the imagination, and the imagination affects the body primarily through vision and hearing.

II

Before taking up these two guilty and tormented senses, however, we should be aware of a torment that afflicts Macbeth's body as a whole. He is subject to excruciating agitation, shak-

---

[2] *The Droomme of Doomes Day* (1576), in *Works*, ed. by John W. Cunliffe (Cambridge, 1910), p. 266.

Pestered Senses · 159

ing, and "starting" of the body. He excuses this affliction at the banquet as "a strange infirmity, which is nothing / To those that know me" (III.iv.85–86), and Lady Macbeth also excuses it as something customary but short lasting. "My Lord," she explains, "is often thus, / And hath been from his youth" (III.iv. 52–53). He is, indeed, "often thus." He looks upon all of living as "life's fitful fever" (III.ii.23). But the fits do not seem to be epilepsy, or even a fever, though epilepsy occurs in *Julius Caesar* and *Othello*, and imagery suggesting the plague is to be found in *Macbeth*. That they are associated with an emotional condition is suggested by his reaction to the news that Fleance has escaped:

> Then comes my fit again: I had else been perfect;
> Whole as the marble, founded as the rock,
> As broad and general as the casing air:
> But now, I am cabin'd, cribb'd, confin'd, bound in
> To saucy doubts and fears.
>
> *(III.iv.20–24)*

When the "fit" is associated with shaking, it is invariably related to guilt, and to fear (usually from guilt). The image of murder which early afflicts him *shakes* his single state of man (I.iii.139–140). Terrible dreams later *shake* him nightly (III.ii.18–19). And in desperation he resolves that he will no longer "*shake* with fear" (V.iii.10). Similarly the word *start* is applied (five times in the play) to Macbeth's guilt or fear. He *starts* guiltily at the prophecy of the Witches (I.iii.51) and fearfully at the sight of the Ghost (III.iv.62). His eyes *start* in painful realization at the sight of the Apparitions (IV.i.116). His Queen in her sleepwalking remembers particularly this trait when she relives the scenes in which he betrays guilty fear: "you mar all with this starting" (V.i.43–44). When he nears utter nervous exhaustion, he observes that "Direness, familiar to my slaughterous thoughts, / Cannot once start me" (V.v.14–15). There is one other use of *start* in the play. Menteith says of Macbeth that his "pester'd senses . . . recoil and start" (V.ii.23); but this passage is useful in explaining the whole theme of "pester'd senses" in the play, and its complex meaning will require fuller attention later.

Because of the prominence of the Witches in the play, we cannot ignore the possibility that they are at least partially responsible for the fits. Certainly his agitated symptoms are almost identical with those widely publicized in contemporary reports of witchcraft. One bewitched girl, suffering from a "fearful starting & pulling together of her bodie," grew "worse & worse falling into often strange & extreame fittes."[3] In another victim the fit would assault first one member and then another, and "alwaies shake the grieved part, as if it had been the palsie."[4] The Witches, moreover, certainly contribute by their frightful visions to the fear that accompanies the convulsions. On the other hand, the superior demons can "tosse" a victim's body when God permits them to, and as a punishment.[5] Human witches were not needed. One divine gives a particularly good explanation for the fits in that it includes an evil spirit and also another common cause, melancholy. Explaining "How Saul was vexed of the evill spirit," Andrew Willet writes that some think that he "was troubled onely with melancholike and frantike fitts." But, he insists, "there was more in Saul, then fittes of melancholy"; rather, "an evill spirit from God vexed him: it was therefore more than a naturall worke." What happened was that first guilt troubled Saul; then he was "tormented with the spirit of envie and ambition, . . . and by this vexation of his minde, he fell into furie and phrensie." Satan "thus disquieting his minde, did worke also upon the distemperature of his bodie, and his melancholy passions might help thereunto," and so "he seemed as it were possessed for the time."[6] Guilt or conscience mistaken as "Melancholy fits" is also discussed by Ephraim Huit.[7] Saul's spiritual ordeal is similar to Macbeth's, and it is at least interesting that a contemporary writer diagnosed his resultant malady as having a supernatural origin. The Witches, at least as human witches, would not be enough to give tragic significance to the fits Macbeth suffers. Only the Devil, working

---

[3] George More, *A True Discourse Concerning the Possession of 7 Persons in One Familie in Lancashire* (1600), p. 12.

[4] *The Most Strange and Admirable Discoverie of the Three Witches of Warboys* (1593), sig. D 4ᵛ; for "twitches," see sig. C 3ᵛ. For convulsions, see Reginald Scot, *Discoverie of Witchcraft* (1584), p. 5.

[5] Henry Holland, *A Treatise Against Witchcraft* (1590), sig. G 4ᵛ.

[6] *An Harmonie upon the Firste Booke of Samuel* (1607), pp. 141–142.

[7] *The Anatomy of Conscience*, pp. 85–86.

through a sense of guilt which in turn takes advantage of melancholy, can be worthy cause for so profound a shaking of a tragic hero. One other Biblical parallel is also suggestive in that it involves a murderer of a kinsman and a bodily shaking from horror of conscience. Cain, one divine notes, "had a marke of God upon him, *Gen.* 4.15."

> And what might that marke be? Chrysostom thinks it was a continuall shaking and trembling of his body. If that were his mark, why might not that trembling come from the horror of his guilty Conscience, following him with a continuall hue and cry for murther, and reproaching him for a bloody murtherer.[8]

In any case, Macbeth's "strange infirmity," like his poetic imagination, is not something that he has had since his youth. It comes as a result of his guilt, which in turn produces, through an evil spirit, fear and trembling.

III

When we come to specific senses, we find that there is no uniform cause for Macbeth's suffering. Some of the tormenting sights and sounds, for example, are purely natural. But often these have supernatural symbolism. And whether the cause is natural or supernatural, Macbeth suffers most, not because of the intrinsic horror or vehemence of what he sees or hears, but because of something within him, usually temptation, evil, or guilt, which agonizes his nervous system. Guilt, in the form of temptation or deed, as a cause of sensory torment is dramatically enhanced in *Macbeth* by contrast with the freedom from pain enjoyed by the innocent. Banquo, only partially innocent, will feel the heavy burden of a guilty summons but will not receive sensory torment. Duncan, entirely innocent, can comment that the air

> Nimbly and sweetly recommends itself
> Unto our gentle senses.
>
> *(I.vi.2–3)*

---

[8] Jeremiah Dyke, *Good Conscience: or, a Treatise Showing the Nature Thereof* (1624), p. 79.

And about the castle itself, before the murder, heaven's breath *smells* wooingly (I.vi.5–6).

The senses themselves have an innocent background in the play. The sense of hearing (which we may take up first) is first mentioned by a human participant when Macbeth resolves to "make joyful / The hearing of my wife" with Duncan's approach (I.iv.45–46). The sentiment, though possibly hypocritical, is a good one, for Duncan, through his virtue, can impress the ear joyfully.

Macbeth and his Lady will not, however, long entertain only virtuous tidings through the ear. Hearing will become one of the first and most important senses to respond to the evil spirits, and it is appropriate that it become a major object of torment. Macbeth hears first the discordant chant, sexually ambivalent and disturbing in coming from women with beards, of the foul Witches, who make seemingly fair prophecies. As Macbeth's reactions show, he is both repelled (by guilt) and tempted by what his ear receives. What they offer him is that mutable good which can produce the pain of sense.

Akin to the Witches in tempting him through the ear with a mutable good is Lady Macbeth. Upon reading his letter, she prepares her strategy for winning him to evil:

> Hie thee hither,
> That I may pour my spirits in thine ear,
> And chastise with the valour of my tongue
> All that impedes thee from the golden round....
>
> *(I.v.25–28)*

The "golden round" represents for her the supreme end of human endeavor and, through its climatic position in the speech, recalls the disappointing climax of the great speech by Tamburlaine ending in "The sweet fruition of an earthly crown."[9] In Renaissance symbolism it was superior to the frivolous rewards of Doctor Faustus's sacrifice, but since for Macbeth it would be a usurpation and hence barren, it must be, beyond question, considered a mutable good. It is Lady Macbeth's strategy, how-

---

[9] 1 *Tamburlaine* II.vii.29, in *Tamburlaine the Great Parts I and II*, ed. by John D. Jump (Regents Renaissance Drama Series), (Lincoln, Neb., 1967).

ever, which is most interesting. She will use the wiles of Milton's Satan and seduce through the ear. In perhaps a more than figurative sense she will, since she is becoming demonic, pour her *spirits* in her husband's ear. And she will chastise his ear with that which will excite him to false manliness and a resolution to bend up each corporal agent: the valor of her tongue. For this task every sense about her will be charged with demonic energy, for she prays to be filled, "from the crown to the toe, topfull / Of direst cruelty" (I.v.42–43). The valor of her tongue is employed with fearful energy in the scene when he needs further temptation, that in which he declares, "We will proceed no further in this business" (I.vii.31). She lashes him with an intolerable series of short, whiplike questions, forcing him to cry, "Pr'ythee, peace" (I.vii.45).

He is assaulted not only through the outer ear but through the ear of his imagination. In anticipatory punishment he hears Duncan's virtues pleading like angels, trumpet-tongued. In the struggle for his soul, it is noteworthy that the forces of good assault his hearing as clamorously as those of evil; and this is true also of his eye. Their assault is not so frequent, but it has greater impact; the tongues of angels are superior to the grotesque chants of the Witches—even to the shrill force of his wife's tongue.

The forces of evil prevail because he is amenable to a lesser good; and once he has bent up each corporal agent, he begins to receive through the ear the ominous sounds that will accompany him through the deed. Since he is committed to the demons, he assents to the import of these sounds, even though they are sinister. They are mainly the sounds of fatal birds and animals. Lady Macbeth, the first to be demonically possessed, had heard, with grim approval, the hoarse raven "That croaks the fatal entrance of Duncan / Under my battlements" (I.v.38–40). The raven is so portentous a symbol that it must be interpreted as a more than natural consort, waiting on, and leading to, Nature's mischief. Similarly with Macbeth. Once he is "resolved," he hears the demonically supplied creatures of evil Nature, notably that sentinel of Murder, "the wolf, / Whose howl's his watch" (II.i.53–54). Like Lady Macbeth he grimly acquiesces in this unsettling music, and does not want to "take the present horror from the time, / Which now suits with it" (II.i.59–60). Even that disturbing sound, a bell at night, "invites" him; and this literal sound takes on a supernatural meaning as a knell that summons Duncan to heaven or to hell.

Once the deed is done, the sounds become not tempting and guiding, but tormenting. The owl "shrieks" and "screams," the crickets "cry," hideous and frightening. The omens are now directed not against Duncan, but against the murderers, though they do not fully acknowledge the fact. Macbeth is unaware that the bell is summoning *him* to hell. And Lady Macbeth is unaware of the applicability to her of another bell that she uses so aptly in her imagery:

> It was the owl that shriek'd, the fatal bellman,
> Which gives the stern'st good-night.
>
> *(II.ii.3–4)*

In 1605 a charity provided a bellman to speak outside the dungeon of condemned prisoners on the eve of their execution "to awake their sleepie senses from securitie." The prescribed speeches had a refrain which was to be accompanied by a tolling handbell.[10]

Then come the appalling voices, the lamentings heard in the air, the strange screams of death, and, for the benefit especially of the murderers, the prophesying with accents terrible. A voice will repeatedly "cry," and cry "to all the house" (II.ii.34–35). Holinshed is silent about the source of this voice. Buchanan's Latin *History*, which Shakespeare may have read, identifies it as either an audible voice from heaven or the suggestion of Macbeth's guilty mind.[11] Lady Macbeth did not—nor did anyone except Macbeth—hear the voice which cried to all the house; and Shakespeare is noncommittal about it, as he is about most of the supernatural happenings in the play. It could be a demonic voice, speaking now that God has abandoned Macbeth and the Fiend is soon to claim his own. But probably it is not entirely the gloating voice of triumphant evil, but the voice of regretful

---

[10] John Russell Brown, note to his edition of *The Duchess of Malfi* (The Revels Plays), (London, 1964), p. 125.

[11] Kenneth Muir, *Shakespeare's Sources*, I, *Comedies and Tragedies* (London, 1957), p. 170, following Mark H. Liddell's 1903 edition of *Macbeth*.

Pestered Senses · 165

good forces leaving Macbeth. As such, it could be the voice of conscience making perhaps its last articulate statement to Macbeth. It derives partially from what the Book of Job says of the wicked man: "A sound of feare is in his eares, & in his prosperitie the destroyer shal come upon him" (15:21), and from the sound of Cain's blood which cries from the ground (Genesis 4:10). Referring to both these texts, Calvin describes the sound as "not the voyce of man nor of beast: but a deaf sound, which God sendeth them even when al things are at rest." Cain, he goes on, "had no rest, and yet who pursued him? ... he quaked like the leafe of a tree. And wherof came that? Even of the secrete voyce, of the voyce that was not herd with the eare, but yet was the same a dreadful noise...."[12] This seems to be the voice of the conscience, which is God speaking through the imagination of man, which in turn refers it to the senses. Appropriately in *Macbeth* the conscience speaks this message through the ears, for these cries, seemingly throughout the house, are the beginning of the larger repercussions that will forever, trumpet-tongued, deprive Macbeth of the sleep he has murdered.

The next strong assault upon the murderers' ears is a suggestion, like Macbeth's pangs of conscience, that their life has become an image of hell. The knocking at the gate is, at first thought, a purely natural sound. Macbeth's first reaction to it is that of a nervous system which can endure no more strain, particularly that of sound:

> Whence is that knocking?—
> How is 't with me, when every noise appals me?
> *(II.ii.56–57)*

But the knocking has seemingly a more than natural persistence. Even the drunken Porter complains, "Knock, knock. Never at quiet!" (II.iii.17), and more than an antic drunkenness inspires him to enact the role of the porter of Hell-Gate. It is surely one of the most impressively symbolic episodes in the play, demonstrating how a monotonous sound, if placed in a scene of dark evil and terrible tension, can evoke the sensation carrying a major moral message of the play. The knocking, as much as the

[12] *Sermons of Master John Calvin upon the Booke of Job*, trans. by Arthur Golding (1574), p. 279a.

mysterious voice, is evidence that the judgment of the heavens is beginning to make man tremble. The act of loud and repeated knocking at night has always been deeply connotative. In Elizabethan times, it could signify death knocking at the door.[13] The form that death took was often the plague, and a modern scholar has suggested that the Jacobean audience, having just suffered through a major plague in which authorities pounded on doors to seek out dead to bury, would have trembled at the sound.[14] The knocking could also signify divine justice assailing the conscience. According to *The French Academie*, "divine justice rappeth continually at the doore of their [the wicked men's] conscience, as it were an Apparitor or Sergeant, calling them to judgement."[15] Christ also pounds at the door of man's conscience. Hooker, citing Revelation 3:20—"I stand at the door and knock"—observes, "Nor doth he only knock without, but also within. . . ."[16]

But Christ does not always knock invitingly to save man through his conscience; and I am not so fortunate as G. R. Elliott as to find any evidence that following the murder of Duncan the possibility of Macbeth's salvation is ever a real one.[17] If Christ is knocking here, it is not to save Macbeth but to assault the door of Hell-Gate, which Inverness has become. The scene is very close, even in the role of the Porter as the character Rybald, to the playlet within the Miracle Cycles depicting "The Harrowing of Hell." Glynne Wickham has pointed to parallels that place the scene unmistakably in hell:

> On the medieval stage hell was represented as a castle, more particularly as a dungeon or cesspit within a castle, one entrance to which was often depicted as a dragon's mouth. . . .

---

[13] Myles Coverdale, "A Most Frutefull Pythye and Learned Treatyse, How a Christen Man Ought to Behave Hymselfe in the Daunger of Death" [1550]. In *Remains of Myles Coverdale*, ed. by Rev. George Pearson (Parker Society), (Cambridge, 1846), p. 51.

[14] John Webster Spargo, "The Knocking at the Gate in *Macbeth*: An Essay in Interpretation," in *Joseph Quincy Adams Memorial Studies* (Washington, D. C., 1948), p. 277. Spargo further interprets this sound as the third in "a crescendo of three ominous portents of death," the first being the wolf's howl and the second the owl's screech.

[15] Pierre de La Primaudaye, *The French Academie* (1594), II, 580.

[16] *The Laws of Ecclesiastical Polity*, Book VI, in *Works*, "compleated" by John Gauden (1662), p. 140.

[17] See *Dramatic Providence in Macbeth* (Princeton, 1960).

Its gate was guarded by a janitor or porter. Christ, after his crucifixion, but before his resurrection, came to this castle of hell to demand of Lucifer the release of the souls of the patriarchs and prophets. The setting for this play was either the interior of the gate-house or the courtyard of the castle: Christ's arrival was signalled by a tremendous knocking at this gate and a blast of trumpets.[18]

Even thus early in the play Macbeth is the "fiend of Scotland," and the pounding at the door means that his tyranny over hell castle will ultimately be ended for the virtuous victims. Most germane to our purpose here are the sounds that Wickham finds to be emblematic:

> Thunder, cacophony, screams and groans were the audible emblems of Lucifer and hell on the medieval stage. Those same aural emblems colour the whole of II, iii of *Macbeth* and, juxtaposed as they are with thunderous knocking at a gate attended by a porter deluded into regarding himself as a devil, their relevance to the moral meaning of the play could scarcely have escaped the notice of its first audiences.
>
> *(P. 73)*

I especially value this interpretation because, coming as it does from so respected a student of the stage, its endorsement of symbolic and "moral meaning" of spectacle lends authoritative support to my endeavor in the whole of this study. I would add to Wickham's account what I have discussed elsewhere, the dreadful impact and significance of the alarum-bell which awakened the sleepers of the house. It becomes for Lady Macbeth a "hideous trumpet," prophetic not only of the Harrowing of Hell but of Doomsday. Even as merely a bell it would "call to parley" the guilty pair, with their already taut nerves. Moreover, Shakespeare had only recently used a frightful alarum-bell at night in Othello, and in both plays it signals the beginning of disaster for the protagonists. In *Macbeth* it is appropriately Macduff, the liberator of Scotland, who commands, "Ring the alarum-bell" (II.iii.75).

---

[18] "Hell-Castle and Its Door-Keeper," *Shakespeare Survey 19* (Cambridge, 1966), pp. 68–69. For an earlier article on this subject, see John B. Harcourt, "I Pray You Remember the Porter," *Shakespeare Quarterly*, XII (1961), 393–402.

Not all of the aural torment is to be that of mere sound, however symbolic. As the sleepers of the house gather, Lady Macbeth is to suffer a subtler kind of agony through the ears. Macduff would spare her the report of the murder:

> O gentle lady,
> 'Tis not for you to hear what I can speak:
> The repetition, in a woman's ear,
> Would murder as it fell.
>
> *(II.iii.83–86)*

It would be satisfyingly ironic that this "gentle" lady, who had poured her spirits into Macbeth's ear, should in turn be murdered by a repetition of the crime in her own ear. This almost in fact happens, for she faints when her husband graphically relives for her the scene of the murder, emphasizing that which caused her unnerving—the blood. Macbeth later recalls for us this episode when he says that "murders have been perform'd / Too terrible for the ear" (III.iv.76–77). Murder in this play is almost throughout made terrible to and through the ear. It is not done so, however, in one conspicuous exception. We have already noticed that, unlike most stage ghosts, that of Banquo is silent. But its silence is more disconcerting to Macbeth than words, even those thrilling ones of the Ghost in *Hamlet*, could be.

Unmistakably supernatural sounds return to torment Macbeth when—in a recommitting scene not entirely unlike that in *Faustus*—he deliberately seeks out the Witches. These creatures provide again seemingly fair omens, but the Apparitions are ominously accompanied by thunder. The Second Apparition, moreover, speaks thunderously as it cries, "Macbeth! Macbeth! Macbeth!" for Macbeth complains, "Had I three ears, I'd hear thee" (IV.i.77–78). After all the buffeting his ears have received and after his sleeplessness, it is the more understandable that he should resolve to take a bond of Fate that he might "sleep in spite of thunder" (IV.i.86). Peals of thunder have rolled through the play from the very opening, and usually it is associated with the Witches. But, like the knocking, the thunder that keeps Macbeth sleepless is heard also within. The thunder in *King Lear* may, or may not, be the wrathful voice of the heavens; we are still, despite William Elton's formidable *King Lear and the Gods*, not sure about the role of the gods in that play in which torment may be meaningless and strange phenomena without heavenly portent. In *Macbeth*, a play in which both evil and suffering have meaning, this is simply not the case. The thunder that tortures Macbeth the most is the voice of God, speaking through his conscience. *Thunder* had this connotation in works that closely enough bear upon Macbeth's spiritual state. In *A Warning for Faire Women* (ca. 1599) the murderer asks, "What sound was that?" It could not be that of the slain man.

> Who was it then that thundred in mine eares,
> The name of Jesu? Doublesse twas my conscience,
> And I am damn'd for this unhallowed deede.
> *(Sig. F 1ʳ)*

Of all tortures, Calvin writes, "neither the horse, neither the racke, nor any kinde of torment, is so violent to urge malefactors, as was this thunder of Gods voyce, to strike Caine, and to overthrowe him to confusion."[19] Both of these instances suggest that the thunder, even if it speaks the name of Jesus, need not imply the attempted salvation of the culprits. The murderer recognizes that he is damned, and Calvin sees the purpose of the thunder of God's voice as overthrowing Cain to confusion. According to Christian doctrine, to be sure, Macbeth would not be necessarily damned at this point, any more than Faustus was when he re-enacted his pact with Lucifer. But Macbeth's reaction to the torments is one of fear and desperation rather than repentance.

There is further auditory distress for Macbeth in this second encounter with the Witches. As the caldron sinks, he cries out, "what noise is this?" (IV.i.106). This recalls his earlier state of nerves when he had asked, "How is 't with me, when every noise appals me?" The "noise" in this case is the innocent one of hautboys, and the word here means simply a small consort of the instruments. *Every* sound now appalls Macbeth. But the

---

[19] *A Commentarie of John Calvine upon the First Booke of Moses Called Genesis*, trans. by Thomas Tymme (1578), p. 140. According to John Woolton, conscience speaks "with the noyese of the thunder, as it is sayde in the Psalme." *Of the Conscience* (1576), sig. E 3ʳ.

music of the Witches may additionally be eerie, designed to accompany their grotesque dance. Thus one of them offers to "charm the air to give a sound, / While you perform your antic round" (IV.i.129–130). Macbeth is himself almost charmed; he stands "thus amazedly" at the awful sights he has seen. The eerie music is offered as something to "cheer . . . up his sprites," but in actuality it is, like the sights he has seen, something to lead him through his frayed nerves toward desperation.

This stage seems to be reached late in Act V. There is a hair-raising cry offstage. Again Macbeth is to ask, "What is that noise?" (V.v.7). He learns "It is the cry of women, my good Lord." But his nerves are now virtually dead, in contrast to the time when his "senses would have cool'd / To hear a night-shriek" (and he has heard many a one). He reaches this stage at the time when he most needs to respond to a human experience. His wife is dead. The cry is the most human one in the play, yet probably the most uncanny. The unidentified cry of women strikes far back into the primordial experience and sorrow of man. Coming from offstage, and without words, it is almost as mysterious as the voice which had cried much earlier. There could be no fitter musical setting for Macbeth's major human experience in the play or for the darkly sinister manner of Lady Macbeth's death.

It is immediately following this cry, and his inability to react emotionally to its horror, that he makes his most desperate comment upon life. Appropriately this comment has, as one of its most deeply felt expressions—truer to tangible experience than to abstract imagery—"full of sound and fury, / Signifying nothing" V.v.27–28).

In the final scenes Macbeth, though his nervous resources may be nearly spent, hears a sound that speaks commandingly to his increasing desperation: an insistently ominous music. It seems to be an explainably natural kind of music. Leading his army against Dunsinane, Macduff commands:

> Make all our trumpets speak; give them all breath,
> Those clamorous harbingers of blood and death.
> *(V.vi.9–10)*

We have already noticed, as far back as the trumpet-tongued angels, that the trumpet in this play connotes something more than natural. But it mainly connotes a vigorous, open challenge, suitable for the very human aspect of the onslaught upon Macbeth. It is similar to the trumpet which sounds the return of Edgar in *King Lear*. For the more covert and mysterious approach of divine justice upon Macbeth, Shakespeare needed a different kind of music, and for this purpose he chose the offstage drum. This instrument had at least as much supernatural connotation as the trumpet.

It could, as in Gascoigne's *The Droomme of Doomes Day*, signify the approach of the Last Judgment. Shakespeare also, like other dramatists, used it frequently in the muffled beat of the Dead March which ended tragedies. But usually it connoted Nemesis overtaking the wicked. The supernatural source of the drum announcing vengeance could be the Devil, if the Devil happened to be the agent of punishment. According to Lavater, the Demon, with God's permission, "can make a noyse & reare a clamour & crie, as it were of a great Armie in the ayre, and play as it were on a Drum, and do other such things, whiche al Hystoriographers affirme with one voyce, have oftentimes chaunced."[20]

The vengeful Ghost, perhaps the Devil, in *Caesar's Revenge* (ca. 1595) demands the drum's "gastly musicke" to accompany the death of his assassins:

> Let sterne Maegera on her thundering drumme,
> Play gastly musicke to consort your deathes.[21]

In *The Battle of Alcazar* (ca. 1589) the drum is that of Nemesis summoning the Furies:

> Now Nemisis upon her doubling drum,
> Movde with this gastly mone, this sad complaint,
> Larumes aloud into Alectos eares,
> And with her thundering wakes whereas they lie....[22]

---

[20] Ludwig Lavater, *Of Ghostes and Spirites Walking by Nyght*, Englished by R. H. (1592), ed. by J. Dover Wilson and May Yardley (Oxford, 1929), p. 166.
[21] Malone Society Reprints (1911), III.i.2070–2071. I draw for my discussion of the drum partially upon my *Shakespeare's Military World* (Berkeley and Los Angeles, 1956), pp. 31–34.
[22] Ed. by John Yoklavich, *The Dramatic Works of George Peele* (New Haven, 1961), II, Presenter, 288–291. See also I, Presenter, 37, where Nemesis "With thundering drums awakes the God of Warre."

In *Julius Caesar* Shakespeare had effectively experimented with the offstage drum suggesting Nemesis. "Low alarums"—that is, drums heard from a distance—accompany the closing in on Brutus. When he has twice seen Caesar's Ghost and has been beaten "to the pit," the low alarums underscore his request that Volumnius kill him (V.v.23). Then, with "Alarum still," the sense of hastening doom is heightened as Clitus cries, "Fly, fly my lord; there is no tarrying here" (V.v.29–30). And finally, after the stage direction "*Alarum. Cry within,* Fly, fly, fly!" (V.ii.42), the identity of the human Nemesis becomes prosaically clear with the arrival of the victorious enemy, whose presence onstage is far less impressive than the atmospheric suggestiveness of their distant drums.

In *Macbeth*, Shakespeare used the drum with consummate effectiveness. We should expect him to do so because of his improved artistry in sensation generally and because *Macbeth* has from the beginning been more mysterious in supernatural retribution. Most of the fifth act of *Macbeth*, from the second scene through the eighth, is drawn tensely together by the now intermittent, now steady, beating of drums. "Drum and colours" appear prominently in most of these scenes, announcing the appearance of army after army to a Dunsinane which Macbeth "strongly fortifies" but which cannot shut out the sound of Nemesis. Just as Brutus had been told, "there is no tarrying here," so Macbeth comes to the deeper realization that "There is nor flying hence, nor tarrying here" (V.v.48). But from most reading editions of the play (the Pelican excepted), with their constant scene divisions, one has no awareness of the drum music which beats this truth home; for the scene ends within some four lines, and the reader is not likely to anticipate the approaching music announced at the beginning of the next scene (the sixth): "Enter, with drum and colours, Malcolm, Old Siward, Macduff, etc., and their army, with boughs." Actually, of course, these scenes were continuous on the stage, and their continuity and its impact upon Macbeth were strengthened by the cumulative effect of drums. Only with concentration will the reader appreciate one of the finest sensational achievements of the play, for it is now hidden in inconspicuous directions for alarums which should powerfully increase near the end. Within the thirty-nine lines which comprise scenes six and seven, are the following musical directions: "Drum and colours," "Alarums continued," "Alarum," "Alarum," and finally the full force of all the armies, "Alarums." Macduff, like Octavius Caesar, may be a prosaic instrument of Nemesis for Macbeth, but not so the relentless sound with which, in more than a military sense, he announces divine retribution.

IV

Despite the persistent thunder and drums, the sense of sight is the object of a more excruciating torment than the ear. The episodes are less frequent but more intense. They serve to substantiate our feeling of agonizing vision in the imagery of the play, and they contribute to the common impression that Macbeth is Shakespeare's supreme poet of the visual imagination. It should be recognized, in partial support of the explanation for the visual emphasis which underlies much of this book, that Shakespeare had just completed, in *King Lear*, an even more intense, but largely physical, representation of ocular torment. The once lustful Gloucester, as we have observed, is blinded for a reason that his captors do not know. The ethical spokesman Edgar tells Edmund of the profoundly condign nature of the punishment (related possibly to Christ's commandment to pluck out the offending eye):

> The gods are just, and of our pleasant vices,
> Make instruments to plague us.
> The dark and vicious place where thee he got
> Cost him his eyes.
>
> *(V.iii.170–173)*

But there are few sensational sights in this play. Sight becomes mainly a philosophical part of the imagery, pointing toward a more interior form of seeing. In *Macbeth*, the mental "seeing" is there, but much less impressively so than in *King Lear*. What Macbeth sees serves mainly to tempt him to damnation and to torment him. Sight in *King Lear* is precious and, even in its loss, creative; in *Macbeth* it is almost purely horrible.

There are not, as there are with sounds, any pleasant sights near the beginning of the play to contrast with the dark ones to follow. Later, however, two allusions to the eye assure us of its native virtue. Macbeth, asking Night to scarf up "the tender eye of pitiful Day" (III.ii.47), reveals that he knows both the sensitivity of the eye and its proper kinship with good things of day rather than with night's black agents; and at this late stage in the play he also makes the audience aware of how much his own tender eye has suffered. And Lady Macbeth's reference to "the eye of childhood," though scornful like the rigor of her proffered sacrifice of the nursing baby, shows that she, too, has known innocence. Before it has been sophisticated by experience and rebuked by convention, the eye is curious, open, impressionable, and vulnerable. Possibly Macbeth has by nature, in unusual degree, this kind of eye, which is really the poet's eye as Theseus defines it in *A Midsummer Night's Dream*. His wife seems to think that he does, and his lively reaction to objects both outwardly and inwardly visible suggests that he sees with painful clarity and even, with unfamiliar objects, some of the freshness of childhood.

But his eye is not, I think, assaulted so specifically and violently primarily because it is the eye of childhood. It is assaulted, above all other senses, because it has been directed by Macbeth to acquiesce in evil, because one member of the body cannot be morally innocent of what another member does. The crucial speech in which Macbeth consecrates his eye to evil occurs just after he has made his first real gesture toward murder:

> Stars, hide your fires!
> Let not light see my black and deep desires;
> The eye wink at the hand; yet let that be,
> Which the eye fears, when it is done, to see.
> (I.iv.50–53

As I have observed earlier, there will occur exactly that which Macbeth here requests. The eye will see, after the deed, what it will fear to see. It is almost a Faustian kind of contract, simply postponing the inevitable penalty. But though Macbeth soon realizes that the horrid deed will be blown into every eye, he does not come close to foreseeing the effect upon his own eye. If his tears did drown the wind, we should have an entirely different kind of play, much closer to *King Lear* in the protagonist's growing awareness of the pity of the human condition. Instead, the torture of Macbeth's vision leads mainly, though not exclusively, to the shrinking effect of nervous exhaustion and futility. This diminution of his human sensibilities is evident, as with his hearing, in his reaction to one horrid sight after another.

The first sight, the bloody dagger, both tempts and appalls him. He is sensitive to the blood on it, which he had not anticipated, but he pursues the vision nonetheless. He even rationalizes it as of purely physiological origin, as a creation of "the heat-oppressed brain" (II.i.39). This explanation was logically plausible. Thomas Nashe had written that "from the fuming melancholly of our spleene mounteth that hot matter into the higher Region of the braine, whereof manie fearfull visions are framed."[23] But the more fearful supernatural cause of the dagger is that the Devil, according to one divine,

> can vitiate and corrupt the organe of sight the eye by tempering the humours in such sort, as things shall appear like as the humour is: as when all appeareth outwardly like blood, when some bloodie humour is mixed with the sight.[24]

Macbeth is tragically shallow in not recognizing the metaphysical meaning of the phenomenon. He tremblingly pursues the dagger without responding morally to its menace.

The next sight which he comments upon is his bloody hands after the murder: "This is a sorry sight" (II.ii.20); and his Lady, though she is not comparably tortured through the eye, reveals in her hysterical reaction to the naming of the horror that she, too, is suffering: "A foolish thought to say a sorry sight." She, however, will mainly *feel* the blood. Macbeth regards the sight of the hands as most appalling. During this scene the two should probably not look at each other's eyes. Macbeth's fascinated attention should be upon his hands: "What hands are here? Ha! they pluck out mine eyes" (II.ii.58). The eye was to have

---

[23] *The Terrors of the Night Or, A Discourse of Apparitions* (1594), in *Works*, ed. by Ronald B. McKerrow, with corrections and supplementary notes by F. P. Wilson (Oxford, 1958), I, 354.

[24] Andrew Willet, *An Harmonie upon the First Booke of Samuel* (1607), p. 327.

winked at the hand. This cannot successfully happen. The eye cannot say to the hand, I have no need of thee. The hand will return, with bloody instructions, to plague the inventor; and Shakespeare may, in picturing the bloody hands plucking out the eyes, be led to the later image of the "bloody and invisible hand," in conjunction with "tender eye," which cancels and tears to pieces (III.ii.47–49). But the image of the hand plucking out the eye comes most obviously from Mark 9:47:

> And if thine eye cause thee to offende, plucke it out: it is better for thee to go into the kingdome of God with one eye, then having two eyes, to be cast into hel fyre. . . .[25]

For the audience this famous passage, so unmistakably suggested, serves as a compelling clue to Macbeth's spiritual crisis. But Macbeth himself seems to be aware only of the plucking hands as independently vengeful agents, almost compulsively reflexive. It is not he who directs them to pluck out an offending eye. Moreover, as with the dagger, he is aware only of the physical horror of the sight and not its moral meaning.

He has also had to expose his eye to the body of the murdered Duncan. And again his reaction is simply physical panic. The sight of Duncan's body is kept vague visually until he later describes it, with some degree of control, to the assembled guests. At first, and basically, he feels a dumb horror. He will not return to the murder scene.

> I'll go no more:
> I am afraid to think what I have done;
> Look on 't again I dare not.
>
> *(II.ii.49–51)*

Obviously the physical fact of the sight, his most sensitive and tormented sense, is what most paralyzes him. But he is also afraid to think about the deed. When he does describe to the guests his less nervous reaction, it is to explain his slaying of the grooms.

---

[25] The image of the eye of the wicked being tormented is frequent in the Bible. One of the passages most quoted by Renaissance commentators is Proverbs 30:17: "The eye that mocketh his father, and despiseth the instruction of his mother, let the ravens of the valley picke it out, and the yong egles eat it." See also Job 11:20; Joshua 23:13; Zechariah 14:12: Deuteronomy 28:32,65; Leviticus 26:16.

Only in "the wine of life" reflection, intended to deceive and not to express his real feelings, does he rise from nervous ordeal to thought about the deed. Lady Macbeth diagnoses his response as fear:

> The sleeping, and the dead,
> Are but as pictures; 'tis the eye of childhood
> That fears a painted devil.
>
> *(II.ii.52–54)*

The imagery of the diagnosis seems impeccably logical. Charron, in a book that Shakespeare probably read in the French original before writing *King Lear*, says of fear that "it tormenteth us with masks and shewes of evils, as men feare children with bug-beares; evils that have nothing but a simple appearance."[26] But neither of the two criminals is in a position, spiritually or nervously, to respond logically to the violated body of a sainted king. The underlying assumption of Lady Macbeth's observation is that pictures have no life. But these are speaking pictures, especially for those whose sight is to be tormented. Lady Macbeth had earlier contradicted her statement when one "picture" of the sleeping was so unnerving for her that she could not carry out her fell purpose: Duncan resembled her father as he slept. And Macbeth will later picture Duncan, with lively force, as sleeping well after life's fitful fever. Moreover, the pictures of the dead assume terrifying eloquence for both the murderers in the shape of the victims. The image of Banquo's Ghost, for instance, cannot be exorcised simply by "Unreal mockery, hence!" Nor does Lady Macbeth take into account the invariable, and sometimes retributive, triumph of youthful innocence in the play. The "eye of childhood" proves to be another ironic instance of the underrated power, even terror, of the weak and vulnerable baby. Had, moreover, Macbeth responded to the deed with more of the eye of childhood, had Pity like the naked

---

[26] *Of Wisdome* (ca. 1606), p. 103. Pierre Le Loyer, *A Treatise of Specters or Strange Sights*, trans. by L. Jones (1605), says that infancy "(by the authoritie of Aristotle, and daily experience) is most subject to perceive false visions" (fol. 91ᵛ). Lavater also states: "They say that sometimes Children doe see certaine things, whiche other men see not" (p. 90). Although Shakespeare probably had read all three books, Charron is the closest to Lady Macbeth's speech, yet I have never seen its influence or parallel noted.

new-born babe blown the deed in his eye, his spiritual vision might not have atrophied and his own tears might have saved him by drowning the wind.

The sight of the murdered Duncan proves to be Macbeth's last chance to receive torture through the eye as a saving rather than a seductive or punitive agent. All of the remaining sights are demonically caused, and they serve either to lead Macbeth to his confusion or to torment him. Increasingly they parallel the function of the tormenting sounds in auguring the approach of Nemesis.

The sight of Banquo's Ghost leads him to no reflection on the guilt that caused the murder. Surely there is no remorse or compassion in his response. If we ourselves are aware of any poignancy in his predicament, it is in his total isolation from the rest of humanity. Besides sheer panic at the nature of the vision, his principal emotional reaction is an almost pathetic need to make his Queen and guests share his suffering and to appreciate his manliness in looking at the Ghost. In reply to Lady Macbeth's cold "Are you a man?" he protests that he is "a bold one, that dare look on that / Which might appal the Devil" (III.iv.57–59). She again resorts to her strategy of reducing the nature of seeing by telling him that he looks "but on a stool." He can answer only by pleading with her to *see*:

> Pr'ythee, see there!
> Behold! Look! lo! how say you?
> *(III.iv.67–68)*

He becomes a stranger even to his own disposition when he thinks that others are beholding without terror what he sees (III.iv.111–113). A stranger to himself and to others, he is on his way to the isolation whose torment we shall examine in the next chapter. But what he sees cannot really be shared with others, for it is the uniquely appropriate and lonely torment that cannot be felt by others. Even for his wife there will be a torment of a different kind, one that likewise separates her from others.

The final supernatural torture of his eyes is arranged, through his own deliberate conjuration, by the Witches and their "masters." He wants to learn his fate, and he goes, against all Biblical injunction, to sorcerers. Their evil purpose in presenting him with visual auguries is well expressed by Hecate. Although her speech may be apocryphal, it was written by a contemporary whose interpretation of the play is of some value. A distilled drop from the moon, Hecate tells the Witches,

> Shall raise such artificial sprites,
> As, by the strength of their illusion,
> Shall draw him on to his confusion.
> He shall spurn fate, scorn death, and bear
> His hopes 'bove wisdom, grace, and fear.
> *(III.v.27–31)*

These artificial spirits will, then, serve the purpose of drawing Macbeth to his confusion. But, like the equally demonic Ghost of Banquo, they will also provide a diabolical bonus in the form of mockery and torment.

The three Apparitions are foul in form but fair in promise; and, as with the sight of the Witches themselves, Macbeth accepts without expressed pain what he is forced to see. It is different with the Show of Kings. These figures are, except for the blood-boltered Banquo, fair in form but terrible in promise. The Witches present them with glee.

> *1. Witch.* Show!
> *2. Witch.* Show!
> *3. Witch.* Show!
> *All.* Show his eyes, and grieve his heart.
> *(IV.i.107–110)*

"Why," Macbeth cries, "do you show me this? A fourth? Start, eyes!" (IV.i.116). The image of eyes "starting" is not of course unusual. It is found, however, most appositely in a passage from Thomas Nashe:

> Ambition, Ambition, harken to mee, there will be a blacke day when thy Ambition shall breake hys necke, when thou shalt lie in thy bedde as on a Racke stretching out thy joints; when thine eyes shall start out of thy head, & every part of thee be wrunge as with the wind-chollick.[27]

[27] *Christs Teares over Jerusalem* (1593), in *Works*, ed. by McKerrow, II, 92. Nashe is the prose writer most worthy in lively detail of Shakespeare's imitation. The torture described in *The Unfortunate Traveller* is probably the most horrible in Elizabethan literature.

What makes the passage noteworthy in reference to *Macbeth* is that the subject matter is ambition and its punishment; the Show of Kings is terrible to Macbeth primarily because it means the death of his ambition in the form of issue. The climax of the Show is the irrepressible Banquo, whose "crown does sear mine eye-balls" (IV.i.113). Of Banquo's progeny, Macbeth exclaims "Horrible sight!—Now, I see, 'tis true" (IV.i.122). After the Show, he pleads, "But no more sights!" (IV.i.155).

Although Macbeth says, "I see, 'tis true," what he sees as true is the threat to his ambition, which had been first given expression by the Witches, and not any repentant or humane observation upon his bloody career. Such an observation upon sin does occur in a play that may have influenced *Macbeth*, for it describes aptly some of Macbeth's visual torment from the Show. In Thomas Hughes's *The Misfortunes of Arthur* (1587), the King says:

> I see (alas) I see (hide, hide againe:
> O spare mine eyes) a witnesse of my crimes:
> A fearefull vision of my former guilte:
> A dreadfull horror of a future doome:
> A present gaule of minde. O happie they,
> Whose spotlesse lives attaine a dreadlesse death.[28]

Unlike Arthur, Macbeth recognizes in the visions no witness of his crimes, no fearful vision of his guilt, but only a partial horror of a future doom. He sees only what he has feared all along, the threat of Banquo to his ambition. What the Witches make him see will, as they intend, provide the basis for a later philosophical view of life, but that view will be the Devil's doctrine of despair. Gloucester in *King Lear* had learned to "see feelingly," and under the benign guidance of Edgar he successfully fought off despair. Macbeth's torment is simply torment. Unless it is de-

---

[28] Cunliffe, V.i.98–103. For a possible verbal influence of this play upon *Macbeth*, see II.ii.44–45: To Mordred's statement, "Chaunce hath made me king," Gawin replies, "As Chaunce hath made you King, so Chaunce may change." Cf. *Macbeth* I.iii.144–145:
> If Chance will have me King, why, Chance may crown me,
>   Without my stir.

I find this parallel noted in no edition of *Macbeth*.

served, it lacks meaning, and this is one of the dangers of so dark a play.

V

Shakespeare does make Macbeth's torture of the senses deserved. I have said earlier that although there are several possible causes for the various tortures, symptomatic concentration upon specific senses can be explained meaningfully, and probably most of the general torment proceeds from supernatural, often diabolically administered, punishment for guilt. The sounds and sights are not so horrible in themselves as in the way they speak to something evil in Macbeth.

I should like to look a little more deeply into this conclusion in view of the one important generalization Shakespeare makes upon Macbeth's torment. It comes from a minor character, it is not clear in meaning, and it is echoed nowhere else in the play. Nevertheless students of Shakespeare have learned to be grateful for, while still remaining wary of, any kind of commitment Shakespeare deigns to offer. The generalization is made by Menteith in the course of Macbeth's nervous torment:

> Who then shall blame
> His pester'd senses to recoil and start,
> When all that is within him does condemn
> Itself, for being there?
> *(V.ii.22–25)*

Despite its limitations, the passage deserves explication. That which is "within him" could well be his conscience, for this would condemn itself for being there. According to Thomas Rogers, the consciences of malefactors will "continually object unto their senses most horrible sights of strange things which wyl at no tyme suffer them to be at reast."[29] And according to Bishop Hooper, "where sin is thoroughly felt in the conscience, the feeling sinner is not only troubled within in spirit, but also outwardly in all the members and parts of his body."[30] And

---

[29] *Anatomie of the Mind* (1576), p. 36.
[30] *Later Writings of Bishop Hooper, Together with His Letters and Other Pieces*, ed. by Rev. Charles Nevinson (Parker Society), (Cambridge, 1852), p. 314.

Shakespeare had read that on the night before Bosworth Field, Richard III saw "diverse images like terrible divels, which so pulled and haled him, not suffering him to take anie quiet or rest." This "was no dreame, but a punction and pricke of his sinfull conscience."[31] Conscience is, then, a strong possiblility, but there is a real question as to whether or not "sin is thoroughly felt in the conscience" of Macbeth after he has heard the voice crying at night.

Certainly many of Macbeth's symptoms are those which the Renaissance commonly ascribed to a guilty conscience. What is lacking, in terms of Renaissance criteria for an active conscience, is something that goes steadily beyond physical symptoms to an awareness of having sinned. Thomas Becon asks, "What is an evil conscience? It is an inward boiling heat, and tossing of the mind, for a man's wickedness, and when for pure anguish of the sight and horror of sin the heart fainteth and faileth him."[32] Besides "the sight of sinne," William Perkins, a major authority on the conscience, mentions another almost invariable characteristic of the conscience-troubled man: he has "the sense of Gods wrath."[33] Macbeth is lacking in both these characteristics. The most that can be safely said of his conscience has been expressed by Willard Farnham, who, however, elsewhere argues well for its vividness:

> His conscience is little if anything more than a self-centered fear and therefore it is a grossly imperfect sense of right and wrong. It has no power to make him see why his crimes are horrible, however much it shakes his single state of man, and no power to conquer his pride.[34]

---

[31] Holinshed, *The First and Second Volumes of Chronicles*, III, (1587), "Historie of England," p. 755. See also John Woolton, *A Treatise of the Immortalitie of the Soule* (1576), sig. I 1ᵛ.

[32] "The Demandes of Holy Scripture," in *Prayers and Other Pieces of Thomas Becon, S.T.P.*, ed. by Rev. John Ayre (Parker Society), (Cambridge, 1844), p. 604.

[33] *Cases of Conscience* (1608), p. 194. This is specified by Samuel Hieron, *Davids Penitentiall Psalme Opened* (Cambridge, 1617), p. 259.

[34] *Shakespeare's Tragic Frontier: The World of His Final Tragedies* (Berkeley and Los Angeles, 1950), p. 119. G. R. Elliott says that the "fear with which his conscience plagued him before his first crime (I.iii.135 ff.) has continued to torture him (III.ii.21) throughout his career in ever new ways, ways varying in accordance with the dire expedients employed by him to banish that fear" (p. 194).

In its advanced stages of deterioration after the murder, Macbeth's conscience would possibly have been defined by the Renaissance as "seared," a favorite term for the condition in which it "becomes dead, and is no longer informed by the soule; so continuance in sinne, deprives Conscience of all life in the truth."[35] The seared conscience, or hardness of heart, is regarded by Perkins (citing Deuteronomy 28:28) as a punishment, and thus becomes an important way in which sin is punished by sin.[36]

Rather than an active conscience, therefore, we may well look for something else to explain what is within Macbeth that would fit Menteith's diagnosis. I would suggest that it is something evil, perhaps even an evil spirit. Bishop Hooper is again helpful. A clean spirit within a man, he writes, "strengtheneth so every member, that they will be given to nothing so much as to the service of God. But if the spirit be wicked, doubtless the outward members cannot be quiet."[37] A philosophical dramatist of the time, writing in about 1600, adds further evidence for thinking the inner cause to be something evil. Fulke Greville's Alaham, seeing "visions of horror," with "shapes, and figures like to that of death," speculates upon their meaning:

> Things seeme not as they did; horror appeares.
> What sinne imbodied, what strange sight is this?
> Doth sense bring backe but what within me is? [38]

Sense brings back merely "what within me is," and that is "sinne imbodied." Applied to Macbeth, this view would explain how the senses receive condign punishment. Macbeth feels through the senses a horrible figuring of his inner evil, as with the dagger. We might even extend this explanation to refer to the demonic inhabitation of Macbeth's body. All the good characters have

---

[35] Huit, p. 317. See also William Perkins, *Works* (1603), pp. 568–569; *The Sermons of John Donne*, ed. by G. R. Potter and Evelyn Simpson (Berkeley and Los Angeles, 1959), IV, 221; and King James I, *The Basilicon Doron*, ed. by James Craigie (Edinburgh and London, 1944), p. 43. Frequently it was called a cauterized conscience.
[36] *Works*, Chapter XIV: "Of the Punishment of Sinne," p. 16.
[37] John Hooper, *Certeine Comfortable Expositions*, ed. by Rev. Charles Nevinson (Parker Society), (Cambridge, 1852), p. 329.
[38] *Alaham*, in *Poems and Dramas of Fulke Greville, First Lord Brooke*, ed. by Geoffrey Bullough (New York, 1945), p. 209, 11. 78–80.

by now placed him confidently in hell, as "this fiend of Scotland" and "hell-kite."

The passage is difficult, and no explanation is satisfactory to the exclusion of others. But we may briefly notice what clearly is in him at the time. One thing is his "distemper'd cause," which he cannot buckle within the belt of rule (V.ii.15–16). Another is the horror that he has supped full with (V.v.13). Still others suggest a darkened conscience groping for expression. He doubtless feels, though he is referring to Lady Macbeth, the bosom "stuff'd" with "that perilous stuff / Which weighs upon the heart" (V.iii.44–45). And he tells Macduff later, "my soul is too much charg'd / With blood of thine already" (V.viii.3–4). Once more *King Lear*, so closely antecedent, is helpful. Lear commands:

> Close pent-up guilts,
> Rive your concealing continents, and cry
> These dreadful summoners grace.
> *(III.ii.57)*

Perhaps Macbeth's close pent-up guilts, though not adequately recognized by the conscience, are breaking through into full bodily exposure. As Bishop Hooper would have it, if the spirit "be troubled, the outward members cannot be quiet."

But I would not limit to one ambiguous, and probably not authoritative, passage the interpretation of so complex a theme in the play. Underlying the theme is a shifting complex of causes: conscience, though flawed; the doctrine of condign punishment; internal evil expressing itself externally; much activity, tempting and penal, of the instruments of Darkness; and, as a general theological formulation, the pain of sense. Whatever may be the precise explanation, *Macbeth*, in its sensory torment, is certainly one of the most persuasive images of a physical hell in all literature.

Chapter X

Torture of the Mind

If pain of sense is the criterion, *Macbeth* must be ranked as Shakespeare's supreme picture of a physical hell. I am only somewhat less easy in my enthusiasm when I propose that *Macbeth* is also Shakespeare's supreme picture of a mental hell, perhaps the supreme picture in English drama. It is less ambitious to claim for a tragedy incomparable assault upon a nervous system. Fewer sensitive toes are stepped on than to move into the very center of tragedy and claim for a play its supremacy in torture of man's highest faculty. Mental agony is the very substance of Shakespeare's tragic power, and the source of his finest poetry.

But I am making a more guarded claim for *Macbeth*, one that will not impinge unduly upon the claims that must be made for *Hamlet* and, especially, *King Lear*. It is a claim that is congruent with the central thread of this study. Macbeth in mental ordeal is not so beautiful as Hamlet or so grand as King Lear, but he does suffer steadily, and without relief, from kinds of agony more exquisitely designed for hell than those of the other tragic heroes. He is, after all, the only major protagonist who is certainly damned. Macbeth's mental suffering is more clearly a punishment than is that of the other heroes. It destroys or reduces the man. It is not so constructive, so creative, in terms of life's fuller meaning, as the ordeals suffered by Hamlet or Lear. This punishment limits Macbeth's own tragic vision to the appropriate passion that dominates him. Other heroes are also

186 · OUR NAKED FRAILTIES

limited by passion.[1] Although he finally rises above passion, Hamlet mainly transforms one passion into another; Othello tries, with much less success, to do so; only Lear succeeds in transmuting passion into compassion. Although all are more or less limited by the one torment that beats upon their mind, Macbeth, rivaled only by Othello, is especially limited by what he suffers, and we shall constantly be aware of his limitations. But what he suffers has the sensory impact, and the penal quality, and the unrelieved pain, that we associate with hell. Even the limited dimension of his mental suffering gives it uncommon force. It has a thematic concentration and thereby is appropriate to infernal monotony and specialization of punishment. Tantalus, Ixion, and Sisyphus have only one form of punishment. Macbeth's mental punishment takes almost wholly the form of fear. Much of his sensory torment, as we have just seen, produces a panic fear. And most of his mental torment, caused by the rack of fear, has a sensory basis. In fact, it is very difficult in Macbeth's case to separate somatic from psychosomatic suffering. But this is what we should expect in this play. And we should also expect that the passion which principally afflicts the hero, fear, is the passion which has the closest relationship to the nervous system. Fear is perhaps man's primal passion, the one which he shares with animals, and it is the one which most agitates the body. It is the passion which, inevitably, Shakespeare used to sensational advantage in a play dealing with temptation, crime, and punishment.

II

Before taking up the thematic meaning of fear in the play, I shall first look at some aspects of Shakespeare's techniques in depicting mental suffering. It is appropriate to do so because the techniques are basic to theme and meaning. Most obvious, perhaps, is the device of making Macbeth feel through the body what he suffers in the mind. Expressions like "sick at heart" are

[1] But not, some critics would insist, so much as proposed by Lily B. Campbell in the strong, but sometimes misunderstood, book to which I am glad to acknowledge much indebtedness, *Shakespeare's Tragic Heroes: Slaves of Passion*. I agree with her about the importance of fear in *Macbeth*, but my interpretation of fear in this chapter differs radically from hers.

of course found in all of Shakespeare's suffering protagonists. And the body is always important. King Lear, especially, learns much about himself through the body.[2] But his suffering is not expressed mainly in sensory terms. He himself explains what distinguishes his form of agony:

> When the mind's free,
> The body's delicate; the tempest in my mind
> Doth from my senses take all feeling else
> Save what beats there.
>
> *(III.iv.11–14)*

The tempest in his mind not only is not felt in his senses; it takes away feeling from the senses. The imagery of his mental torment is that of storms, of beasts, of woman's body, and not, except for passing reference to being struck to the heart and being cut to the brain, of his own body. Hamlet likewise expresses his most deeply felt pain in such terms as rank vegetation, rottenness, death, and law courts. It is not his own body which torments him so much as Gertrude's. His most painful image is perhaps "honeying and making love / Over the nasty sty" (III.iv. 93–94). For both Hamlet and Lear the pain is translated into external symbols; Macbeth is much more confined to what he privately and directly feels.

His mind is "full of scorpions" (III.ii.36). There are "rancours in the vessel of [his] peace" (III.i.66). His concept of a troubled soul is that of "hurt minds" that need a "balm" (II.ii. 38) or of a heart that is weighed down with "perilous stuff" (V.iii.44–45). His symptomatic reaction to fear is extraordinarily physiological. His hair is unfixed (I.iii.135); his seated heart knocks at his ribs (I.iii.136) and throbs (IV.i.101); his fears "stick deep" (III.i.49); and his heart sags with doubt (V.iii.10). He repeatedly turns pale and is, as we noticed, subject to fits, flaws, and starts. Terrible dreams "shake" him nightly (III.ii. 18–19). He has known "the taste of fear" (V.v.9); he is "tainted" by it (V.iii.3), and is "bound in / To saucy doubts and fears" (III.iv.23–24). (Both *tainted* and *saucy* in the last two references were live images, *tainted* meaning not just mor-

[2] See Winifred M. T. Nowottny, "Lear's Questions," *Shakespeare Survey 10* (Cambridge, 1957), p. 92.

ally but physically stained, and *saucy* carrying still, if not the flavor of salt, at least something pungent.) Macbeth makes terrible faces and has "rugged looks" (III.ii.27). The instances are almost endless. There is scarcely a sorrow, a regret, a fear that is felt independently of the body. In fact, his strongest general statement of mental suffering uses an image of his whole body lying on a rack:

> Better be with the dead,
> Whom we, to gain our peace, have sent to peace,
> Than on the torture of the mind to lie
> In restless ecstasy.
>
> *(III.ii.19–22)*

Undeniably this concentration on the body is due partly to his way of thinking, which is more limited than Hamlet's. But it is also connected with a uniquely successful extension by Shakespeare of the pain of sense throughout Macbeth's whole being. It is also due to concentration on fear. Almost all of Macbeth's emotions are tinged by fear, as in the general malaise of the "perilous" stuff which weighs upon the heart, the guilt that makes him "start," the jealousy of Banquo, and even the vacuity of life which results when fear takes on its ultimate form of despair.

The poignant and vehement feeling that is thus achieved through direct symptoms in the body is not achieved without some sacrifice. It does not lend itself to larger, more abstract speculations about humanity, such as we find in Hamlet ("What is a man . . . ?") and in Lear ("Poor, naked wretches").[3] Fear, moreover, is a reductive rather than enlarging passion.[4] It makes a man urgently aware of what seems most

---

[3] Theodore Spencer aptly writes: "In *Macbeth*, as in *King Lear*, the individual, the state, and external nature are seen as interrelated parts of a single whole . . . —and yet the atmosphere and tone of the two plays are very different; we may say *Lear* is a play that opens out, whereas *Macbeth* is a play that closes in." *Shakespeare and the Nature of Man* (New York, 1942), p. 143.

[4] So it was characterized in Renaissance psychology. According to *The French Academie* (1594), II, 261, ". . . Feare is not onely a fantasie and imagination of evill approching, or a perturbation of the soule proceeding from the opinion it hath of some evill to come, but it is also a contraction and closing up of the heart. . . ."

immediately to threaten him, and him alone. It becomes ultimately selfish.

For whatever reasons, Macbeth's most moving observations are those that proceed almost entirely from his own experience and his immediate situation. And because his experience is mainly sensory, they express a general idea in terms of the senses, in terms of what Macbeth is almost literally feeling. Such is the case with his beautiful lament for murdered sleep, a "balm" that he needs physically. Sleep is felt from his bodily anguish and exhausted condition as "sore labour's bath" (II.ii.37), and it is expressive of his immediate, personal, and bodily situation. Similarly with his lament for the aridity of life wthout grace: "my way of life / Is fall'n into the sere, the yellow leaf" (V.iii.22–23). This poignant speech describes a mood that many persons temporarily experience, but for Macbeth it proceeds immediately from his own deprived and withered soul, and it is not temporary and general but lasting and personal. He cannot here really speak for all humanity because he is—unlike Hamlet or Lear—now barren of certain human qualities, forfeited by his sin. He can see only what a hollow man sees. Again, Macbeth's description of a mind diseased is as beautifully sensitive a one as we shall ever know. But although the speech is prompted by his wife's illness, Macbeth really knows and cares very little about that. He is describing his own mind, with its "rooted sorrow" in the memory and the "written troubles" in the brain (V.iii.41–42). And, as with his need for a physical balm for hurt minds and a bath for sore labor, he characteristically thinks of a medicinal cure for the mental illness: "some sweet oblivious antidote" that will "Cleanse the stuff'd bosom" (V.iii.43–44). He can speak so feelingly about mental illness because he has felt its anguish in the fullest physiological sense. But there must be acknowledged in these speeches, beyond the poignancy that personal experience gives, a cadence, a music, and a melancholy solemnity that lifts suffering into poetry. This is especially true of his most famous observation on life, the "To-morrow, and to-morrow, and to-morrow" speech. This speech I have already discussed as the disenchanted comment on a life of futile labor.[5]

[5] Roland Mushat Frye has helpfully discussed this speech in terms of Macbeth's spiritual condition and emphasizes that the point of view is

It is also, as we shall see, the comment of a soul stricken with despair because of separation from God. But again, although both suffering and sensory feeling inform this speech, they do not account for its full beauty. The miracle in this speech is Shakespeare's ability to feel, at a particular moment, the tormented vision of a particular character and to give it expression—no more profound or universal than befits the man—in a verbal music that is greater than, but not different from, the soul of the protagonist.

Shakespeare, then, made Macbeth a less universal but not necessarily less moving commentator upon mental torment than Hamlet or Lear. He covers a smaller spectrum in terms of all humanity, but he comments upon a remarkable span of experience in short space. He moves, without ranging as widely as Hamlet or Lear, through almost a complete career of a sinning soul on earth. This remarkable span is achieved by linear rather than spatial movement, by unusual compression of episodes, and by the highest intensity of sensational moments. It involves a technique that Shakespeare had not used since *Titus Andronicus*, that of supplying almost unmitigated gloom. There may be brief exhilaration for Macbeth as he rises to his wife's demands for love before the murder. Otherwise, he has not a pleasant moment.

So dark a texture has its dangers. We are impelled along from one speech of agony to another. Audiences laugh excessively at the Porter Scene; no play ever needed more such a scene of comic relief. Hell can become too murky for clean, tragic definition of effect; and monotony, the dominant mood of hell, is not ideal for dramatic variety of the kind we get in *Hamlet*.

In still another technique of depicting mental torment *Macbeth* is remarkable, especially in comparison with the tragedy that preceded it. In *King Lear* Shakespeare had made a notable advancement from his dependence, in *Hamlet*, upon the soliloquy and other set speeches to express suffering. Even in *Othello* the soliloquy is relegated primarily to the dramatic needs of

---

Macbeth's and not Shakespeare's. "*Macbeth* and the Powers of Darkness," *Emory University Quarterly*, VIII (1952), 164–174. Frye also has some good insights into *Macbeth* in *Shakespeare and Christian Doctrine* (Princeton, 1963). See particularly comments under "Fear," "Guilt," and "Sin."

Torture of the Mind · 191

the villain, where it had tended to be in earlier drama. The elocutionary aria was useful in permitting total honesty and coherent statement. But in *Hamlet* it was used to unprecedented advantage, and succeeded in no small part because of what earlier might have been considered flaws; I refer to dramatic irregularities, seemingly produced by the speaker's passion and live progress of thought. This development is especially noticeable in the "O, what a rogue and peasant slave am I!" soliloquy, where the discourse changes direction three times, is incoherent, and generally expresses by its form the force of a man in painful, but not prepared, thought. In *King Lear* the soliloquy is generally consigned to Edmund. The King's longer discourses are directed to the elements and the gods. They are designed less to reveal what he really thinks than to express his painful passion, whether of anger, self-pity, or (later) compassion. Most significantly, however, his mind is exposed not in long set speeches but in the seemingly outward form of dialogue with others, mainly the Fool. They are only in appearance on the printed page normal dialogues, since Lear does not seem to listen to what others say. If he responds, it is often much later and out of context. In his essential isolation, his mind is almost always in an extended or highly dramatic soliloquy. The sheer pain of what he is feeling suddenly starts forth from the continuity of what he is saying, as in "To take 't again perforce" (I.v.42). His suffering is too tumultuous to be expressed in an ordered speech such as Hamlet's "To be or not to be." It surfaces in powerful form in sudden outcries, or in shocking form in his madness.

After this triumphant experiment in finding a worthy technique of expression for mental suffering, it is surprising that Shakespeare reverts again in *Macbeth* to the set speech, in soliloquies and in asides that are long enough to be soliloquies. The play has by far the largest proportion of set speeches in Shakespeare's works. For long periods it seems to be one elocutionary aria following another. Long asides, like long parentheses in books, are inserted into scenes of tense dialogue. Extremely important information is entrusted to these speeches, including Macbeth's earliest thoughts about the crime and temptation. To defend the artistry of the depiction of mental suffering in *Macbeth*, one must inevitably defend it in its dominant, almost exclusive, form of soliloquy. It is distinct from the way in which pain of the senses is expressed, by short outcries following sights or sounds. It can, I think, be vindicated in terms of both technique and thematic purpose. The effect an audience receives is certainly one of well-sustained tension, almost excruciating at times, and not one of boredom from monotonous exposure to a single voice.

The earliest long speeches seem to be methodical, and they achieve some of the sense of agony which accompanies an attempt to reason through an almost insoluble problem. In "Two truths are told" (I.iii.127–142) there is a painful effort to resolve a dilemma. And in the "If it were done" soliloquy (I.vii. 1–28) Macbeth's full intellectual powers are expended, in an argument perfectly organized, to fathom the consequences of a deed that cannot ultimately be done. But the tormenting aspect of these speeches is not so much in the arduous thought that goes into a futile inquiry, great though this is, as in the way logic explodes into sensory imagery—into the horrid image that unfixes the hair and into the spectacle of Pity taking on angelic strength.

The contexts of the speeches also contribute to the feeling of tension. We have already seen how the isolated utterances of the protagonists before and during the murder emphasize the separateness of the two, and also how Macbeth's use of ritual gives a chill mystery to his preparation for the deed. These speeches, though long and private, have also an atmospheric and musical quality that seems to belong peculiarly in Shakespeare's artistry to long and private speeches. The context is also important in the rapt manner of the speeches we have just considered. An aside may conventionally give the speaker privacy on the Elizabethan stage. But Macbeth's "Two truths are told" is so long as to require explanation. Banquo comments, "Look, how our partner's rapt" (I.iii.143), and Macbeth himself apologizes:

> Give me your favour: my dull brain was wrought
> With things forgotten.
>
> *(I.iii.150–151)*

His brain was indeed "wrought," but the speech is nonetheless a lie. The aside has become a noticed dramatic pause, not a securely leisured speech to the audience. We are aware even here of the danger that Macbeth's rapt manner, which later worries his wife, can lead to. The "If it were done" soliloquy may seem to be less conspicuous in context, for Macbeth is alone on stage. Nevertheless, though his rapt expression cannot be noticed by others, we are uneasily aware that important time is passing. A banquet is going on, and servants carrying dishes have just passed over the stage. The host is not dining with his royal guest. Duncan has almost supped when Lady Macbeth comes to arouse her husband. It is the first of two highly symbolic banquets that Macbeth will miss, for it is Duncan's last supper and Macbeth's last opportunity, forfeited by a guilty mind in racked thought, to communicate with his fellow men. One recalls his earlier invitation to Banquo:

> Think upon what hath chanc'd; and at more time,
> The Interim having weigh'd it, let us speak
> Our free hearts each to other.
> *(I.iii.154–156)*

The impossibility of Macbeth's speaking his free heart to other men created somewhat of a dramaturgic challenge for Shakespeare and doubtless contributed to the extensive use of soliloquy. One of the reasons for giving the soliloquy principally to villains is that they cannot confide their plans openly to others. Macbeth, as we must never forget, is a villain. But he is not an accomplished villain. He has few plans to confide to others, but he does have urgent griefs to confide. Shakespeare takes full dramatic advantage of his difference from the conventional villain by making it a part of Macbeth's mental torment that he cannot safely or satisfyingly speak his free heart to others. Shakespeare has Lady Macbeth (who also suffers from the same privation) complain to her husband about his increasing withdrawal:

> How now, my Lord? why do you keep alone,
> Of sorriest fancies your companions making,
> Using those thoughts, which should indeed have died
> With them they think on?
> *(III.ii.8–11)*

Unlike Iago, however, he cannot confine his thoughts to the safety of the conventional soliloquy. In a manner worthy of the technique used in *King Lear*, Shakespeare increases naturalness and tension by transmuting the soliloquy. He has both protagonists speak their hearts under strained and revealing circumstances. Macbeth testifies to the naturalness of the technique when he twice comments on his ordeal in having false face hide what the false heart knows (I.vii.83) and on the danger of making his face "vizard" to his heart (III.ii.34).

The danger and the tension are also evident in Macbeth's comments, before the awakened guests, on the murder. In the speech beginning "Had I but died an hour before this chance" (II.iii.91–96), he voices what is a publicly acceptable reaction to the murder; but he also, as we shall later see, gives vent to his own free heart. It is a soliloquy made public and yet, by ambiguous phrasing, precariously kept private.[6] Similarly the "Here lay Duncan" speech (II.iii.111–118) expresses proper horror at the sight of the murdered King, but it continually threatens to go beyond this into his peculiarly private terror of the scene, and some critics have suspected that Lady Macbeth faints to prevent her husband's further exposure. In the Banquet Scene, of course, he does expose himself most perilously. Here is a scene of naked frailties dramatically exposed in a way that is comparable to Lear mad on the heath. It is as personally revealing as a soliloquy, and it even resembles in its broken form Hamlet's "O, what a rogue and peasant slave am I!" But the finest scene of exposure is that of Lady Macbeth's sleepwalking. So far as she is concerned, it is a soliloquy. She, who has been so much alone, has reached a lonely despair and need to express her guilt. As the Doctor says,

> Unnatural deeds
> Do breed unnatural troubles: infected minds
> To their deaf pillows will discharge their secrets.
>
> *V.i.(68–70)*

What she speaks, interrupted for us but not for her by the com-

---

[6] Kenneth Muir differs from John Middleton Murry in believing that "Macbeth was unconscious of the truth of his words." *Macbeth* (new Arden edition), (New York, 1964), note to II.iii.91–96, p. 67.

ments of the two observers, is perhaps Shakespeare's finest achievement in the natural, unconventional use of the soliloquy, broken, incoherent, and pathetically naked.

It is, ironically, Lady Macbeth who has finally been forced to soliloquize to a faintly lighted night and to unsympathetic listeners. For she had earlier been the deaf pillow to her husband's infected mind. He had not been able to tell her his real reasons for not wanting to kill Duncan, and she fiercely scoffs at the lame, but still valid, reason which he dares make public: he will increasingly feel the loss of the "Golden opinions from all sorts of people" (I.vii.33). Immediately after the murder he tries to convey to her the horror he feels at his inability to say "Amen" and at the voice that forever will deprive him of rest. Her response is "Consider it not so deeply" (II.ii.29), "What do you mean?" (II.ii.39), and "You do unbend your noble strength, to think / So brainsickly of things" (II.ii.44–45). And this will be her response through the nightmare of the Banquet Scene. One must not, of course, underestimate the rising dismay that she is feeling, the protest,

> These deeds must not be thought
> After these ways: so, it will make us mad.
> *(II.ii.32–33)*

But whatever her private hell may be, she resolutely withholds any sympathy, any comprehending acknowledgment of what he is suffering. There is, accordingly, a condign punishment in the fact that Lady Macbeth, who has repeatedly refused to share her husband's visions, finally has no mate or friend to share her own. And Shakespeare takes full advantage in dramatic technique of this privation, enlarging the function of the soliloquy as far as it will ever be enlarged.

III

The privation that separates the guilty pair is only a part of a larger privation, one that accounts for much of their torment. We recall that all endeavor is labor which is not used for the King. Similarly all life is meaningless, lonely, and arid which is not consecrated by his grace, which is really the grace he bestows as the Lord's anointed. *Grace* is used frequently in Shakespeare in reference to the higher nobility and to social virtues, but in *Macbeth* it is used almost entirely in a religious sense, to mean the free virtue and blessing bestowed by the King, the divinely appointed qualities of the King, or even the Deity Himself. It is only the legitimate king who can possess and give grace. At the beginning of the play Scotland is blessed with such a king, and life itself is gracious. Duncan gives favors generously, and Macbeth is a major beneficiary. Soon after arriving at Inverness, Duncan tells Lady Macbeth:

> Give me your hand;
> Conduct me to mine host: we love him highly,
> And shall continue our graces towards him.
> *(I.vi.28–30)*

Had Duncan lived, Macbeth would have enjoyed the blessed time of continued grace from the King. When Duncan is dead, grace is dead. Macbeth therefore speaks for all Scotland when he says of the murder:

> Had I but died an hour before this chance,
> I had liv'd a blessed time; for, from this instant,
> There's nothing serious in mortality;
> All is but toys: renown, and grace, is dead;
> The wine of life is drawn, and the mere lees
> Is left this vault to brag of.
> *(II.iii.91–96)*

Scotland will experience a period of "violent sorrow" before it recovers grace in the person of a divinely appointed king, Malcolm. Rosse later describes the separateness and unrelieved darkness of this country suffering privation from God's grace:

> Alas, poor country!
> Almost afraid to know itself. It cannot
> Be call'd our mother, but our grave; where nothing,
> But who knows nothing, is once seen to smile;
> Where sighs, and groans, and shrieks that rent the air
> Are made, not mark'd; where violent sorrow seems
> A modern ecstasy. . . .
> *(IV.iii.164–170)*

But, as we have seen, Macbeth is speaking for himself as well, describing his own future. Without grace, there will be for him nothing serious in mortality: life will lack meaning, and he will be a hollow man without the grace which is the wine of life. Later, too, he adds to his catalogue of penalties for having killed "the gracious Duncan":

> For Banquo's issue have I fil'd my mind;
> For them the gracious Duncan have I murder'd;
> Put rancours in the vessel of my peace,
> Only for them; and mine eternal jewel
> Given to the common Enemy of man,
> To make them kings, the seed of Banquo kings!
> *(III.i.64–69)*

The catalogue includes, besides giving his soul to Satan, the mental torment of having forfeited all hope for successful issue. This speech, however, is especially important in reinforcing the private message of the earlier one. Macbeth knew earlier, though not fully, that he had killed not simply Duncan, but the gracious Duncan.

That Macbeth will be unable to give grace to Scotland, or to have it himself, is dramatically demonstrated in the Banquet Scene. Rosse asks of Macbeth:

> Please't your Highness
> To grace us with your royal company?
> *(III.iv.43–44)*

Macbeth cannot do so. "The table's full." He cannot grace, or even share in, the community of men. The scene in England between Malcolm and Macduff, often omitted in performance, is much concerned with absent grace and the consequent state of Scotland. It is also preparing the country for a revisiting of grace under a new sovereign. Malcolm tells Macduff:

> Though all things foul would wear the brows of grace,
> Yet Grace must still look so,
> *(IV.iii.23–24)*

a clear reference to Macbeth's vain attempt to assume grace and to the uncompromising ideal maintained by Grace itself, or

God. Malcolm also refers to "the king-becoming graces" (IV. iii.91), which he claims not to have but which in reality Macbeth lacks. The scene also contrasts Scotland with "Gracious England" (IV.iii.189) under Edward the Confessor, where "sundry blessings hang about his throne, / That speak him full of grace" (IV.iii.158–159). The play ends with Malcolm promising to restore this quality to Scotland; he will, "by the grace of Grace" (V.ix.38), heal his suffering country.

But though all of Scotland suffers privation throughout most of the play, it is Macbeth for whom it has the most withering and permanent meaning. It underlies the great speeches in which he complains of the barrenness of his own life and the meaninglessness of life in general. More subtly it underlies the lack of comprehension with which he goes through one mental agony after another, particularly fear. Fear is a meaningless compulsion for him, leading not to understanding but to emotional and spiritual blindness. To appreciate the significance of why it is so, and what really causes it, we must revisit hell, and those concepts of divine punishment which are so aesthetically as well as ethically admirable.

IV

Privation, as the loss of God's grace, is essentially equivalent to the pain of loss, which "doth more afflict . . . then all the sensible torment."[7] Pain of loss is the punishment, not of choosing a mutable good, but of rejecting an immutable good, which is God, and it is fittingly the loss of grace. One result of this "withdrawal of grace," according to Aquinas, is "that the mind is not enlightened by God to see aright, and man's heart is not softened to live aright."[8] Drawing upon Aquinas, Henry Bullinger amplifies this doctrine to show the devastating effect of God's leaving man unto himself. The heart of man in its corrupt state is stony and "is made tractable by the only grace of God: therefore the withdrawing of God's grace is the hardening of

---

[7] Ephraim Huit, *The Anatomy of Conscience* (1626), p. 310.

[8] *The Summa Theologica*, trans. by Fathers of the English Dominican Province (London, 1922), Second Number (QQ. XLIX-LXXXIX), vol. VII, pt. II, 390, Q. 79. Art. 3. This concept seems to be based upon Ephesians 4:18–19.

man's heart; and when we are left unto ourselves, then are we hardened."[9] It is a life without pleasure or meaning. Being "deprived of the fruition of the Godhead," writes Latimer, is according to Chrysostom a greater pain than being in hell. It is "pain without pleasure, torment without easement, anguish, heaviness, sorrow, and pensiveness...."[10]

To complete the background in the picture of the wasteland that becomes Macbeth's life, we must note that, in the pain of loss, the dark monotony of the hardened heart[11] is enlivened by one dominant passion: fear. Some of the fearful symptoms are described by Henry Bullinger:

> If God be away from us, how great is the horror in the minds of men? Here therefore, as punishments due to sinners, are reckoned the tyranny of Satan, a thousand torments of conscience, the death of the soul, dreadful fear, utter desperation....[12]

The "tyranny of Satan" can become manifest when God has left men. According to Abernethy, "The devill is busie by his illusions, through Gods permission, to plague the heart of the wicked with many bad and mad feares. As *the spirit of the Lord departed from Saul, and an evill spirit sent of the Lord, vexed him with strange feares*" [1 Samuel 16:14].[13] These demonically supplied fears are intended by Satan to lead the guilty soul to what Bullinger called "utter desperation," the final stage of the pain of loss.

The fear from the pain of loss is usually characterized as vague and unlocalized. Even definite symptoms would be welcome to the man from whom God has turned his face. The

---

[9] "Of Sin, and of the Kinds Thereof . . . the Tenth Sermon," in *Fiftie Godlie and Learned Sermons, Divided into Five Decades* (1587), *The Thirde Decade of Sermons,* ed. by Rev. Thomas Harding (Parker Society), (Cambridge, 1850), p. 381.

[10] *Sermons and Remains of Hugh Latimer*, ed. by Rev. George E. Corrie (Parker Society), (Cambridge, 1845), p. 236.

[11] For emphasis upon this quality in Macbeth's deterioration, see Dolora G. Cunningham, "Macbeth: The Tragedy of the Hardened Heart," *Shakespeare Quarterly*, XIV (1963), 39–47.

[12] "Of Sin, and of the Kinds Thereof . . . The Tenth Sermon," p. 426.

[13] John Abernethy, *A Christian and Heavenly Treatise Containing Physicke for the Soule* (1622; first published 1615), p. 326.

depth of this, the worst malaise known to man, would be much less if it were defined for him, or explicable in terms of tangible objects or persons to fear. Thus Saul, suffering fundamentally from the loss of "the spirit of the Lord," focused his fear on David. But the favorite Renaissance example of a man who suffered inexplicable and continual fear was Cain, who had to fly from the face of God and who believed that anyone who found him would kill him.

Commenting upon Genesis 4:12, "A vagabond and a runnagate shalt thou be in the earth," Calvin writes of Cain's punishment,

> whiche was, that he should not be in securitie and rest in any place whithersoever he came. . . . the proper sense is this, that whither soever Caine should come, he should be unstable and a wanderer: as theeves commonly are, who have no rest or firm abiding. For there is no manner looke or countenaunce of man, which bringeth not a terrour unto them: and the carefulnesse it selfe is also a horrour in them.[14]

Cain's punishment was, he complained, greater than he could bear, but he never learned the actuality of what he feared.

Still one other aspect of the pain of loss is related to fear. In Chapter II I surveyed the doctrine that sin can be punished by sin. The withdrawal of God's grace leaves man morally insensible and defenseless against his passions and diabolical compulsion; and he is impelled to react to one sin by painful pursuit of another. Man left to himself becomes an irresponsible automaton, driven only by passions which, like Cain, he does not understand.

And that Macbeth is left to himself is clear, not only from his real sense of loss at the privation of grace, but from what occurs at the pivotal moment in his career. This is of course his horrified realization—without recognition of why it occurred—that he cannot say "Amen," that "Amen" stuck in his throat. God had turned his face from him and left him to his own devices.

---

[14] John Calvin, *A Commentarie upon Genesis*, trans. by Thomas Tymme (1578), p. 143. For Cain's restless fear, see also Henry Smith, *The First Sermon of the Punishment of Jonah*, in *Works* (1593), p. 150; Thomas Becon, "The Pathwai unto Prayer," in *The Early Works*, ed. by Rev. John Ayre (Parker Society), (Cambridge, 1845), p. 146; Richard Leake, *Foure Sermons Preached in Westmoreland* (1599), p. 56.

Thus abandoned by God, he is befriended by the Devil, to whose service he has consecrated his body. And the evil spirit will vex him, as it did Saul, with "strange feares," making sure that he never profits from, or even understands, the full meaning of his fears.

V

This explanation for Macbeth's fears will not persuade all readers. Some may, for example, pardonably prefer to interpret them as coming from Macbeth's conscience, which like the pain of loss is for him a hell on earth. Certainly "all that is within him," including guilt, causes him to fear. The explanation must at least be a comparably religious one. And whatever its precise nature, all readers must acknowledge the masterful artistry with which Shakespeare depicts Macbeth, his only hero dominated by this unheroic passion, in the throes of fear. The panic fears at sights and sounds we have already observed. The technique that remains for appreciation is that in which Macbeth is made to move from one fear to another, each time almost persuading us that this is his underlying fear, only to lead us to still another urgent one. The technique is as dynamic as the technique of self-discovery in *King Lear*, as the King proceeds from one object of learning to another, from one passion to another. But unlike Lear, Macbeth does not move upward. The series of fears leads to no self-understanding, not even to essentially new experience, but to atrophy of soul, and to despair. The technique is admirably right for the tragedy of Macbeth.

Shakespeare's achievement is the more admirable in that Holinshed had made easily available, and doubtless tempting, to him an obvious reason for Macbeth's fears. After King Kenneth has poisoned Malcolm Duffe, he "could not but still live in continuall feare, least his wicked practise concerning the death of Malcolme Duffe should come to light and knowledge of the world."[15] Shakespeare's Macbeth never mentions such a reason, though Lady Macbeth, whose concern has always been strategy, reveals in her sleepwalking that it has been troubling her:

[15] *The First and Second Volumes of Chronicles* (1587), II, "Historie of Scotland," p. 158.

"What need we fear who knows it, when none can call our power to accompt?" (V.i.36–38). Holinshed gave Shakespeare something closer to what interested him in the following explanation for Macbeth's fear: "For the pricke of conscience (as it chanceth ever in tyrants, and such as atteine to anie estate by unrighteous means) caused him ever to feare, least he should be served of the same cup, as he had ministred to his predecessor" (p. 172). Shakespeare makes much of the idea that Macbeth becomes a tyrant, but he does not, as some Renaissance books did, associate the fear with tyranny.[16] Nor does the conscience of Macbeth, once he has killed Duncan, keep him in fear of reprisal. Concerning the motive that made Macbeth proceed to a career of slaughter, it was in Holinshed simply that "as there were manie that stood in feare of him, so likewise stood he in feare of manie...." And having started to kill, he continued because "he found such sweetnesse by putting his nobles thus to death, that his earnest thirst after bloud in this behalfe might in no wise be satisfied" (p. 174), a far cry from Macbeth's joyless dismay at having stepped too far in blood to return. But what is most interesting about the source as a basis for comparison is that in Holinshed Macbeth's reasons for fear are apparently those of the historian. In Shakespeare, though we can never be sure of the dramatist's intentions, Macbeth is made to seem fearful for unexpressed or wrong reasons.

Shakespeare's Macbeth is subject to agitating fear from his first scene in the play. And from the beginning the cause of his fear is mysterious to us, though at first he himself knows what it is. After Macbeth has heard the fair prophecies, his strange reaction is noted by Banquo:

> Good Sir, why do you start, and seem to fear
> Things that do sound so fair?
>
> *(I.iii.51–52)*

This kind of reaction is well phrased by Horatio in describing the behavior of the Ghost:

---

[16] See, however, Ruth L. Anderson, "The Pattern of Behavior Culminating in *Macbeth*," *Studies in English Literature*, III (1963), 151–173.

> And then it started like a guilty thing
> Upon a fearful summons.[17]
>
> *(Hamlet I.i.148–149)*

The "fearful summons" that causes Macbeth to "start" is the evil in the Witches speaking to his own evil. The fear is the shock of recognition, the shock of having his private and dimly acknowledged evil thoughts so clearly and so publicly uttered. One of the frightening aspects of the Witches may well be that they give accurate embodiment, foul in shape, to the thought that within him had seemed fair.

An important clue to the nature of fear in Macbeth is given by Rosse in describing the thane's courage in battle:

> In viewing o'er the rest o' th' selfsame day,
> He finds thee in the stout Norweyan ranks,
> Nothing afeard of what thyself didst make,
> Strange images of death.
>
> *(I.iii.94–97)*

The strange images of death which Macbeth had made are not merely dead men. They are more vividly figured, possibly as something like iconographical images of Death. They are similar to the "painted devil" that Lady Macbeth later derides. They belong to the imagination and not simply to the bodily eye. And yet Macbeth, supposedly the victim of a hectic imagination, does not fear them. The speech is therefore crucial. It tells the audience that Macbeth, when not subject to evil or guilt, is not characteristically vulnerable to images. It serves as a valuable preparation for Macbeth's first comment on his own fear when he says of the supernatural solicitings:

---

[17] For a similar association of *start*, guilt, and fear, see *The Faerie Queene* I.i.49, in which the Redcrosse Knight awakens to find the false Una:

> In this great passion of unwonted lust,
> Or wonted feare of doing ought amis,
> He started up, as seeming to mistrust
> Some secret ill, or hidden foe of his.

And John Woolton (*Of the Conscience*, 1576, sig. F 3ᵛ) quotes St. Ambrose: "The corrupt Conscience, starteth at every cracke. . . ."

> If good, why do I yield to that suggestion
> Whose horrid image doth unfix my hair,
> And make my seated heart knock at my ribs,
> Against the use of nature? Present fears
> Are less than horrible imaginings.
> *(1.iii.134–138)*

This horrid image does frighten him. It is not the image of Death which he had made in the service of Duncan, but the image of the slaughtered Duncan himself. He is, of course, not entirely clear about the nature of the horrid image, and the vagueness is both artistically effective in troubling the audience and correct in that he had not verbally articulated the nature of the evil. But so far he has not really been mistaken in the realization that it is an evil deed, or its consequences, that frightens him. The last sentence of his speech is, however, morally obtuse. Images may indeed become for him more terrible than corporal actualities, but they do so mainly not because of the chimeras of the imagination but because of the evil that informs them. Virtuous imaginings do not cause fear. And Macbeth will meet many "present fears" that are as horrible as anything the imagination can shape. We must not attribute Macbeth's fearfulness primarily to his imagination, though both guilt and the Demon may work most influentially through that faculty.

Before the murder Macbeth will be most fearful of everything connoted by the horrid image. He will therefore fear to look on what he does. But that fear is allayed for him by his resolution to make the eye wink at the hand. And during the murder his fears are muted by a trancelike state that is probably possession. Afterward, however, he emerges reluctantly from the trance, afraid both to think of what he has done and to look at it. His last accurate view of the fear is therefore that which precedes the murder. After the deed he will tremble at the voice he hears but will not know what it signifies. And henceforth he will think very little about the murder and will not associate it with his fear. Even his recognition that grace is dead does not seem to enlighten him as to the underlying cause for his subsequent career of fear. His punishment will appropriately be that of Cain, a blind fear of everything.

This kind of fear is described by Rosse in terms of the whole of Scotland, for the country, too, now lacks grace and has been subject to the infection of Macbeth's fear, which manifests itself politically in tyranny. Rosse comments:

> But cruel are the times, when we are traitors,
> And do not know ourselves; when we hold rumour
> From what we fear, yet know not what we fear,
> But float upon a wild and violent sea
> Each way, and move.
>
> *(IV.ii.18-22)*

Macbeth no longer knows what he fears, no longer knows himself, no longer knows other people. All persons, in his ungraced state, become strangers and threats to him, and he will float restlessly upon a wild and violent sea.

It is a curious but psychologically profound fact that whomever Macbeth seeks to kill, he first fears. Fear leads to crime, even as one sin is punished by another. Thus fear is, also in psychological terms, perhaps an attempt to localize symptomatically the underlying malaise that tortures him. There is a temporary relief in specific fear and hostility for a disease, whether psychologically or spiritually caused, that floats beneath the consciousness. Coleridge, with his fine psychological intuition, saw much of this unconscious activity working in Macbeth and recognized that Macbeth is not a trustworthy commentator on his own fears. He writes:

> Macbeth mistranslates the recoilings and ominous whispers of conscience into prudential and selfish reasonings, and after the deed, the terrors of remorse into fear from external dangers—like delirious men that run away from the phantoms of their own brain, or, raised by terror to rage, stab the real object that is within their own reach.[18]

The first human object of Macbeth's fears is Banquo. So anxiously and repeatedly does Macbeth mention this menace

[18] *Coleridge's Shakespearean Criticism*, ed. by Thomas Middleton Raysor (Cambridge, Mass., 1930), I, 80. Coleridge correctly sees conscience working before the murder of Duncan; but for what follows the murder, "the terrors of remorse" is possibly too kind a description of Macbeth's mental agony.

that, unless we are divines or physicians accustomed to graphic symptomatic recitals, we are likely to accept his own diagnosis of his spiritual illness. His fears in Banquo "stick deep" (III.i. 48–49). "There is none but he / Whose being I do fear" (III.i. 53–54). He is speaking sincerely when he tells the assassins that every minute of Banquo's being "thrusts / Against my near'st of life" (III.i.116–117). All of his generalized discomforts are related to Banquo. There are the terrible dreams that shake him nightly and the eating of his meal in fear. And above all there is his resolution:

> Better be with the dead,
> Whom we, to gain our peace, have sent to peace,
> Than on the torture of the mind to lie
> In restless ecstasy.
> *(III.ii.19–22)*

Even the "restless ecstasy"—a perfect term for his suffering—is placed in a context that makes its connection for him with Banquo unmistakable. His own explanation for the nightmares, for the torture of the mind, is simply this:

> We have scorch'd the snake, not kill'd it:
> She'll close, and be herself; whilst our poor malice
> Remains in danger of her former tooth.
> *(III.ii.13–15)*

That he is thinking of the threat of Banquo is made absolutely certain by what almost immediately follows:

> O! full of scorpions is my mind, dear wife!
> Thou know'st that Banquo, and his Fleance, lives.
> *(III.ii.36–37)*

And shortly following is his reference to Banquo, or to the Witches' prophecy about Banquo, as "that great bond / Which keeps me pale!" (III.ii.49–50).

Banquo is, to be sure, a real threat to him, especially in all that he symbolizes. But he should not be such a threat as to make him shake nightly, or to make Banquo's continued life intolerable; it is after all Banquo's issue, and not the man himself, that constitutes the real hazard to his ambition. Even threatened ambition should not cause terrible fear, but it seems to do so after news comes that, though Banquo is dead, Fleance has escaped. Macbeth's fit comes again. If only Fleance were dead, Macbeth would be

> Whole as the marble, founded as the rock
> As broad and general as the casing air:
> But now, I am cabin'd, cribb'd, confin'd, bound in
> To saucy doubts and fears.
> *(III.iv.21–24)*

Is this not, one wonders, merely another symptom of his fear? Earlier Fleance had only once been mentioned as an object of fear, but now that Banquo is dead the son achieves the same horrible form as the father. It should be noticed that the localization of the fear has already taken another, though minor, form. It does so in the much disputed person of the Third Murderer, whom Macbeth has sent for the killing of Banquo. The Second Murderer rightly protests of Macbeth that "He needs not our mistrust" (III.iii.2). Macbeth's restless ecstasy simply needs something specific to fear.

At about this point the audience should have begun to recognize that Macbeth's homicidal fear is a hopeless case of sin compulsively plucking on sin. Even before the murder of Banquo he had expressed the substance, without recognizing the meaning, of this kind of punishment. It is with grim resolution and not with spiritual uneasiness that he says, "Things bad begun make strong themselves by ill" (III.ii.55). He again betrays for us the nature of his compulsion when he speaks—as had Richard III in his comment upon sin plucking on sin—of having stepped so far in blood that he must go on. And he betrays it yet again when he tries to diagnose his malady:

> My strange and self-abuse
> Is the initiate fear, that wants hard use:
> We are yet but young in deed.
> *(III.iv.141–143)*

His intended meaning is that he fears because he is a novice in crime and needs only more experience. But for us the lines should be ironic in saying more than the speaker knows. From our vantage point we know that the hard use is needed not to fit him for crime but to satisfy a compulsion caused by the withdrawal of divine grace, thus permitting sin to pluck on sin. How young in deed he actually is, he knows imperfectly, but well enough to make this one of the saddest lines in the play.

The next localization of the fear is Macduff. Although the earliest mention of this fear is the First Apparition's warning, "beware Macduff" (IV.i.71), the fear has been germinating since the loss of an object in Banquo's death and because of the long time it will take for Fleance to mature. Macbeth says, "Thou hast harp'd my fear aright" (IV.i.74), another instance of the way the demons phrase, by his spiritual attunement to their evil, his own thoughts. The Apparitions may, in fact, come to him in the forms that his fears shape, just as the ghosts in *Richard III* take the shape of the King's guilty fears.

Macbeth's fear is dangerous to Macduff; the tyrant resolves to kill him that he "may tell pale-hearted fear it lies" (IV.i.85). But meanwhile his fears float back to an earlier obsession. His "heart / Throbs to know one thing" (IV.i.100–101), whether Banquo's issue will ever reign in Scotland. Though inadequate to justify panic fear in a rational man, the concern over progeny would understandably become an adequate symptom for a man in Macbeth's spiritually sterile state. It does not account for the attempted murder of Macduff, but it may underly the maniacal act of giving

> to th' edge o' th' sword
> His wife, his babes, and all unfortunate souls
> That trace him in his line.
>
> *(IV.i.151–153)*

It does not, however, remain adequate for long. As he nears desperation, the result of living hopelessly without grace ("I have liv'd long enough"), he raises new fears, increasingly inadequate for his state of soul. Malcolm comes to his mind, but is rejected because he is born of woman (V.iii.3–4). The sight of a pallid servant arouses panicky fury (V.iii.11–12). The mention of the word *fear* will be a cause for hanging (V.iii.36). As the symptoms become less compelling and meaningful, so does his whole being. He will fear only as long as he has a vital need to save something, principally that permanent hold upon the throne toward which his wife has driven him. When she dies, though he does not mention it and it may be merely coincidental, a certain motive in life, a need for living intensely, which she had supplied, goes with her. He is drained of purpose, and of fearful symptoms. But the loss of fear is something more serious than merely the loss of his wife could account for.

He cannot, as we have seen, react suitably to the death of Lady Macbeth. Just before he learns of it, as he hears the cry of women, he says that he has almost forgot the taste of fears. He attributes the loss, mistakenly I think, to his having supped full with horrors. His emotional emptiness at her death is really an important clue, which he typically explains symptomatically, to his present spiritual state. It is one of the play's two thematic occurrences of a failure in response. There had earlier been his inability to say "Amen" when blessing was asked during the murder of Duncan. That failure had represented his alienation from God. His inability to respond to his wife's death signifies another major stage in his spiritual deterioration. He has lost not only fear but any kind of hope, purpose, or feeling. The remainder of his life will be desperate, and his withered soul will be nakedly exposed as never before.

VI

Despair is the fate toward which the Witches and Hecate, taking the place left void by grace, had been leading him both by intolerable fear and by false security. According to Robert Burton (who cites Hemmingius as authority), there are two antidotes to despair: "good Hope out of God's Word, to be embraced; perverse Security and Presumption from the Devil's treachery, to be rejected."[19] And according to Myles Coverdale, wretched sinners brought to despair by "inward trembling and doubtfulness" will "cry out to the devil to help them, if God will not ... yet have they no trust nor confidence that the same sin shall be taken from them and forgiven them, but rave and rage and give themselves over to the devil, and so depart

---

[19] *The Anatomy of Melancholy* (1628), ed. by Floyd Dell and Paul Jordan-Smith (New York, 1941), p. 951.

wretchedly out of this world."[20] Macbeth, by going to the Witches, by seeking to make assurance double sure, and by taking a bond of Fate, has tried to fend off despair by drawing "perverse Security and Presumption from the Devil's treachery." He does nothing but "rave and rage," and he will "depart wretchedly out of this world." His spiritual career from guilt, to fear, to melancholy, to despair, had been charted by Kyd's Hieronimo, by no means a professional theologian, and we may well look at this speech once more:

> There is a path upon your left-hand side,
> That leadeth from a guilty conscience
> Unto a forest of distrust and fear,
> A darksome place and dangerous to pass:
> There shall you meet with melancholy thoughts,
> Whose baleful humours if you but uphold,
> It will conduct you to despair and death.[21]

Macbeth's desperation is manifested first in the somewhat nervous confidence he places in the equivocation of the Fiend. The demonic prophecies now replace symptoms of fear in preventing his thinking about perils more fundamental. Even as he despairingly begins to be aweary of the sun, he becomes blindly defiant of danger, content to risk military safety and caution:

> Blow, wind! come, wrack!
> At least we'll die with harness on our back.
> *(V.v.51–52)*

Bearlike he will "fight the course" (V.vii.2).

But what he is by his callous indifference thus risking militarily is trivial compared with what he is risking spiritually. We get a glimpse of this enormous risk in the "Blow, wind! come, wrack!"—a desperate invitation to demonic destruction that he had prepared for by earlier conjuring the Witches: "Though you untie the winds, and let them fight / Against the Churches" (IV.i.52–53).

---

[20] "A Spiritual and Most Precious Pearl" (trans. from Otto Wermullerus), in *Writings and Translations*, ed. by George Pearson (Parker Society), (Cambridge, 1844), p. 150.

[21] *The Spanish Tragedy*, ed. by Philip Edwards (The Revels Plays), (London, 1959), III.xi.13–19.

Torture of the Mind · 211

The spiritual symptoms of his despair account for his most intense and disturbing utterances. But so horrible is despair that its adequate expression provided a real challenge for his dramatic creator. Even so eloquent a student of minds diseased as Robert Burton complained of the difficulty of "describing the Symptoms of Despair":

> imagine what thou canst, fear, sorrow, furies, grief, pain, terror, anger, dismal, ghastly, tedious, irksome, &c., it is not sufficient, it comes far short, no tongue can tell, no heart conceive it. 'Tis an Epitome of hell, an extract, a quintessence, a compound, a mixture of all feral maladies, tyrannical tortures, plagues and perplexities.[22]

In *King Lear* Shakespeare had successfully tried his hand at translating such hyperbole into controlled dramatic language. Gloucester is in a perilous spiritual state when, after his blinding, he makes the famous comment upon life:

> As flies to wanton boys, are we to th' gods,
> They kill us for their sport.
>
> *(IV.i.38–39)*

The utterance is persuasive in its quiet intensity. But that Gloucester is not speaking any philosophical message for the play as a whole is indicated by his later repentance under the tender care of his son Edgar, who comments upon his ministry:

> Why I do trifle thus with his despair
> Is done to cure it.
>
> *(IV.vi.33–34)*

Macbeth is in an even worse spiritual state than Gloucester when he makes his most desperate comment upon life. Though I have previously alluded to this comment, it deserves to be looked at now in its most important context, at the end of Macbeth's mental agony and the threshold of his damnation. The comment follows, much as Gloucester's follows his blinding,

---

[22] *The Anatomy of Melancholy*, p. 946. Burton mentions fear as a symptom, one which Macbeth has lost the taste of. In the general view, fear precedes despair. It is not absent but is transformed into its ultimate form of expression.

the news that his wife is dead. Its desperate protest takes the place of human grief or compassion:

> To-morrow, and to-morrow, and to-morrow,
> Creeps in this petty pace from day to day,
> To the last syllable of recorded time;
> And all our yesterdays have lighted fools
> The way to dusty death. Out, out, brief candle!
> Life's but a walking shadow; a poor player,
> That struts and frets his hour upon the stage,
> And then is heard no more: it is a tale
> Told by an idiot, full of sound and fury,
> Signifying nothing.
> *(V.v.19–28)*

Because Macbeth does not explicitly, as does Doctor Faustus, express lack of faith in God's forgiveness, the speech has not generally been viewed as an exact and binding commitment to despair. It may not be theologically exact—Shakespeare tends to be more interested in the spirit than in the letter of theology—but it does contain sufficient details to make the state of spiritual hopelessness unmistakable. It follows, and is possibly influenced by, the episode in Sidney's *Arcadia* in which Cecropia tries to lead Pamela desperately to atheism. One passage of her speech comments upon the indifference of any supposed god to man's tomorrows, and it also uses the fly in a way that may have suggested Gloucester's comment:

> Yesterday was but as to day, and to morrow will tread the same footsteps of his foregoers: so as it is manifest inough, that all things follow but the course of their own nature, saving only Man, who while by the pregnancie of his imagination he strives to things supernaturall, meane-while he looseth his owne natural felicitie. Bewise, and that wisedome shalbe a God unto thee; be contented, and that is thy heaven: for els to thinke that those powers (if there be any such) above, are moved either by the eloquence of our prayers, or in a chafe by the folly of our actions; caries asmuch reason as if flies should thinke, that men take great care which of them hums sweetest, and which of them flies nimblest.[23]

[23] *The Countess of Pembrokes Arcadia* (1590), ed. by Albert Feuillerat (Cambridge, 1939), pp. 406–407.

Macbeth's speech does not, as do Gloucester's remarks on the flies, charge the gods with malice, but it is desperate in a way close to Cecropia's philosophy in that there would seem to be no divine interest in the way man struts and frets—even as the flies hum sweetly and fly nimbly—on an empty stage.

In writing his "To-morrow" discourse for Macbeth, Shakespeare rejected what must have been a real temptation to make the style convey that quality which Burton emphasizes, excruciating horror. The style of *Macbeth* generally is one of intense, excited statement, tending at times to overstatement. At moments of exceptional crisis, even a Shakespeare must come to the verbal plight which Macduff reaches in "O horror! horror! horror! / Tongue nor heart cannot conceive, nor name thee!" (II.iii.64–65); in his subsequent "Do not bid me speak: / See, and then speak yourselves" (II.iii.73–74); or, in ultimate form, in Macbeth's resorting to pointing, "Pr'ythee, see there! / Behold! look! lo! how say you?" (III.iv.67–68). At its best, of course, this technique of abandoning words can be one of consummate artistry, as in Lear's last question, to express the ineffable:

> Do you see this? Look on her, look, her lips,
> Look there, look there!
>
> *(V.iii.310–311)*

But even in a play so persistently loud as *Macbeth*, Shakespeare did not choose to abandon words for his most intense speech. Nor did he try to howl above the thunder. His mode was, at least in part, suggested to him by Macbeth's state of nervous exhaustion, however lively the pain of despair may have been. The speech is therefore slow and terribly quiet in its rhythms. But this very quality gives it the needed intensity, just as an accomplished speaker commands attention by suddenly lowering his voice. The speech should not be pronounced too wearily. It is in its own way incomparably emphatic.

Not only is the speech given terrible force by its sudden contrast with the greater volume of what has preceded it, but it achieves the power of contrast within itself. The music of the lines is slow and mournful, conveying the hopelessness of human effort. But the diction one listens to against the background of that music is agitated, angry, and bitter in meaning. What Macbeth actually says is far more than a sorrowful acquiescence in the human condition. The passage contains words that are really exclamatory in their bitterness and disillusionment: *petty, fools, brief candle, struts and frets, idiot,* and *sound and fury*. The despair is not calm, but defiant, and it is made to seem emphatically and deliberately so by the remarkable style of the speech.

But we must not neglect its meaning for Macbeth's life. Essentially it is a denial of everything in this life which might give meaning or hope. There is surely no God, no hereafter, no possibility of redemption in "lighted fools / The way to dusty death," in "a tale / Told by an idiot," in "then is heard no more," or in "signifying nothing." Like Cecropia's discourse, Macbeth's is a testament of atheism. Its desperation is dangerous less in its gloomy view of man than in its implicit comment upon any God who might preside over this tragicomic stage spectacle. It is, in substance, the most blasphemous utterance that Shakespeare ever wrote. But it is of course safe in its blasphemy because it is placed so securely in dramatic context. Macbeth is damned, and we are not Macbeth.

VII

Although it is presently unwise to look too nicely into the salvation or damnation of Shakespeare's characters, Macbeth is unquestionably damned. But his damnation is manifested upon this earth, just as his hell is here. His damnation is manifested most appallingly, I think, in the basic meaning of the word. *Damnum* means loss; and *poena damni* is the pain of loss. Macbeth's real tragedy consists in the meaning of all he has lost. Loss is the essence of the two tragedies which immediately precede *Macbeth*. Othello is most tortured by the awareness that he "threw a pearl away / Richer than all his tribe" (V.ii.347–348), and our pity for him comes largely from our sense of this loss. Lear has lost and suffered much more, but still his final agony is for the loss of Cordelia: "I might have sav'd her; now she's gone for ever! / Cordelia, Cordelia! stay a little" (V.iii.270–271). Shakespeare in his mature tragedy seems to have come to the

Torture of the Mind · 215

realization that not the fact of death, but the loss occasioned by death, makes the greatest appeal to the hearts of men.

But Macbeth is almost uniquely afflicted by loss, by the loss of more than life, and I think that our pity for him comes almost entirely from the awareness of how much he has forfeited. Because of his great evil, and the rightness of his great punishment, we must be especially careful to keep in mind the pity of his loss. Even Richard III, with whom his evil has most in common, appeals to us momentarily by calling to our attention that he has lost something which he had earlier tried to scorn and which now apparently means everything to him:

> I shall despair. There is no creature loves me,
> And if I die no soul shall pity me.
> *(V.iii.200–201)*

Macbeth, much more human, grieves much more than Richard that he has lost human ties. He had foreseen that he would have to give up the "Golden opinions from all sorts of people" which he had bought. But he had not foreseen the completeness of his human loss:

> And that which should accompany old age,
> As honour, love obedience, troops of friends,
> I must not look to have.
> *(V.iii.24–26)*

For him there can be no more communion with his human kind at banquets. He will lose the one person whom he truly loves, the woman who never caresses him with any fond terms, but whom he calls "my dearest partner of greatness" (I.v.11–12); "My dearest love" (I.v.58), "Love" (III.ii.29), "dear wife" (III.ii.36), and "dearest chuck" (III.iii.45). He has lost the innocent sleep which he murdered and the solace of labor used for the King. More terrible are the spiritual losses: "mine eternal jewel / Given to the common Enemy of man" (III.i.67–68), and above all the resultant pain of loss, carrying with it the death of renown and grace and, ultimately, of human feeling.

It is the loss of feeling which is the most peculiar to Macbeth and which is, afflicting him, especially ironic and pitiable. For he is the tragic hero whose life as we see it has been most persistently and intensely one of sensation. For him, although sensation had been a source mainly of torment, it had also been potentially good. It had made possible the vividness with which his conscience pictured all the virtuous, the holy, the innocent things in life. Even in torment it had been the source of his deepest, most vital existence. Uniquely active in him are those sensible faculties which Shakespeare's Claudio had dreaded to lose, "This sensible warm motion to become / A kneaded clod" (*Measure for Measure* III.i.120–121).

How much pity we owe a tragic hero who is a "butcher" (V.ix.35) and "this fiend of Scotland" (IV.iii.233) depends perhaps upon each one of us. But we must acknowledge that he takes us upon one of the most profoundly violent, most vividly felt experiences of life that we shall ever know. Through his tortured mind and senses we experience a range of sensation extending through the excited inception of shared ambition and hope, through plausible temptation, through reluctant evil, through hopeless labor, through racked nerves and restless fears, to a blasphemous negation of a life robbed of meaning.

But the whole experience is securely placed for us by dramatic context. Macbeth is damned, and we are not Macbeth. Or are we?

Chapter XI

Epilogue in Hell

The critic who has made confident, unequivocal statements about the art and meaning of *Macbeth* must be prepared to live ever after on the torture of the mind in restless ecstasy. The play itself is contrived to damn him. There is a theatrical legend that performances of the play have been repeatedly hexed, doubtless by the malice of the Witches. And critics, beguiled by its "simplicity," have lived to curse the equivocation of the fiend that lies like truth.

In my own study I am uneasily aware of an assertiveness of thesis, for I know that no Shakespearean play can be "solved" by the search for a controlling idea. My concern with condign punishment would be deplored by a critic like C. J. Sisson, who finds in such an approach "no place for pity."[1] I have, on the contrary, found much pity in the play—as much as I presently feel for myself. One cannot vividly experience so much suffering, however merited, without compassion. However, I find less pity in this play than in *Othello* or *King Lear*. Condign punishment may not, I am further aware, be so thoroughly applicable as I have made it to be. But to me, in my present estate, it is the only theory that makes Macbeth's suffering tolerable and my reaction to it not blasphemous. If I have erred, it is in taking Shakespeare at his word. I was profoundly convinced by Mac-

[1] *Shakespeare's Tragic Justice* (Scarborough, Ontario, Canada, 1961), p. 26.

beth's own explanation: that he teaches bloody instructions which return to plague the inventor, and that an "even-handed Justice" commends the ingredients of the poisoned chalice to his own lips. There was for me an irresistible statement of condign punishment by the voice which cried:

> Glamis hath murder'd sleep, and therefore Cawdor
> Shall sleep no more, Macbeth shall sleep no more!

Nevertheless, anyone who today, in the middle of warring armies of critics, ventures upon a theological approach to Shakespeare must say of his venture, "I am afraid to think what I have done; / Look on 't again I dare not."

I have also sinned by venturing to define limits to the achievement of the play and the dimensions of its hero. I have argued, with Curry, that Macbeth has a worsening character and, I add to Curry's view, a shrinking character. Because of the nature of his evil and its reductive effect on him (much as is the case with Satan in *Paradise Lost*), he becomes a less various, less reliable commentator on life than Hamlet or Lear, or than he himself had been early in the play, and becomes much closer to Othello. The play itself suffers, as a result, from the limitations of what is said within it, but not from any limitations on what, as a total work, it is. I may also be said to have robbed Macbeth of his splendor as a poet by trying to find an explanation for his imaginative excitement in his dramatic situation. (This pain of sense is beyond belief!) Other critics, notably L. C. Knights and Kenneth Muir, have sinned in a similar way, but they find the explanation solely in Shakespeare's own poetic genius. That I put more emphasis upon dramatic situation than upon innate character should not be taken to mean that I do not think Macbeth to be, even out of the context of this play, a totally different personality from Hamlet, Othello, and Lear. Unfortunately we never see him in anything like a "normal" situation, but all available evidence would suggest that he is by temperament not unduly fearful or imaginative and that he has many of the warrior qualities typically given by Shakespeare to generals.[2] The

---

[2] For Macbeth's basically warlike nature, see Alan S. Downer, "The Life of Our Design—The Function of Imagery in the Poetic Drama," *Hudson Review*, II (1949), 252-254; and, as an unsettling diversion,

testimony of his wife and his own satisfaction in "Golden opinions from all sorts of people" suggests a man who values the prosaic virtues of worldly achievement, morally attained. I therefore impenitently insist that many of Macbeth's striking features in this play come from demonic inspiration, from the spirits poured in his ear by his wife, and above all from the terrible torments of sense and mind visited upon him by condign punishment for a deed of supreme evil.

If, as apparently I am, I am damned for my deed, for making Macbeth something less than a Romantic poet, I hope that the punishment will not be that of pain of loss, at least not in the form of alienation from those scholars whose work on *Macbeth* has most helped me: Walter Clyde Curry, Willard Farnham, and Kenneth Muir.

One final *suspirium de profundis*. I would not recommend to others years devoted to the study of *Macbeth*. The gloom of the play, with the constant menace of the heresy of fatalism, closes in upon one. It makes one morose, and given to exclaiming in the evening, "O! full of scorpions is my mind, dear wife!" The rightness of divine justice is not a source of euphoria; nor is the severed head of the criminal an adequate memento of the tortured imagination that once gave it life and a kind of grandeur. Fortunately the incomparable, deeply sorrowful music of the verse lingers with one, a testimony to the way Shakespeare's art can give a dark beauty to, even while still making firm comment upon, the victims of life's fitful fever.

Mary McCarthy, "General Macbeth," *Harper's Magazine*, June, 1962, pp. 35–39. Reprinted in *The Tragedy of Macbeth*, ed. by Sylvan Barnet (The Signet Classic Shakespeare), (New York, 1963), pp. 229–240.

INDEX

Aaron (*Titus Andronicus*), 7–8, 10, 130
Abernethy, John
  Christian and Heavenly Treatise, Containing Physicke for the Soule, A, 199
Acts and Monuments. See Foxe, John
Adams, Henry Hitch
  English Domestic Or, Homiletic Tragedy 1575 to 1642, 22 n. 21
Aeneas (*Hamlet*), 59–60, 62, 68
Alger, W. A.
  Life of Edwin Forrest, The, 92n. 33
Altick, Richard D.
  "Symphonic Imagery in *Richard II*," 88 n. 31
Ambrose, Saint, 203 n. 17
Anatomie of the Mind, The. See Rogers, Thomas
Anatomy of Conscience, The. See Huit, Ephraim
Anatomy of Melancholy, The. See Burton, Robert
Anderson, Ruth L.
  "Pattern of Behavior Culminating in *Macbeth*, the," 202 n. 16
Andrea (*Spanish Tragedy, The*), 33
Angus (*Macbeth*), 92, 158
Antony and Cleopatra, 11, 12, 144
Antony, Mark: in *Julius Caesar*, 77; in *Antony and Cleopatra*, 144
Apologie for Poetrie, An. See Sidney, Sir Philip
Apology for Actors, An. See Heywood, Thomas
Apparitions (*Macbeth*), 64, 105, 106, 208; armed head, 106, 208; bloody child, 91, 93, 106, 168; child crowned with a tree in his hand, 106. See also Show of Kings
Aquinas, Saint Thomas
  Contra Gentiles, 34–35
  Summa Theologica, The, 36–37, 38, 157, 198
  See also *poena damni*; *poena sensus*
Arden of Feversham, 74, 127
Aristotle, 15, 32, 77

Arondell, Thomas, 34
Arte of English Poesie, The. See Puttenham, George
Arte of Rhetorique, The. See Wilson, Thomas
Arthur (*King John*), 103
Ate (*Locrine*), 115
Atin (*Faerie Queen, The*), 143
Atreus (*Thyestes*), 61
Ayre, Rev. John
  Prayers and Other Pieces by Thomas Becon, S.T.P., 30 n. 41
  Early Works of Thomas Becon, The, 200 n. 14

Babes, 25; symbolic interpretation of, in *Macbeth*, 94–96, 103; slaughter of, in popular writings, 96–101; triumph of, in Shakespeare's history plays, 101–103. See also Innocence
Bad Angel (*Doctor Faustus*), 29
Baker, Howard
  Induction to Tragedy, 11, 20
Balthezer (*First Part of Hieronimo, The*), 73
Banquo (*Macbeth*), 2, 45, 88, 103–104, 107, 117, 119–120, 146, 150, 151, 208; comments on the nature of evil in *Macbeth*, 42–43; participates in Macbeth's evil, 135–136, 161; representative of fruitful labor, 154–155, 180; Macbeth's fear of, 205–207. See also Ghost
Barnet, Sylvan
  Tragedy of Macbeth, The, 218 n. 2
Bartholomaeus. See *Batman uppon Bartholme*
Bartholomeusz, Dennis
  Macbeth and the Players, 3 n. 2, 68 n. 7
Basilicon Doron, The. See James I
Bassianus (*Titus Andronicus*), 8, 75
Batman uppon Bartholome, his Booke De Propietatibus Rerum, 16 n. 5, 7
Battenhouse, Roy W.

222 · Index

Marlowe's Tamburlaine: A Study in Renaissance Moral Philosophy, 30 n. 40
Shakespearean Tragedy. Its Art and Its Christian Premises, 100 n. 9
Battle of Alcazar, The. See Peele, George
Beard, Thomas
  Theatre of Gods Judgements: Or, a Collection of Histories out of Sacred, Ecclesiasticall, and Prophane Authours, Concerning the Admirable Judgements of God upon the Transgressours of His Commandements: 37, 40, 78–79; as authority for condign punishment, 33–34
Beaty, Jerome, and William H. Matchett
  Poetry from Statement to Meaning, 141–142 n. 1
Becon, Thomas
  "Demands of Holy Scripture, The," 30, 36, 66, 182
  "Pathwai unto Prayer, The," 200 n. 14
Bedford, Duke of (1 Henry VI), 127
Beelzebub (Doctor Faustus), 99
Bethell, S. L., 4
  "Shakespeare's Imagery: The Diabolic Images in Othello," 139
Bible, 12, 26–27, 27–28, 54; books of: Proverbs, 26, 32–33, 66, 99, 176 n. 25; Psalms, 33, 142; Wisdom of Solomon, 34, 128; Romans, 39, 57; John, 53–54; Genesis, 55, 79, 89, 161, 165, 200; Matthew, 66; Corinthians, 66; Revelation, 80, 137; Isaiah, 86; Numbers, 89; Habakkuk, 90; Joshua, 90 n. 32, 176 n. 25; Kings, 99; Deuteronomy, 99, 176 n. 25, 183; Joel, 137; Mark, 137, 176; Zephaniah, 137 n. 30; Job, 142, 153, 167, 176 n. 25; Ecclesiasticus, 153; Leviticus, 155, 176 n. 25; Jeremiah, 154 n. 12; Zechariah, 176 n. 25; Samuel, 199. See also Babes; Blood; Cain and Abel; Calvin; Herod; James I; Judas; Nebuchadnezzar; Pilate; Saul
Blood: sight of bloody hands as torment for the murderers, 65, 175–176; pervasiveness of, in Renaissance writings, 70–74, 78–79, 82–83; Shakespeare's apprenticeship to, 74–78; theme of, presented in the Bible, 79–80; bleeding Captain introduces the theme of, 81–82; widening of, 84, 85–87, 88, 90–93; as major symbol of murderous discovery, 87–88; Macbeth's vision of, on dagger, 175
Boas, Frederick S.
  Works of Thomas Kyd, The, 73 n. 10
Bolingbroke, Henry (Richard II), 76
Book of Martyrs. See Foxe, John
Bradbrook, M. C.
  "Sources of Macbeth, The," 116
Bradley, A. C.
  Shakespearean Tragedy, 4, 12, 42, 45, 52, 71
Brooke, C. F. Tucker
  Shakespeare Apocrypha, The, 115 n. 3
Brooks, Cleanth
  "Naked Babe and the Cloak of Manliness, The," 95–96
Brown, John Russell
  Duchess of Malfi, The, 164 n. 10
Brutus (Julius Caesar), 61, 77, 78, 172
Buchanan, George
  Rerum Scoticorum Historia, 164
Buckingham, Duke of (Richard III), 103
Bullinger, Henry
  "Of the Second Precept of the Second Table, Which Is in Order the Sixth of the Ten Commandments, Thou Shalt not Kill," 80
  "Of Sin, and of the Kinds Thereof ... the Tenth Sermon," 198–199
Bullough, Geoffrey
  Poems and Dramas of Fulke Greville, First Lord Brooke, 183 n. 38
Bundy, M. D.
  "'Invention' and 'Imagination' in the Renaissance," 18
Burke, Kenneth
  Philosophy of Literary Form, The, 142 n. 1
Burton, Robert
  Anatomy of Melancholy, The, 17, 26, 209, 211, 213

Caesar, Julius, 130. See also Ghost
Caesar, Julius (Caesar's Revenge), 73, 113–114
Caesar, Octavius (Julius Caesar), 173

Caesar's Revenge, 73, 73 n. 10, 83, 113–114, 171
Cain: and Abel, 55; associations with blood, 76, 78, 79; punishment of, 161, 165, 169, 200, 200 n. 14, 204
Calpurnia (*Julius Caesar*), 130
Calvin, John, 30
   Commentarie of John Calvin upon the First Booke of Moses Called Genesis, A, 31, 79, 169, 200
   Sermons of John Calvin upon the Fifth Booke of Moses Called Deuteronomie, The, 79–80, 86–87
   Sermons of Master John Calvin upon the Booke of Job, 143, 165
Cambises. See Preston, Thomas
Campbell, Lily B.
   Shakespeare's Tragic Heroes: Slaves of Passion, 3 n. 3, 34 n. 50, 186 n. 1
"Candelmas Day & the Killynge of the Children of Israell," 100 n. 9
Captain (*Macbeth*): bleeding Captain's speech, 44, 72, 73–74, 82 n. 20, 111, 140–141, 146; introduces the theme of blood, 81–82; symbolic role of, 83
Carlisle, Bishop of (*Richard II*), 76
Casca (*Julius Caesar*), 130
Cases of Conscience. See Perkins, William
Cassius (*Julius Caesar*), 130
Cecropia (*Countess of Pembrokes Arcadia, The*) 212–213, 214
Certeine Comfortable Expositions. See Hooper, John
Charlton, H. B., and L. E. Kastner
   Poetical Works of Sir William Alexander, The, 20 n. 17
Charney, Maurice
   "Persuasiveness of Violence in Elizabethan Plays, The," 14–15
Charron, Pierre
   Of Wisdome, Three Bookes, 16 n. 6, 17 n. 8, 35 n. 54, 177
Christ, 53–54, 100, 173; and man's conscience, 166–167. See also Duncan
Christian and Heavenly Treatise, Containing Physicke for the Soul, A. See Abernethy, John
Christmas, Rev. Henry
   Works of Nicholas Ridley, D.D., The, 57 n. 18
Christs Teares over Jerusalem. See Nashe, Thomas

Chrysostom, 161, 199
Clarke, C. C.
   "Darkened Reason in *Macbeth*," 53 n. 14
Claudio (*Measure for Measure*), 29, 216
Claudius (*Hamlet*), 37, 68, 78, 149
Clemen, Wolfgang
   English Tragedy before Shakespeare: The Development of Dramatic Speech, 15
Clitus (*Julius Caesar*), 172
Cole, Douglas
   Suffering and Evil in the Plays of Christopher Marlowe, 38 n. 59
Coleridge, Samuel Taylor, 3
   Coleridge's Shakespearean Criticism, 205
Compendium Maleficarum. See Guazzo, Francesco Maria
Conscience: of Macbeth, condemns itself, 181–182; characteristics of a guilty, as depicted in Renaissance writings, 182–183. See Macbeth: Thunder
Contra Gentiles. See Aquinas, Saint Thomas
Cordelia (*King Lear*), 138, 214
Coriolanus, 12, 49 n. 12
Cornelia. See Kyd, Thomas
Corrie, Rev. George E.
   Sermons of Hugh Latimer, 28 n. 36
Countess of Pembrokes Arcadia, The. See Sidney, Sir Philip
Coverdale, Myles
   Hope of the Faithful, The, 28 n. 36
   "Most Frutefull Pythye and Learned Treatyse, How a Christen Man Ought to Behave Hymselfe in the Daunger of Death, A," 166 n. 13
   "Spiritual and Most Precious Pearl, A," 209–210
Craigie, James
   Basilicon Doron, The, 183 n. 35
Creon (*Oedipus*), 123
Cunliffe, John W.
   Droomme of Doomes Day, The, 28 n. 36
   Early English Classical Tragedies, 72 n. 6
Cunningham, Dolora G.
   "Macbeth: The Tragedy of the Hardened Heart," 199 n. 11
Curry, Walter Clyde, 219
   Shakespeare's Philosophical Pat-

terns, 3 n. 6, 43 n. 5, 122, 125, 134, 218

Daemonologie. See James I
Dante
 Divine Comedy of Dante Alighieri, The, 56, 56 n. 17, 58, 79
Davidson, Clifford
 "Full of Scorpions Is My Mind," 54 n. 16
Davids Penitentiall Psalme Opened. See Hieron, Samuel
Davies, John, of Hereford
 Mirum in Modum, 18 n. 13
Day, Thomas
 Wonderfull Straunge Sightes Seene in the Element, over the Citie of London and Other Places . . . : Most Strange and Fearefull to the Beholders, 25 n. 28, 26
Declaration of Egregious Popish Impostures, A. See Harsnet, Samuel
Dekker, Thomas, 19
Dell, Floyd, and Paul Jordan-Smith
 Anatomy of Melancholy, The, 17 n. 11
Deloney, Thomas
 Strange Histories, of Kings, Princes, Dukes, Earles, Lords, Ladies, Knights, and Gentlemen, 113
Demonolatry. See Remy, Nicolas
Dent, Arthur
 Sermon of Repentaunce, A, 27–28, 28 n. 36
De Quincey, Thomas, 4, 59
 "On the Knocking at the Gate in *Macbeth,*" 69 n. 8
Desdemona (*Othello*), 62, 67, 77
Devil, 3, 74, 124, 128; symbolic representation of, in *Macbeth,* 12, 124–125, 133, 171; operation of, on the imagination, 17, 35, on the body and spirit, 160–161, 175; relationship of to witches, 24, 118–119, 121, 145; Macbeth's pact with, 57, 64–65, 67, 200–201; and despair, 180, 199, 209–210
Dialogue Concerning Witches and Witchcraftes, A. See Gifford, George
Discord (*Caesar's Revenge*): ominous role of, 113–115
Discourse of the Conscience, A. See Woolton, John
Discourse of the Damned Art of Witchcraft, A. See Perkins, William
Discoverie of Witchcraft, The. See Scot, Reginald
Divine Comedy. See Dante
Doctor (*Macbeth*), 194
Doctor Faustus. See Marlowe, Christopher
Donalbain (*Macbeth*), 46
Donne, John
 Sermons of John Donne, The, 30 n. 40, 183 n. 35
 "Sermon Preached at White-hall, April 21, 1616, A," 36, 37
Doomsday, 12, 25, 112, 134, 137–138, 167. See also Gascoigne, George
Dorey, T. A., and Donald R. Dudley
 Roman Drama, 20 n. 17
Downer, Alan S.
 "Life of Our Design—The Function of Imagery in the Poetic Drama, The," 218 n. 2
Downey, June E.
 Creative Imagination: Studies in the Psychology of Literature, 142 n. 1
Droome of Doomes Day, The. See Gascoigne, George
Drums: symbolic interpretation of in Renaissance writings, 170–172; announce the coming of divine retribution in *Macbeth,* 172–173
Duessa (*Faerie Queene, The*), 120
Duncan (*Macbeth*), 45, 46, 151; murder of, 39, 60, 68, 69, 71, 87, 111, 176–177; elements reflect the death of, 44, 135–136, 164; betrayal of, 51–52; and divine grace, 51–52, 195–197; Christlike qualities of, 53–54, 60, 87–88; as innocent victim, 55, 94, 108, 109, 161–162, 163, 195; informed by the bleeding Captain, 81; labor of, as contrasted with Macbeth's, 148, 149, 150, 154–155; body of, as source of visual torment for Macbeth, 178, 194
Dyke, Jeremiah
 Good Conscience: or a Treatise Shewing the Nature, Meanes, Marks, Benefit, and Necessity Thereof, 28, 30, 161

Edgar (*King Lear*), 138, 173, 180, 211
Edmund (*King Lear*), 77, 171, 173, 191
Edward, Prince of Wales (*3 Henry*

VI), 102
Edward II. See Marlowe, Christopher
Edwards, Philip
   Spanish Tragedy, The, 31 n. 44
Eliot, T. S., 20 n. 18
Eliphas (*Job*), 142
Elliott, G. R.
   Dramatic Providence in Macbeth, 3 n. 2, 4 n. 9, 166 n. 17, 182 n. 34
Elton, William
   King Lear and the Gods, 169
Evans, Gareth Lloyd
   "Shakespeare, Seneca, and the Kingdom of Violence," 19–20
Evil, 6, 9, 116: critical interpretation of in *Macbeth*, 3–4, 41–42; demonic nature of, 43–44; reversal of values as source of, 45–46; blurring of, 47–51; awareness of in the protagonists, 51–57. *See also* Banquo; Nature, ambiguous role of; Witches
Exton, Sir Pierce of (*Richard II*), 76

Faerie Queene, The. See Spenser, Edmund
Farnham, Willard
   Shakespeare's Tragic Frontier: The World of His Final Tragedies, 6, 122, 182, 219
   Medieval Heritage of Elizabethan Tragedy, The, 11
Faustus, 29, 57, 84, 99, 162, 169, 212
Fear, 253 n. 22; as form of punishment, 186–188, 199–200; reasons for Macbeth's, 201–204; Macbeth's response to, 203–205; specificity of Macbeth's, 205–209. *See also* Despair; Punishment
Fergusson, Francis
   "*Macbeth* as the Imitation of an Action," 152
Feuillerat, Albert
   Countess of Pembrokes Arcadia, The, 212 n. 23
First and Second Volume of Chronicles, The. See Holinshed
First Part of Hieronimo, The, 73
Fitzgerald, Percy
   Life of David Garrick; From Original Family Papers, and Numerous Published and Unpublished Sources, The, 84 n. 26
Fleance (*Macbeth*), 135, 136, 159, 207, 208
Foakes, R. A.

   Macbeth, 3 n. 5
Fool (*King Lear*), 191
Forman, Simon, 4
   Bocke of Plaies and Notes thereof per Formans for Common Pollicie, The, 86
Foxe, John
   Volume of the Ecclesiastical Historie, Conteining the Acts and Monuments of Martyrs, The, 21, 99
Fraunce, Abraham
   Arcadian Rhetorike, The, 47
French Academie, The. See La Primaudaye, Pierre de
Frye, Roland Mushat
   Shakespeare and Christian Doctrine, 54, 100 n. 9, 189 n. 5
   "*Macbeth* and the Powers of Darkness," 139, 189 n. 5
Furnivall, F. J.
   Digby Plays, The, 100 n. 9

Gardner, Helen
   Business of Criticism, The, 95–96
Gascoigne, George
   Droomme of Doomes Day, The, 28 n. 36, 30, 38, 158, 171
Gauden, John, 166 n. 16
George, Duke of Clarence (*Richard III*), 9
Gertrude (*Hamlet*), 50, 187
Ghost: of Banquo, 15, 21, 89, 111, 122–124, 177, 178–179; in *Locrine*, 115; in *Hamlet*, 28–29, 63, 122–123, 124–125, 168; in *Oedipus*, 123; in *Caesar's Revenge*, 171; in *Julius Caesar*, 172. *See also* Lavater, Ludwig
Gifford, George
   Dialogue Concerning Witches and Witchcraftes, A, 118 n. 9, 121
Gismond of Salerne, 72, 115
Gloucester, Earl of (*King Lear*), 37–38, 173, 180, 211–212, 212–213
Golding, Arthur
   Metamorphoses, 98
Good Conscience: or a Treatise Shewing the Nature, Meanes, Marks, Benefit, and Necessity Thereof. See Dyke, Jeremiah
Gorboduc. See Norton, Thomas, and Thomas Sackville
Grace: loss of Divine, 4, 36–37, 52, 195–196; effects of loss of, on Macbeth, 197–198, 200–201, 207–

226 · Index

209; withdrawal of, as the equivalent of pain of loss, 198–201. *See also* Duncan
Granville-Barker, Harley
On Dramatic Method, 42
Greek drama: contrasted with Elizabethan tragedy, 14–15
Greville, Fulke
Alaham, 183
Grosart, A. B.
Complete Works of John Davies of Hereford, The, 18 n. 13
Guazzo, Francesco Maria
Compendium Maleficarum, 24 n. 24, 34–35 n. 51, 119 n. 15, 145 n. 5
Guyon (Faerie Queene, The) 143

Hamlet, 5, 12, 68, 124, 218; and the emotional engagement of tragedy, 27, 28; sense of condign punishment in, 37; language of, 49–50, 59–69, 62; suffering of, compared with Macbeth's, 185–186, 187, 188, 189, 190, 191, 194
Hamlet, 2, 10, 11, 68, 116, 140, 190; sensation in, 9–11; poetic justice in, 37, 53; as bloodless tragedy, 77–78; use of soliloquy in, 190–191. *See also* Ghost
Hankins, John E.
"Pains of the Afterworld: Fire, Wind, and Ice in Milton and Shakespeare, The," 29 n. 37
Harbage, Alfred
William Shakespeare: The Complete Works, 3 n. 4
William Shakespeare: A Reader's Guide, 48
Harcourt, John B.
"I Pray You Remember the Porter," 167 n. 18
Harding, Rev. Thomas
Fiftie Godlie and Learned Sermons Divided into Five Decades, 199 n. 9
Harmonie upon the First Booke of Samuel, An. See Willet, Andrew
Harsnet, Samuel
Declaration of Egregious Popish Impostures, A, 118
Hazlitt, William, 4, 5
Hecate *(Macbeth),* 179, 209
Heilman, Robert B.
" 'Twere Best not Know Myself," 51 n. 13
Hell: Renaissance concept of, 27–28,
38; punishments of, 28, 142, 186; on earth, 29–32; as represented in *Macbeth,* 29, 31–32, 133, 139, 164, 165–167, 185–186, 190. *See also* Punishment
Hemmingius, Nicolaus. *See* Hemmingsen, Niels
Hemmingsen, Niels (Hemmingius), 209
Henry VI, 7, 9, 102, 116; *part 1,* 127, 129; *part 2,* 74, 129, 133 n. 27; *part 3,* 76–77, 101–102, 133 n. 27
Henry VIII, 152
Herod, 99–100, 100 n. 9
Heywood, Jasper
Troas: "The Argument" to, 96–97
Heywood, Thomas
Apology for Actors, An, 40 n. 63, 70
Hieron, Samuel
Davids Penitentiall Psalme Opened, 182 n. 33
Hieronimo *(Spanish Tragedy, The),* 127, 210
Hippolytus. See Seneca
Holinshed
First and Second Volumes of Chronicles, The, 113
"Historie of Scotland," 71, 94, 117, 120, 125–126, 135, 164, 201–202
"Historie of England," 182
Holland, Henry
Treatise against Witchcraft, A, 119 n. 15, 160 n. 5
Holloway, John
Story of Night, The, 81 n. 19
Homicide *(Two Lamentable Tragedies),* 82–83
Hooker, Richard
Laws of Ecclesiastical Polity, The, 166
Hooper, John
Certeine Comfortable Expositions, 26 n. 31, 283, 184
Later Writings of Bishop Hooper, Together with His Letters and Other Pieces, 181
Hope of the Faithful, The. See Coverdale, Myles
Horatio *(Hamlet),* 9–10, 37, 202–203
Horrible Creuel and Bloudy Murther, A, 23, 70
Horrible Murther of a Young Boy of Three Yeres of Age, The, 100 n. 11
Howe, P. P.

Complete Works of William Hazlitt, The, 5
Hughes, Thomas
  Misfortunes of Arthur, The, 21, 73, 180
Huit, Ephraim
  Anatomy of Conscience, The, 157, 160, 183 n. 35, 198 n. 7
Humphrey, duke of Gloucester (*2 Henry VI*), 74, 86
Hunter, G. K.
  Macbeth, 2

Iago (*Othello*), 39, 194
Imagery: sensationalism of, in *Macbeth*, 1–2, 15, 53, 55; Doomsday, 25, 137–138, 164; blood, 71–73, 74–78, 90–91; of violated Innocence, 95–96, 108; of night, 131–132; of hell, 139; of futile labor, 140–141, 152–153; kinaesthetic, 141–142; of leaping, 149–150; of pursuit, 150–151; of running, 151–152; of implantation, 154–156; sensory, 157–158, 173–174, 192; of mental torment, 186–188. *See also* Language
Imagination: Renaissance view of the, 16–19. *See also* Devil; Macbeth
Innocence, 21, 55, 58, 94, 96, 99, 100, 101–102; treatment of, in *Macbeth*, 94–96; symbols of, 103–106; Macbeth and his Lady as victims of, 106–109. *See also* Babes; Duncan; Malcolm, Pity
Innocent III, 38
Insatiate Countess, The. See Marston, John
Ixion, 186

Jack, Jane H.
  "*Macbeth,* King James, and the Bible," 137 n. 30
James I, 23, 71, 118, 137 n. 30
  Daemonologie, 64 n. 4, 116, 118, 119 n. 15, 124, 145 n. 8
  Basilicon Doron, The, 183 n. 35
Jocasta, 73
Johnson, Francis R.
  "Shakespearian Imagery and Senecan Imitation," 86 n. 29
Jorgensen, Paul A.
  "Deed Without a Name, A," 47 n. 8
  Shakespeare's Military World, 171 n. 21
Judas, 53–54

Julius Caesar, 9, 61, 77, 116, 130, 131, 133, 159, 172
Jump, John D.
  Doctor Faustus, 29 n. 38
  Tamburlaine the Great Parts I and II, 162 n. 9

Kent, Earl of (*King Lear*), 138
King Edward the Second (*Edward II*), 59
King John, 75, 103
King John, 75, 103
King Lear, 5, 138, 189, 213, 218; self-awareness of, 12, 131, 201; suffering of, 184, 185–186, 187, 188, 194, 214
King Lear, 118, 138, 171, 177, 217; compared with *Macbeth*, 2, 77, 175, 180, 201; sensationalism of, 10, 11, 116, 130–131, 168–169; mental torment as depicted in, 37–38, 173, 184, 185, 190, 191; Nature in, 44; dramatic language of, 211
Kirschbaum, Leo
  "Shakespeare's Stage Blood and Its Critical Significance," 70 n. 1
Kittredge, George Lyman
  Tragedy of Macbeth, The, 32 n. 47
Knight, G. Wilson, 4
  Imperial Theme, The, 3 n. 7
  Wheel of Fire, The, 3 n. 7, 41
Knights, L. C., 4, 218
  Explorations, 3–4 n. 8, 45
  "Shakespeare's Imagery," 142 n. 1
Knocking: symbolic of Macbeth's entry into Hell, 165–167. *See also* Macbeth, punishment of through senses
Knowles, Sheridan, 92
Kocher, Paul H.
  "Lady Macbeth and the Doctor," 83–84
Kyd, Thomas
  Spanish Tragedy, The, 7, 31 n. 44, 33, 127, 210
  Cornelia, 73 n. 9

Labor: futility of, 140–142, 144; and its association with evil, 142–143; as represented in *The Faerie Queene,* 143–144; doubling of, 145–148; kinds of, Macbeth undertakes, 148–153
Lady Macbeth, 112, 136, 148, 193, 203, 215; commitment to evil, 45, 51–

52, 56, 65, 133, 150–151; and the blurring of evil, 47–49, 50, 51, 52; ordeal of, 61, 184; estrangement of from Macbeth, as a result of evil, 63, 67–68, 178, 193, 195; and the murder of Duncan, 67–68, 68–69, 108; reaction of to blood as compared with Macbeth's, 72, 85–87; inability of to wash away blood, 84, 85–86, 91–92, 175; sleepwalking scene of, 85–86, 92, 194–195, 201–202; classical models for unpitying cruelty of, 97–99; and helpless babes, 95, 104–105; "naked frailties" of, 104; and the willful destruction of Innocence, 106–107, 109, 174; closeness in spirit to the Witches, 120, 153–154, 162–163; influence of on Macbeth's futile labor, 146–148; sterility of, 153–154, 156; punishment of, through senses, 157–158, 162, 163, 164, 168, 175, 177; role of in tempting Macbeth, 162–163, 219; death of, 209

Lady Macduff (*Macbeth*), 46, 92, 93
Laertes (*Hamlet*), 37, 95
Laius (*Oedipus*), 123
Language, 52, 59, 61, 148–149; evasiveness of, in *Macbeth*, 47–49; Renaissance sensitivity of to names, 49, 50–51; mature achievement of, in *Macbeth*, 49–50; of evil, 49–51; of individual speeches, 52–53, 55, 62–63, 104, 132, 153, 189, 213–214; of Aeneas's tale to Dido (*Hamlet*), 59–60, 62, 68; Renaissance connotation of strangeness of, 110–112; use of "start" to demonstrate Macbeth's fear, 159–160. *See also* Imagery; Murder, as ritual; Soliloquy; Witches
La Primaudaye, Pierre de
French Academie, The, 17 n. 9, 166, 188 n. 4
Later Writings of Bishop Hooper, Together with His Letters and Other Pieces. See Hooper, John
Latimer, Hugh
Seven Sermons of the Reverend Father M. Hugh Latimer, The, 28 n. 36
Sermons and Remains by Hugh Latimer, Sometime Bishop of Worcester, Martyr, 142, 199

Lavater, Ludwig
Of Ghostes and Spirites Walking by Nyght, 124–125, 134–135, 171, 177 n. 26
Lavinia (*Titus Andronicus*), 75
Laws of Ecclesiastical Polity, The. See Hooker, Richard
Leake, Richard
Foure Sermons Preached in Westmoreland, 200 n. 14
Leavis, F. R., 4
Le Loyer, Pierre
Treatise of Specters or Straunge Sights, 177 n. 26
Lennox (*Macbeth*), 110–111, 133–134, 136–137
Lex talionis, 32, 32 n. 48
Liddell, Mark H.
Macbeth, 164
Locrine, 115
Lucas, F. L.
Seneca and Elizabethan Tragedy, 20 n. 17
Lucianus (*Hamlet*), 60
Lucifer (*Doctor Faustus*), 169
Luther, Martin, 30

Macbeth, 23, 103–104; imagination of, 4, 5–6, 142; experiences Hell on earth, 12–13, 31–32; as victim of the imagination, 16–18, 163, 203–204; attention of given to this life, 29, 43–44; moral dilemma of, 46, 141; and the blurring of evil, 46–49, 50–51; awareness of evil, 51, 52, 54–56; receives condign punishment, 53, 88, 104, 174; and despair, 54, 90, 93, 170, 188, 190, 209–215; conscience of, 55, 181–182, 183–184; damnation of, 55–56, 214; commits himself to evil, 56–57; moving in "rapt" manner toward the murder of Duncan, 62–65, 67, 68; possessed by the Devil. 64–65, 67. 125; and the averted eye, 65–67; separation of, from Lady Macbeth, 67–68; initiates the spread of blood, 84, 87, 88–89, 91; and the inescapability of blood, 86–87; inability of to conceal murder, 89–91, 92–93; violates Innocence, 94–95, 103, 106. 107. 108–109; tormented by sleep, 107–108; and strange phenomena, 110–112; reaction of to the Witches, 118, 120, 122, 178; response of to Banquo's ghost, 122–124; and the futility of labor, 146, 147, 148–153; barrenness of, 153–156, 208; punishment of, through senses, 157–158, 161–162, through tormenting sounds, 162–173, through tormenting sights, 104, 173–181; subject to bodily fits, 158–161; response of to Lady Macbeth's death, 170, 251; mental suffering of, 185–186; suffers through the body what he suffers in mind, 186–190; as commentator on suffering, 190, 191–195; and the affliction of loss, 197, 198, 199, 200–201, 215–216; innate character of, 218–291. *See also* Fear; Grace; Hell, Soliloquy; Witches

McCarthy, Mary
"General Macbeth," 218 n. 2
Macduff (*Macbeth*), 50, 91, 137, 138, 168, 208; and Malcolm, 46, 197–198; and the theme of Innocence, 93, 105–106, 108–109; as object of Macbeth's fear, 95, 151, 205–207; as instrument of Nemesis, 138, 170, 173
McGee, Arthur R.
"Macbeth and the Furies," 133 n. 28
McKerrow, Ronald B.
Works of Thomas Nashe, The, 27 n. 33
McManaway, James G.
Shakespeare 400, 51 n. 13
McNeir, Waldo F., and Thelma N. Greenfield
Pacific Coast Studies in Shakepeare, 47 n. 8
Mahood, M. M.
Shakespeare's Wordplay, 49
Mair, G. H.
Arte of Rhetorique, 19 n. 16
Malcolm (*Macbeth*), 91, 111, 137, 149, 196, 208; and Macduff, 46, 197–198; as symbol of Innocence, 105–107
Malegar (*Faerie Queen, The*), 143
Manly, John Matthews
Specimens of the Pre-Shaksperean Drama, 82 n. 23
Marlowe, Christopher
Doctor Faustus, 29–30, 38, 125, 168
Edward II, 59

Tragedy of Dido Queen of Carthage, The, 60
Tamburlaine, 70, 73 n. 10, 162
Marston, John
Insatiate Countess, The, 127
Martius (*Titus Andronicus*), 8
Maxwell, J. C.
"Ghost from the Grave: A note on Shakespeare's Apparitions, The," 124 n. 19
Medea. See Seneca
Megaera (*Gismond of Salerne*), 115
Mehl, Dieter
Elizabethan Dumb Show: The History of a Dramatic Convention, The, 82 n. 21
Menteith (*Macbeth*), 159, 181
Mephostophilis (*Doctor Faustus*), 29–30, 84, 125
Messenger (*Macbeth*), 111
Metamorphoses. See Ovid.
Midas, 33
Middleton, Thomas, 24
Midsummer Night's Dream, A, 174
Milton, John, 29 n. 37
Paradise Lost, 163, 218
Mirror for Magistrates, A, 34 n. 50
Mirum in Modum. See Davies, John, of Hereford
Misfortunes of Arthur, The. See Hughes, Thomas
Mordred (*Misfortunes of Arthur, The*), 73
More, George
True Discourse Concerning the Possession of 7 Persons in One Familie in Lancashire, A, 160 n. 3
Morris, Harry
"Macbeth, Dante, and the Greatest Evil," 56 n. 17
Most Cruell and Bloody Murther Committed by an Inkeepers Wife, Called Annis Dell, and Her Sonne George Dell, Foure Yeeres Since, The, 22 n. 22, 70, 100 n. 11
Most Horrible & Detestable Murther Committed by a Bloudie Man upon His Owne Wife, and Most Strangely Revealed by His Childe that Was under Five Yeares of Age, 23 n. 23, 74 n. 12, 90, 101
Most Horrible and Tragicall Murther of the Right Honorable, the

230 · Index

Vertuous, and Valerous Gentleman, John Lord Burgh, The, 22, 128
Most Strange and Admirable Discoverie of the Three Witches of Warboys, 24 n. 26, 160 n. 4
Most Wicked Worke of a Wretched Witch, A, 64 n. 3
Mowbray, Thomas, Duke of Norfolk (*Richard II*), 76
Mroz, Sister Mary Bonaventure
  Divine Vengeance: A Study of the Philosophical Backgrounds of the Revenge Motif as It Appears in Shakespeare's Chronicle History Plays, 32 n. 48
Muir, Kenneth
  Macbeth, 7 n. 12, 65, 86 n. 28, 89, 133 n. 27, 194 n. 6
  "Image and Symbol in 'Macbeth,'" 95 n. 3
  Shakespeare's Sources, I, Comedies and Tragedies, 164 n. 11
Mundy, Anthony
  View of Sundry Examples Reporting Many Straunge Murthers, Sundry Persons Perjured, Signes, and Tokens of Gods Anger Towards Us. What Straunge and Monstrous Children Have of Late Been Borne, A, 25 n. 27
Murder: as ritual, 59–63; staging of, in *Macbeth,* 68–69; of babes, in classical and Renaissance writings, 96–101. *See also* Babes; Duncan; Macbeth
Murder (*Cambises*), 82
Murderers (Macbeth), 150, 207
Murder tracts: general discussion of, 21–23; sensationalism of, 74, 100–101; use of darkness in, 127–128
Murray, W. A.
  "Why was Duncan's Blood Golden?" 88 n. 31
Murther (*Warning for Faire Women, A*), 82

"Naked frailties," 2, 103–104
Nashe, Thomas
  Christs Teares over Jerusalem, 27, 179
  Terrors of the Night Or, A Discourse of Apparitions, The, 126, 128, 131, 132, 175

Unfortunate Traveller, The, 179 n. 27
Nathan, Norman
  "Duncan, Macbeth, and Jeremiah," 154 n. 12
Natural History. See Pliny
Nature, 56, 58, 88, 89, 132, 153; ambiguous role of, in *Macbeth,* 44–45
Nebuchadnezzar, 35
Neilson, William Allan, and Charles Jarvis Hill
  Complete Plays and Poems of William Shakespeare, The, 7 n. 12
Nemesis, 171, 178; in *Battle of Alcazar, The,* 115, 171, 171 n. 22; in *Julius Caesar,* 172; Macduff as instrument of, 173
Neoplatonism, 16
Nevinson, Rev. Charles
  Later Writings of Bishop Hooper, Together With His Letters and Other Pieces, 181 n. 30
  Certeine Comfortable Expositions, 26 n. 31
Newes from Scotland, 119 n. 15
Newton, Thomas
  Seneca: His Tenne Tragedies Translated into English, 20 n. 19
Night: as aspect of unnatural world of nature, 125–126; as literary convention, 126–128; associations with evil, 88, 128, 133–135; thematic usage of in Shakespeare, 129–131; descriptions of in *Macbeth,* 131–133; symbolic function of in *Macbeth,* 135–137
Noble, Richmond
  Shakespeare's Biblical Knowledge, 54 n. 15
Norton, Thomas, and Thomas Sackville
  Gorboduc, 20, 21, 72–73, 82, 83
Nosworthy, J. M.
  "Bleeding Captain Scene in 'Macbeth,' The," 82 n. 20
Nowottny, Winifred M. T.
  "Lear's Questions," 187 n. 2

Oedipus. See Seneca
Of Ghostes and Spirites Walking by Nyght. See Lavater, Ludwig
Of Wisdome. See Charron, Pierre
Old Man: in *Macbeth,* 12, 112, 134, 136; in *Doctor Faustus,* 112

Othello, 77, 218; suffering of, 37, 186, 214; manner of murder, 61–62, 67
Othello, 39, 159, 217; sensationalism of, 10, 77, 116, 167; language of, 61–62; soliloquy in, 190–191
Ovid, 20, 98
  Metamorphoses, 115 n. 5

Pamela (*Arcadia*), 212
Paradise Lost. See Milton, John
Paul, Henry N.
  Royal Play of Macbeth, The, 3 n. 2
Paul, Saint, 57, 66
Pearson, Rev. George
  Remains of Myles Coverdale, 28 n. 36
  Writings and Translations of Myles Coverdale, 210 n. 20
Peele, George
  Battle of Alcazar, The, 70–71, 82
Perkins, William
  Treatise of Mans Imagination, A, 17, 43
  Discourse of the Damned Art of Witchcraft, A, 35 n. 53
  Cases of Conscience, 182
  "Of the Punishment of Sinne," 183
Phillips, James E.
  "Renaissance Concepts of Justice and the Structure of *The Faerie Queene*, Book V," 32 n. 48
Pilate, 86–87, 144
Pilkington, James
  "Exposition upon Certain Chapters of Nehemiah," 26 n. 29
Piteous Lamentation of the Miserable Estate of the Church in England, A. See Ridley, Nicholas
Pity, 55, 95, 101, 102, 103–104, 105, 107, 134, 192
Player (*Hamlet*), 77–78
Play of the Sacrament, The, 100
Pliny
  Natural History, 133
Poena damni. See Punishment
Poena sensus. See Punishment
Porter (*Macbeth*), 139, 147, 190; symbolic significance of, 165–167
Potter, G. R., and Evelyn Simpson
  Sermons of John Donne, The, 30 n. 40
Presenter: in *Battle of Alcazar, The*, 82, 115, 171 n. 22; in *Caesar's Revenge*, 114

Preston, Thomas
  Cambises, 82, 98–99
Procne (*Metamorphoses*), 98
Punishment: as it appears in Renaissance religious writings, 27–39; condign, 32–39, 40, 53, 95, 183, 217–218; of and through the imagination, 34–35; of sin by further sin, 36–37, 207; pain of sense (*poena sensus*), 38–39, 57, 157–158, 162, 184, 185, 188, 192; pain of loss (*poena damni*), 38–39, 57, 198–201, 214–215. See also Hell; Lady Macbeth; Macbeth; Saul
Puttenham, George
  Arte of English Poesie, The, 18
Pyrochles (*Faerie Queene, The*), 143

Queen Margaret (*3 Henry VI*), 76, 102
Quintus (*Titus Andronicus*), 8

Ransom, John Crowe
  "On Shakespeare's Language," 85 n. 27
Rape of Lucrece, The, 129, 133 n. 27
Raysor, Thomas Middleton
  Coleridge's Shakespearean Criticism, 205 n. 18
Redcrosse Knight (*Faerie Queene, The*), 203
Reese, Jack E.
  "Formalization of Horror in *Titus Andronicus*, The," 7 n. 13
Rehearsall Both Straung and True, of Hainous and Horrible Actes Committed by Elizabeth Stile, A, 24 n. 24
Remy, Nicolas
  Demonolatry, 43 n. 4, 118–119, 145 n. 7, 153
Rerum Scoticarum Historia. See Buchanan, George
Revenge (*Spanish Tragedy, The*), 115
Reynolds, John
  Triumph of Gods Revenge, The, 40
Ribner, Irving, 32 n. 47
Richard, Duke of Gloucester (*Richard III*), 36, 37, 75, 103, 182, 207, 215
Richard II, 49 n. 12, 75–76, 78, 79
Richard III, 9, 37, 75, 102, 102–103, 208

Ridley, Nicholas
Piteous Lamentation of the Miserable Estate of the Church in England, A, 57
Rogers, Thomas
Anatomie of the Mind, The, 181
Rosse *(Macbeth)*, 88, 110, 136, 141, 197, 203; comments on the state of Scotland, 46, 111, 136–137, 196, 205
Rossky, William
"Imagination in the English Renaissance: Psychology and Poetic," 18
Rouse, W. H. D.
Shakespeare's Ovid, 98 n. 5
Rudierd, Edmund
Thunderbolt of Gods Wrath against Hard-Hearted and Stiff-Necked Sinners, The, 26–27
Rutland: in *3 Henry VI*, 76, 101–102; referred to in *Richard III*, 102

Sackville, Thomas. *See* Norton, Thomas, and Thomas Sackville
Satan. *See* Devil
Saul: punishment of, 31, 160, 199–200, 201
Scholefield, Rev. James
Works of James Pilkington, B. D., 26 n. 29
Scot, Reginald
Discoverie of Witchcraft, The, 118, 119 n. 11, 145 n. 6, 154 n. 11, 160 n. 4
Seaton, Ethel
Arcadian Rhetorike, The, 47 n. 9
Seneca, 7, 9, 11–12, 61, 72, 73, 86, 96; Elizabethan reactions to, 19–21; *Thyestes*, 61; *Hippolytus*, 72; use of Innocence as victim in *Troas*, 96–97; in *Medea*, 97–98; in *Oedipus*, 123. *See also* Sensation
Sensation: and the artistry of *Macbeth*, 1–2, 4–7; uses of in earlier Shakespearean plays, 7–11; in Elizabethan drama, 14–15; Senecan influence upon, 19–21; Renaissance attitude toward, 16; in Renaissance writings, 21–27. *See also* Punishment; Strangeness
Senses, punishment through the. *See* Macbeth
Sermon of Repentaunce, A. *See* Dent, Arthur

Sermons: sensational, in Renaissance, 26–27. *See also* Punishment
Sermons and Remains by Hugh Latimer, Sometime Bishop of Worcester, Martyr. *See* Latimer, Hugh
Seven Sermons of the Reverend Father M. Hugh Latimer, The. *See* Latimer, Hugh
Seyton *(Macbeth)*, 111
Sheavyn, Phoebe
Literary Profession in the Elizabethan Age, The, 14
Show of Kings *(Macbeth)*, 82 n. 21, 123, 179–180
Siddons, J. H.
Memoirs of a Journalist, 68 n. 7
Siddons, Sarah, 68 n. 7, 92
Sidney, Sir Philip, 19, 54
Apologie for Poetrie, An, 20, 21
Countess of Pembrokes Arcadia, The, 212
Sisson, C. J.
Shakespeare's Tragic Justice, 217
Sisyphus, 186
Smith, G. Gregory
Elizabethan Critical Essays, 18 n. 14
Smith, Grover
"Naked New-born Babe in Macbeth: Some Iconographical Evidence, The," 95 n. 3
Smith, Henry
First Sermon of the Punishment of Jonah, The, 200 n. 14
Smith, J. C., and E. De Selincourt
Poetical Works of Edmund Spenser, The, 132 n. 26
Smith, Lucy Toulmin
York Plays, 138 n. 31
Snyder, Susan
"Left Hand of God: Despair in Medieval and Renaissance Tradition, The," 30 n. 39
Soliloquy: as expression of mental suffering in: *Hamlet*, 190–191, 194; in *King Lear*, 191, 194; in *Macbeth*, 191–195
Spanish Tragedy, The. *See* Kyd, Thomas
Spargo, John Webster
"Knocking at the Gate in *Macbeth*: An Essay in Interpretation, The," 166 n. 14

Spencer, Theodore
Shakespeare and the Nature of Man, 188 n. 3
Spenser, Edmund
Faerie Queene, The, 32 n. 48, 86, 120, 132 n. 26, 143–144, 203 n. 17
Sprague, Arthur Colby
Shakespearian Players and Performances, 92 n. 33
Spurgeon, Caroline, 71
Stirling, Brents
"Or else Were this a Savage Spectacle," 61
"Look, How Our Partner's Rapt," 61 n. 2
Strange and Miraculous Accident Happened in the Cittie of Purmerent, on New-yeeres Even Last Past, 1599, A, 101 n. 12
Strange Histories, of Kings, Princes, Dukes, Earles, Lords, Ladies, Knights, and Gentlemen. See Deloney, Thomas
Strangeness: as a quality of Renaissance writings, 24–26; as form of sensation in *Macbeth,* 110–113, 125–126; of unnatural figures appearing in plays preceding *Macbeth,* 113–115. *See also* Doomsday; Ghost, of Banquo; Night; Witches
Strange Newes, The, 26
Strange Report of Sixe Most Notorious Witches, A, 24 n. 25, 119 n. 13
Studley, John
Medea, 97–98
Summa Theologica, The. See Aquinas, Saint Thomas
Summers, Rev. Montague
Compendium Maleficarum, 24. n. 24
Demonolatry, 43 n. 4
Symonds, John Addington
Shakespeare's Predecessors in the English Drama, 14

Tamburlaine. See Marlowe, Christopher
Tantalus, 144, 186
Terrors of the Night See Nashe, Thomas
Theatre of Gods Judgements. See Beard, Thomas
Thunder: as the voice of God speaking through Macbeth's conscience, 168–169
Thunderbolt of Gods Wrath against Hard-Hearted and Stiff-Necked Sinners, The. See Rudierd, Edmund
Thyestes. See Seneca
Titus Andronicus, 61
Titus Andronicus, 130, 190; sensationalism of, compared with *Macbeth*'s, 2, 7–9, 10; symbolism and imagery of blood in, 75, 77, 87
Towneley and York cycles, 100 n. 9
Tragedie of Caesar and Pompey. See *Caesar's Revenge*
Tragedy of Dido Queen and Carthage, The. See Marlowe, Christopher
Tragedy of Ferrex and Porrex, The See *Gorboduc*
Traversi, D. A.
Approach to Shakespeare, An, 3 n. 7, 46 n. 7
Treatise against Witchcraft, A. See Holland, Henry
Treatise of Mans Imagination, A. See Perkins, William
Treatise of Specters or Straunge Sights. See Le Loyer, Pierre
Treatise of the Immortalitie of the Soule, A. See Woolton, John
Triumph of Gods Revenge, The. See Reynolds, John
Troas, See Seneca
Troilus and Cressida, 144
True and Most Dreadfull Discourse of a Woman Possessed with the Devill, A, 25
True Discourse Concerning the Possession of 7 Persons in One Familie in Lancashire, A. See More, George
Two Lamentable Tragedies. See Yarington, Robert
Two Most Unnaturall and Bloodie Murthers, 23 n. 23, 70
Tymme, Thomas
Silver Watch-Bell, A, 28 n. 36
Tyndale, William
"Exposition uppon the V. VI. VII. Chapters of Matthew, An," 66 n. 6
Tyrrel, Sir James *(Richard III),* 102

Ulysses *(Troilus and Cressida)*, 144
Una *(Faerie Queene, The)*, 143, 203 n. 17
Unfortunate Traveller, The. See Nashe, Thomas

View of Sundry Examples Reporting Many Straunge Murthers, Sundry Persons Perjured, Signes, and Tokens of Gods Anger Towards Us, A. See Mundy, Anthony
Virgil, 33

Waith, Eugene M.
  "Metamorphosis of Violence in *Titus Andronicus*, The," 7
Walker, Roy
  Time Is Free: A Study of Macbeth, The, 3 n. 2, 53–54, 56 n. 17
Waller, Rev. Henry
  Expositions and Notes on Sundry Portions of the Holy Scriptures, 66 n. 6
Warning for Faire Women, A, 61 n. 1, 74, 82, 127, 169
Wellek, René, and Austin Warren
  Theory of Literature, 142 n. 1
West, Robert H.
  "Night's Black Agents in *Macbeth*," 116–117
Wickham, Glynne
  "Hell-Castle and Its Door-Keeper," 166–167
Willet, Andrew
  Harmonie upon the First Booke of Samuel, An, 31 n. 46, 160, 175 n. 24
Wilson, F. P., 27 n. 33
Wilson, J. Dover, and Mary Yardley
  Of Ghostes and Spirites Walking by Nyght, 124 n. 20
Wilson, Thomas
  Arte of Rhetorique, The, 19
Witches, 15, 63, 81, 111, 112, 114, 136, 149, 154; as demonic incarnations, 12, 13, 64, 121–122, 139; in Elizabethan witch tracts, 23–24; unidentified nature of, 43, 116–118; contribute to the evil in *Macbeth*, 43, 45, 50–51, 120–121; verbal trickery of, 45–46, 106; vocabulary of, 50–51, 84, 91; Lady Macbeth's affinity with, 105, 146–147, 148, 153–154, 162–163; serious manner of presentation of, in *Macbeth*, 115, 116; appearance of, 118–120; and the doubling of Macbeth's labor, 141, 143, 145–146; contribute to Macbeth's punishment, 159–161, 169–170, 178–181, 209–210; as embodiments of Macbeth's own evil, 203. *See also* Devil; Gifford, George
Witherspoon, A. M.
  Influence of Robert Garnier on Elizabethan Drama, The, 20 n. 17
Wonderfull Straunge Sightes Seene in the Element, over the Citie of London and Other Places . . . See Day, Thomas
Wood, H. Harvey
  Plays of John Marston, The, 127 n. 24
Woolton, John
  Discourse of the Conscience, A, 30, 169 n. 19, 203 n. 17
  Treatise of the Immortalitie of the Soule, A, 35, 182 n. 31

Yarington, Robert
  Two Lamentable Tragedies, 22, 74, 82
Yoklavich, John
  Dramatic Works of George Peele, The, 70 n. 3
York, Richard Plantagenet, Duke of *(3 Henry VI)*, 102
York Plays. The Plays Performed by the Crafts or Mysteries of York on the Day of Corpus Christi in the 14th, 15th, and 16th Centuries, 138

www.ingramcontent.com/pod-product-compliance
Lightning Source LLC
Chambersburg PA
CBHW021703230426
43668CB00008B/709